"There is a difference between _____ money and money having you." Bro. Richardson.

Freedom is an attitude of the mind.

The voice of people is not usually the voice of God.

THE PASTOR
and His Work

THE PASTOR
and His Work

By

HOMER A. KENT, SR.

MOODY PRESS
CHICAGO

Library of Congress Catalog Card Number: 63-14563

ISBN: 0-8024-6338-X

Second Printing, 1966

Third Printing, 1967

Fourth Printing, 1969

Fifth Printing, 1970

Sixth Printing, 1971

Seventh Printing, 1973

Eighth Printing, 1974

Ninth Printing, 1974

Printed in the United States of America

Dedicated to
all the former students who
sat in my classes studying to become
good ministers of Jesus Christ

CONTENTS

Part IV

THE PASTOR AND HIS VISITATION AND COUNSELING OPPORTUNITIES

PREFACE

THE MINISTRY OF PASTORAL THEOLOGY is as varied as the need of man. A good pastor is interested in every phase of the lives of the members of his constituency—physical, social, and spiritual. It is evident that no one volume can be expected to deal with all of the problems, responsibilities, tasks, and privileges that belong to the pastor. The many volumes which have been written on these subjects have not solved all of the problems which ministers have faced or given the final word on every aspect of ministerial practice, and no one volume ever will.

It is the purpose of this present volume to deal with a selected number of phases of pastoral work which have appealed to the author as of special importance. Through an extended pastoral experience these have come under his observation, and thus he is persuaded of their importance. When the last chapter has been read, it will be evident that much more could have been written. Other writers will doubtless attempt this task.

The author wishes to acknowledge his indebtedness to many others who have already written on various aspects of pastoral theology. The use which has been made of their writings is partially indicated in the documentation scattered through the book and in the selected bibliographies appearing at the close of most of the chapters.

He is especially indebted to the First Brethren Church of Washington, D.C., of which he was pastor for fifteen years, for the many lessons in pastoral theology he learned there. Without this relationship this volume could never have been written.

He is also greatly indebted to Grace Theological Seminary, in which he has been permitted for many years to teach classes in pastoral and practical theology. These experiences in fellowship with earnest students in preparation for the pastoral relationship as well as other types of Christian service have enriched the writer's life and have confirmed in his mind what is written in this volume. It goes forth with the hope and prayer that it may be helpful to those who have been called into the glorious ministry of our Lord Jesus Christ.

HOMER A. KENT, SR.

Winona Lake, Indiana

"Study to shew thyself approved unto God, a workman that needeth not to be ashamed, rightly dividing the word of truth" (II Timothy 2:15).

Part I

THE PASTOR AND HIS PERSONAL AFFAIRS

Chapter 1

HIS PERSONAL LIFE

IF THE PASTOR is to be effective in the pulpit and in the parish, he must carefully guard his personal life. His great responsibilities and the influence he exerts as a minister of God argue loudly for such care. "Take heed unto thyself," said the veteran preacher to young Timothy (I Tim. 4:16). More literally, this passage may be translated "Keep on paying attention to thyself." Hence the man of God ever needs to be on the alert to keep himself a vessel fit for the Master's use.

His Devotional Life

In his busy round of duty the pastor must ever be on guard lest he devote all his time to feeding the souls of others and have no time left to nourish his own soul. The truth is that no minister is fully qualified to help others spiritually until first he has been in close touch with God. There is a tragic statement in the Song of Solomon, which may apply to any minister who neglects his devotional life: "They made me the keeper of the vineyards: but mine own vineyard have I not kept" (1:6). Doubtless this is a sad commentary on the lives of many pastors.

There are problems involved in maintaining this devotional life. The pastor will discover that the press of duties in the realm of the church and the home and reliance on his long years of Biblical preparation will tempt him to neglect the devotional aspect of his life. He must make time for it if he would be what he ought to be. To dispense with this source of spiritual power will diminish the glow of his ministry.

Devotional Reading of Scripture. Every pastor should take time daily to read the Scriptures devotionally for his own benefit with no thought of preaching or teaching in mind. Feasting on the manna from Heaven will cause the man of God to grow strong, and continuance in this practice will inevitably result in his becoming like the Book in his daily ministrations. The very expressions from his lips will reflect its tone.

Each minister must choose his own plan for Scripture meditation. Some like the plan of reading the Bible through year after year. Dr. Harry Ironside followed this plan with the result that his pulpit expressions and his writings were permeated with the Word of God. Others have followed the plan of reading selected books in their devotional periods, say one from the Old Testament and then one from the New Testament so that there is no prolonged time when either Testament is neglected. Some other plan may have a greater appeal to the reader. But some plan ought to be chosen and followed consistently lest he experience spiritual barrenness. Hit-and-miss reading seldom brings satisfaction or the greatest spiritual blessing. Whatever portion of the Word is read at a particular time, it should be read in a meditative spirit with a determination to find out God's directive for the day. Let the minister ask himself after reading a passage, What is there in this portion of Scripture for me? Let him realize that God does speak to the individual from His Book.[1]

Prayer. The pastor should have a definite time each day to pray. In most cases, the best time is in connection with the reading of God's Word. Prayer ought to be conceived of as a two-way experience. It is like a conversation with a friend. Two parties are involved in the conversation. In the Word God speaks to man. Prayer is never complete apart from listening to the voice of God. In what we usually think of as prayer, man speaks to God. Both are essential to devotional development. The minister ought to have a prayer list. He should pray definitely. Too many prayers are characterized by indefiniteness. God is pleased when his ministers come before Him with definite burdens upon their hearts, definite matters of petition.

Probably few ministers are engaging in the ministry of intercession as they ought. Thus lack of fruitage results. The Apostle Paul in writing to Timothy, the young pastor, wrote, "I exhort therefore, that, *first of all,* supplications, prayers, intercessions, and giving of thanks, be made for all men; for kings, and for all that are in authority; that we may lead a quiet and peaceable life in all godliness

[1]Several books discuss devotional methods of Bible study. See, for instance, Lloyd M. Perry and W. Howard, *How to Study Your Bible;* Wilbur M. Smith, *Profitable Bible Study;* and H. F. Vos, *Effective Bible Study.*

and honesty. For this is good and acceptable in the sight of God our Saviour" (I Tim. 2:1-3). God thus assigns a prominent place to the ministry of prayer in the lives of His servants. He wants His ministers to be men of prayer.

[*Worship.* The pastor should also learn to worship with his people in the public services of the church. He should be so well prepared when he gets to the pulpit on Sunday that he can worship even as he expects his people to do.] Some ministers conceive of their responsibility as only to direct the worship of others. This is a faulty conception and is liable to result in superficiality or the putting on of an act. The minister should cultivate the practice of wholeheartedly entering into the service of worship himself for his own benefit. In this way he will not only benefit himself but will "be an example of the believers, in word, in conversation, in charity, in spirit, in faith, in purity" (I Tim. 4:12). The congregation will quickly sense the nature of the minister's public exercises, whether he is putting on an act or sincerely entering into the presence of God as he exhorts his people to do.

Reading of Devotional Materials. In order to keep his heart aglow with a warm devotional spirit, the pastor ought from time to time to read some devotional books and articles. He needs to get in contact with other men who have walked with God in order that he may profit from their experiences. The man of God will enrich his life and ministry by reading such works as *Memoirs of McCheyne, Pilgrim's Progress* by John Bunyan, *The Preacher and Prayer* by E. M. Bounds, and the series of "Quiet Talks" by S. D. Gordon. There are countless others of equal value. Nothing will bless the heart more than the reading of biographies of such missionary heroes as David Livingstone, J. Hudson Taylor, John G. Paton, and Jonathan Goforth. The reading of such literature is certain to warm the preacher's heart, stimulate his zeal, and give him a fund of powerful illustrations that will make his ministry more attractive.[2]

Charles Spurgeon is said to have read through *Pilgrim's Progress* a hundred times and he continually read much other devotional literature, such as Matthew Henry's commentary on the Holy Scriptures. Doubtless this was responsible to a large degree for his success as a warm-hearted preacher. Such reading tends to keep the

[2]For additional titles, see the list appended to Chapter 3.

minister from becoming spiritually dull and uninteresting in the pulpit.

Attendance at Spiritual Retreats. The pastor will do well also to attend Bible conferences and spiritual retreats. They will refresh the minister's soul and will keep him from getting into a rut. Every church owes it to its minister to help him to attend conferences where his soul can be fed and where he can learn how other men are accomplishing things for God. All things being equal, the pastor will return from such retreats with new enthusiasm, new ideas, and new material with which to bless his congregation. Thus both the pastor and the church will benefit from the pastor's attendance at such meetings.

In summary, let us be reminded of Paul's admonition to Timothy that the man of God must exercise himself unto godliness (I Tim. 4:7). If he is to mature in this divine characteristic, he must give attention to it unceasingly.

The Pastor's Health

The minister also needs to pay attention to his physical welfare. Who needs a strong body more than the busy pastor? His physical well-being affects his mental and spiritual condition. He needs to remember, as does every Christian, that his body is "the temple of the Holy Spirit" and that he must treat it accordingly (I Cor. 6:15-20). The minister's body is not his own. It belongs to God. Therefore he ought to treat it as he should treat the things of God.

In accordance with this truth, there are several things to which the minister needs to give earnest attention:

Rest at Night. He should obtain sufficient rest at night. Not all men have the same sleep requirements, but most ministers need seven or eight hours of sound sleep if they are to be at their best in their day-by-day ministry. Dr. Theodore L. Cuyler, whom Dr. W. B. Riley referred to as the ideal pastor, has some interesting remarks on this point. Said he, "Sleep as soundly as possible all night if you want to keep your congregation awake on Sunday. The Irishman's rule for good sleeping was 'to pay attention to it.' The men who live the longest, and do the most effective work, are commonly good sleepers. If they cannot secure enough rest at night, they make it up during the day. When a man who has so much strain on his brain and his sensibilities as the pastor has, goes to his bedroom, he should school himself to the habit of dismissing all thoughts about outside matters. If this costs him some difficulty, he should pray for Divine help to do it. Too many ministers toil at their sermons until eleven or twelve o'clock, and then retire with throbbing heads to their sleepless beds. The man who invented 'midnight oil' deserves a purgatory of endless nightmare. My own rule is never to touch a sermon by lamplight. One hour in the morning is worth five at night."[3]

Relaxation. The pastor should find some time for relaxation during the week. In these complex days most ministers find it difficult to take a whole day off each week with regularity. Certainly they cannot have a weekend rest like many others. This is the time when their labors reach a climax. From the observation and experience of the writer, it seems best for the minister to arrange for half-day periods of relaxation each week. Some find Saturday afternoon a satisfactory time for this. With the preparations for Sunday complete and the need for a bit of refreshment before the arduous duties of Sunday are undertaken, Saturday afternoon has definite advantages. And, weary from the responsibilities of Sunday, the preacher finds a half day of relaxation on Monday very beneficial.

Others prefer to find their relaxation during the middle of the week in order to break the tension that builds up at that time. Each minister should settle upon a plan most satisfactory to himself and do his best to abide by it. While we are not living under the law of the Old Testament Sabbath in this dispensation, yet there is a principle involved in setting aside one day in seven for rest and recuperation which will benefit the minister if he will adhere to it. A minister's efficiency can be reduced tremendously by a tired body. It can keep him from being a radiant witness for Christ and can result in his making poor decisions. The faithful pastor expends an enormous amount of energy in his labors of preaching and parish ministrations and is entitled to some time of relaxation during the week. He owes it to himself, his family, and his church, and he will be a better preacher because of taking such time.

Vacation. Somewhat related to the above matter is the minister's vacation. Every minister deserves a vacation at some time during the year. He needs a change of scenery at least once a year. There are some ministers who prefer to divide their allotted vacation time

[3]Theodore L. Cuyler, *How To Be A Pastor* (New York: The Baker and Taylor Co., 1890), pp. 56-57.

into two periods, feeling that this plan helps to keep the man of God fresh throughout the year. Some churches feel that it is to their advantage to give their ministers, in addition to a summer vacation, a week or more of vacation after the heavy Christmas activities are over. But whatever the plan, the right kind of vacation will minister benefits to the pastor's body, mind, and spirit. He will come back to his work with a new attack. He will be a better preacher, and thus his congregation will appreciate him more.

During his vacation, the minister should seek to do something different from his regular round of duty during the rest of the year. He ought to do something he likes to do. He ought to look on new scenes, meet new people, and enjoy new experiences. Of course, the desires of the minister's family must be taken into consideration in planning the vacation.

It would be impossible here satisfactorily to outline the proper kind of vacation for all ministers. We differ so greatly in our tastes. What would appeal to one minister would bore another. Our families, too, are different in size and desires. Some have greater means than others. The time allotted by our churches for vacations varies. Each minister should use the wisdom he has to work out for himself and his family what will be the most feasible and profitable vacation. By all means take a vacation. And don't spend the whole vacation preaching elsewhere!

Exercise. The minister should provide for himself some sort of suitable exercise. Without it he will become sluggish and unfit for his best work. [Many times when the pastor feels depressed and his work becomes irksome, he will gain a new perspective if he will get away from his study and take a walk or engage in some other kind of physical exercise.]

There are some who discount the value of this sort of thing because of Paul's word to Timothy, "Bodily exercise profiteth little" (I Tim. 4:8). But when properly understood, this statement is no argument against bodily exercise. A study of the entire verse makes it clear that Paul is contrasting things temporal with things eternal. It is true that, compared to eternal things and godliness which makes them glorious, the exercise that ministers only to the physical body "profiteth little" or "for a little time." But it is also true that while we are in the flesh bodily exercise is beneficial because it ministers to physical health. And it is important since it is necessary to ministry in this world to keep the body fit.

The type of exercise the pastor should engage in depends largely upon his desires and his age. If possible, his exercise should be pleasurable, but it must become his age if it is to be profitable. Some ministers like sports such as golf or fishing. Others are satisfied to get their exercise working in the garden or about the home, keeping it a pleasant place in which to live. Other ministers find pleasure in walking. Still others have availed themselves of the facilities of the local Y.M.C.A., which sometimes offers these facilities to ministers free of charge or at a reduced rate.

The minister who is forty years of age or older should refrain from the more vigorous types of exercise. Known to the author was a minister who appeared in the best of health and thought he could keep up with his sons of high school age athletically. In doing so, he dropped dead doing a round on the track.

If the minister takes up some form of exercise like golf, he will need to be careful lest he spend too much time on the fairways! Too many afternoons devoted to this sort of thing can lessen the minister's usefulness. Analyze your needs and select the type of exercise which will benefit you the most.

Good Eating Habits. The minister should seek to eat properly. This is one of the areas where the virtue of self-control needs to be employed (Gal. 5:22-23). With all the information available to-day, there is no reason why the minister should be uninformed as to what constitutes a balanced diet. Proper eating will contribute to keeping him physically fit for his arduous duties. Overweight, for instance, may cause the minister to become listless and a prey to physical ailments which will impair his ministry. How can the minister with consistency criticize the drinker and his bottle if he cannot control himself in relation to his icebox? He ought to enlist the help of his wife in this matter and determine, in spite of the many temptations that will face him, to eat properly.

Physical Examinations. Finally, on this point, the minister ought to have a thorough physical checkup annually. This is especially important after he has reached the age of thirty-five. By these regular examinations he may ward off serious difficulties by discovering diseases or malfunctions in an incipient form when they may be easily corrected.

The Minister's Home

The Scripture says of the bishop (or pastor) that he should be "one that ruleth well his own house, having his children in subjection with all gravity; (For if a man know not how to rule his own house, how shall he take care of the church of God?) " (I Tim. 3:4-5) .

The minister's home—call it parsonage, manse, rectory or whatever you will—is a marked home in the community. Everybody knows where the preacher lives and expects a type of life there that conforms with the message from his pulpit. Where this conformity is not evident, the spiritual progress of the church is affected.

The minister's children also should be a credit to the minister, well-behaved in and out of the church. The ministry of some pastors has been reduced in effectiveness because of failure at this point. This is not usually the case, however. By and large, the children of the parsonage are a credit to the pastor and his wife. But it is the responsibility of every pastor to exercise care in the development of his homelife so that his children will not bring reproach upon his ministry. The minister's home should be at least a partial reflection of what he would like to see in his church families.

Devoting Time to the Home. If the minister's home is to be what it ought to be the minister must take time for his family. He must not leave all of this responsibility to his wife. Being the head of the home, he has a definite responsibility to guide it in the right way. The pastor must not be so busy with the affairs of his church that be becomes a mere boarder in his own home, almost a stranger to his children! But the minister must not give too much time to his home either. Some preachers spend so much time puttering around the house that they have scarcely any time left for the work of the ministry. The pastor should not be expected to do the work that his wife is perfectly capable of doing.

Characteristics of the Pastor's Homelife. There are several characteristics that should certainly mark the homelife of the pastor.

One of them is *unselfishness.* If he is selfish and crabbed at home, he surely will be far from manifesting the character of his Lord. If his preaching on the Christian virtues is to be well received, he must practice them at home.

The characteristic of *cheerfulness* should also permeate the minister's home. If he is not careful, the pastor is likely to allow the burdens which he must bear to cast a gloom over his home. This ought not to be. The home of the pastor should be a happy place, radiant with Christian joy. His home should be an example for the church and the community in this regard. Many missionary leaders are coming more and more to advocate missionary families on the foreign field in order to teach the natives how a Christian home should be conducted. In like manner, the pastor's home should be an example in the homeland, a place where others will delight to come and where God's presence is a reality.

Another characteristic of the pastor's home should be that of *devotion*. The family altar should be a vital part of his household. A spiritual atmosphere should prevail. A stream will rise no higher than its source. If a warm devotional life is not exemplified in the pastor's home, how can it be expected that the homes of the membership will rise very high in this respect?

The grace of *hospitality* should also characterize the pastor's home. In the pastoral epistles Paul twice speaks of this grace as essential for the pastor. In I Timothy 3:2 Paul says that a bishop, among other things, *must* be "given to hospitality." And in Titus 1:8 the apostle says that a bishop must be "a lover of hospitality." He must not only exercise it as his responsibility, but he must *love* to manifest it. The welcome mat is always out at the true pastor's home. Sometimes the frequency of visitors may disrupt the ways of the household, but the blessings of hospitality far outweigh its inconveniences. Above all, the pastor and his wife should be impressed with the fact that it is the will of God that their home should be a hospitable place and, therefore, do all that they can to make it so.

Let the minister's home, then, be a place where the Christian virtues are beautifully portrayed. Of the English Bishop Hooper's home it was said, "In every corner thereof there was some smell of virtue, good example, honest conversation, and reading of holy Scripture."[4]

The Minister's Personal Appearance

The man of God ought to be careful of his personal appearance, keeping himself neat and clean. It is unthinkable that the representative of the Lord Jesus Christ would appear otherwise in his public ministrations. Dr. Andrew W. Blackwood has set forth this

[4]James M. Hoppin, *Pastoral Theology* (New York and London: Funk & Wagnalls Company, 1901), p. 193.

aspect of the minister's life in the following statement: ["Both in appearance and in dress the servant of God should keep as neat and clean as any man in uniform. With self-imposed discipline, the minister at home should be as careful as any lieutenant under the watchful eyes of his captain and colonel. Surely our Lord expects no less of his local representative than the country requires of an army or navy commander."[5]

The minister's clothing should be spotless. He needs to watch his linens in particular. It is well-nigh unpardonable for a preacher to bring forth a used or wrinkled handkerchief in public. He will beware of wearing his shirts too long, and should see to it that his wife knows how to iron them. There is a knack to producing a well-ironed shirt that not every woman has. But it can be acquired. Since a tie is about the only ornament the preacher wears, he ought also to make sure that it is unspotted.

The pastor needs to exercise care to keep his suits pressed. Baggy trousers are no commendation for the minister. [He need not wear fine clothing, but what he does wear should be kept pressed, cleaned, and brushed.] His clothes ought not to be flashy but in good taste, for the eyes of many people are upon him. He should not dress to draw attention to himself, especially when he is in the pulpit. A few ministers dress so gaudily that their hearers find it difficult to center attention upon the message being proclaimed.

The minister should keep his shoes polished. Nothing more quickly reveals slovenliness than dusty, muddy, or dingy shoes in the pulpit. The same goes for the parlor. The general makeup of many ministers can be detected by a look at their shoes.

[Not only should the minister's heart be clean but His hands also should be clean.] His fingernails should be kept clean and trimmed. This cleaning and trimming should not be done in public. This is a breach of etiquette of which the pastor should not be guilty.

It goes without saying that the minister needs to practice extreme care in keeping his teeth clean. Such neglect has been appalling in some cases, with resulting unsightliness and halitosis. If he wears glasses, he ought to make sure that they are cleaned regularly. Not only is this good for the eyes, but he should remember that there are people who are quick to notice carelessness in such matters. It

[5]Andrew W. Blackwood, *Pastoral Work* (Philadelphia: The Westminster Press, 1945), p. 23.

is sad when a church has reason to be ashamed of its pastor because of his carelessness about his appearance.

The pastor should also give careful attention to his hair. It should be kept clean, trimmed, and combed. He must be careful about dandruff and falling hair. It is most distasteful to see a coat collar and lapels covered with dandruff flakes and falling hair. Also, the minister should appear clean-shaven when in public, even if he has to shave twice a day. At this point, it is not out of place to warn ministers against an excessive use of highly-perfumed lotions, which may be offensive to some people, especially to someone in a sickroom.

One of the best ways to keep clean and fresh is to bathe frequently. This should be a must for every minister. There is much truth in the statement, "Cleanliness is next to godliness."

Finally, the minister should constantly remember that he is a representative of Jesus Christ. We cannot imagine that He was ever slovenly in appearance or lacking in cleanliness. No, He was the One "altogether lovely." Therefore, let His representatives be careful to maintain an attractive personal appearnce.

His Social Conduct

As the minister moves in and out among people, he at all times should act the part of the Christian gentleman. He will separate himself from bad manners in every form, having a sincere regard for the feelings and situations of others. [Arthur Wentworth Hewitt has graphically set forth this matter in a negative way: "When a man contradicts others with a know-it-all finality, when he monopolizes the conversation or the program, when he speaks incessantly or even unnecessarily of himself, when he looks bored or impatient while others are talking, he is seven light-years away from being a gentleman."[6]] There are many other considerations worthy of thought in this matter of ministerial correctness in his social contacts.

Good Etiquette. For one thing, he ought to observe the common rules of etiquette. For instance, he should immediately stand to his feet when a lady or elderly gentleman enters the room, and remain standing until the person is seated. When dining with a woman, he will help seat her at the table. He will refrain from using his napkin to wipe off his silverware after he sits down to the table. This is a first-class way to insult the hostess! Neither will the minis-

[6]Arthur W. Hewitt, *Highland Shepherds* (New York: Harper & Brothers, Publishers, 1939), p. 201.

ter tuck his napkin under his chin. Elbows on the table are certainly taboo. And after the meal is over he will not be found using a toothpick in the living room.

It would be a good thing if all ministers would take a little time to read Emily Post or some similar work. People are quick to observe when ministers fail in some point of etiquette. This is especially true where the minister moves among a group of cultured people.

Courteous Dealings. He should always be courteous in his dealings with others. [Politeness is an attractive characteristic and often breaks down barriers of resistance which may confront the pastor.] Courtesy should be manifest even in the minister's dealings with his enemies. If a minister fails to be courteous, it is soon noised about and is a poor testimony. The Apostle Paul exemplified the finest courtesy, even before those who had him in their custody, such as Felix, Festus, and King Agrippa. Hear him as he addresses the Roman governor, Festus, who had accused Paul of being insane in his convictions. He said, "I am not mad, most noble Festus; but speak forth the words of truth and soberness" (Acts 26:25). In Paul's other dealings with rulers while he was in prison, he acted in a similar dignified and courteous manner.

There are some ministers, however, who do not follow Paul's example. The minister may become easily irritated when people do not agree with him or when they encroach upon his time. He may cut short conversations with salesmen, insurance agents, and others of like occupation in a manner that clearly betrays his irritation. If the telephone operator gives the wrong number he manifests impatience and is very discourteous. This ought not be. The minister will be richly repaid if he always practices the grace of courtesy. He will feel better in his own soul and promote smoother relationships in the church and a better testimony in the community.

Sympathetic Spirit. He ought always to possess a sympathetic spirit. Jesus always had compassion on the crowds of His day, for He saw them as sheep not having a shepherd. He knew their sins and their sorrows. As the minister learns about the sins and the sorrows and the heartbreak of people all about him, no matter who they are, he should be like his Master. [Jowett said, "When we cease to bleed we cease to bless."] The world needs sympathy. [The sympathetic touch of the man of God is one of Heaven's benedictions to this needy world.]

Sobriety of Attitude. He should refrain from undue levity. The pastor is not called to be a clown. A few pastors have so given themselves to foolish jesting that no one ever thinks of them in serious terms. That is a tragedy. Those with burdens hesitate to come to such a pastor, fearing they and their burden may be treated lightly.

It is right and proper for ministers to be jolly and cheerful, full of the joy of the Lord. But it is unbecoming for them to be glaring examples of the thing that Paul speaks against in Ephesians 5:4: "foolish talking" and "jesting." The word for "foolish talking" in the Greek is the word from which comes the word "moron." Christians, and ministers especially included, should not be guilty of moronic talking. The word "jesting" carries the connotation of all sorts of low-type conversation, including shady jokes which are supposed to be funny but are unwholesome. Lay people should be impressed with the minister's seriousness, not with his superficiality and levity.

Good Listening Habits. [The minister needs to be a good listener. People who have burdens are helped if they can talk to someone about their troubles. Many times the best thing the minister can do is to listen sympathetically to the stories of broken and perplexed men and women.] The late Dr. George W. Truett, the great Baptist preacher of Dallas, Texas, said he had a chair in his study which he called the trouble chair. In it people of all walks of life sat down to unburden themselves to him. He just listened.

Some preachers make the mistake of thinking that they must do all of the talking. Job's so-called comforters probably helped most when they kept silence. If the pastor is to be really helpful in counseling, he needs to hear what is upon the hearts of those who come to him. [Dale Carnegie gives six rules for getting people to like you, and one of them is, "Be a good listener."]

Exemplary Financial Practices. The pastor should learn to live within his means. [It has been said that two things have destroyed more ministers than anything else, debts and women.] Ministers should pay their way as they go. This means that some pastors will have to live very frugally because the provision of their churches is not as generous as it might be. Of course, some churches are not able to pay an adequate salary. There are some cases where the pastor will be forced to add to his income by working outside the church. But whatever the situation may be, the pastor should allow no scandal to arise because of his laxity in money matters.

Punctuality in Keeping Appointments. He should be punctual in keeping his appointments. In this matter, he needs to follow His Lord who made appointments and always kept them. Our Lord has made some appointments for the future, and He will keep each one. His undershepherds have responsibility in this matter both in the church and out. A minister who is lax in keeping his appointments in his church will get nowhere. He should be prompt in starting all the services of the church. He should be unfailing in meeting appointments with individuals and committees of the church. He should meet the deadlines for newspaper announcements. He should be on time in meeting the schedule he has set for his own study program. Then he must keep his business appointments outside the church. If he fails to keep them, he will lose the confidence of the people he is seeking to reach for Christ. Let each pastor discipline himself to promptitude in all of these matters. The minister's business is the most important business in the world and deserves nothing less than punctuality.

It is fitting to conclude this chapter on the pastor's personal life by calling attention to a fivefold characterization of the elder as found in the Pastoral Epistles: (1) he should be without reproach, a man of integrity (I Tim. 3:2; Titus 1:7); (2) he should be a man of good behavior (I Tim. 3:2; II Tim. 2:22); (3) he should be a man of good report (I Tim. 3:7); (4) he should be a pattern of godliness, a man of God (I Tim. 6:11); and (5) he should be a man of self-control (Titus 1:8).

RECOMMENDED READING

BLANCHARD, CHARLES A. *Getting Things from God.* Wheaton, Ill.: Sword of the Lord Publishers, 1953 (reprint).

DAVIS, ADELLE. *Let's Eat Right to Keep Fit.* New York: Harcourt, Brace and World, Inc., 1954.

ERDMAN, CHARLES R. *The Work of the Pastor.* Philadelphia: The Westminster Press, 1924.

FULLER, DAVID OTIS (condensed and abridged by). *Spurgeon's Lectures to His Students.* Grand Rapids: Zondervan Publishing House, 1945.

HEWITT, ARTHUR W. *Highland Shepherds.* New York: Harper & Brothers, Publishers, 1939.

HOGUE, WILSON T. *A Handbook of Homiletics and Pastoral Theology.* Winona Lake, Ind.: Free Methodist Publishing House, 1946.

HOPPIN, JAMES M. *Pastoral Theology.* New York and London: Funk & Wagnalls Co., 1901.

JOWETT, J. H. *The Preacher, His Life and Work.* Garden City, N. Y.: Doubleday, Doran and Co., Inc., 1929.

PATTISON, T. HARWOOD. *For the Work of the Ministry.* Philadelphia: American Baptist Publication Society, 1907.

PAUL, the Apostle. *The Pastoral Epistles* (I Timothy, II Timothy, and Titus) .

POST, EMILY. *Etiquette.* New York: Funk & Wagnalls Co., 1950, 10th rev. ed.

RICE, JOHN R. *Prayer: Asking and Receiving.* Wheaton, Ill.: Sword of the Lord Publishers, 1942.

RILEY, MARIE ACOMB (Mrs. William B.) . *Handbook of Christian Etiquette.* Chicago: Moody Press, 1956 (11th ed.) .

RILEY, WILLIAM B. *Pastoral Problems.* New York: Fleming H. Revell Co., 1936.

SCHUETTE, WALTER E. *The Minister's Personal Guide.* New York: Harper and Brothers, 1953.

TURNBULL, RALPH G. *The Minister's Obstacles.* New York: Fleming H. Revell Co., 1946; paperback ed.; Revell, 1959.

VANDERBILT, AMY. *New Complete Book of Etiquette.* New York: Doubleday & Co., Inc., 1963.

Chapter 2

HIS STUDY

A NOTED ENGLISH BARRISTER, Lord Bowen, once said, "Cases are won in chambers." The success or failure of the lawyer is determined by the research he does in his own private office more than by the extempore wit or appeal which he may display in the public court. It is very much the same with the minister of the Gospel. His success or failure in the pulpit is largely determined by the attention he gives to his study. Faithful and continued study habits will result in a constructive and growing preaching ministry. On the other hand, neglect at this point is bound to manifest itself in a shallow pulpit ministry that smacks of superficiality. As a result of failure in study habits some preachers, as they stand behind the sacred desk on Sunday morning, remind one of a football game played in a fog. The congregation knows something is going on, but they don't know exactly what! The pulpit ministry is worthy of finer treatment than this.

The Place

The pastor needs a dedicated *place* for his study. If possible, this place should be at the church. In the minister's home, especially if there are growing children in the family, it is difficult to obtain the necessary privacy. But it is possible, and if it is necessary to have the study in the home, it should be made as private as possible. The other members of the family should come to respect this place and help to maintain its privacy. In his study the pastor should have gathered about him all the things necessary for his study and work, such as books, desk, library, telephone, typewriter, filing cases, records, and stationery. There should be a few chairs in the room for visitors who come to interview the pastor and for committee meetings of various kinds. It should be a well-provisioned office set apart for the carrying on of the most important business in the world. This office need not be large, but it should be large enough to include the items mentioned without the appearance and feeling of being oppressively crowded.

The pastor's study should be made as attractive and cheerful as possible, for here the faithful man of God will be spending many precious hours. Then, too, the visitors who come to counsel with him should find a place set in order and worthy of the great business of the church. Because the pastor spends so much time reading and studying, his study should have adequate sources of light. See to it that there is good ventilation in the study. This will help to keep the pastor alert as he engages in his labors. Attention should be given to the temperature of the room. It should be cool in the summer and warm in the winter. The minister will be unable to give full attention to his studies if he has a hot head or cold feet! The study should be a comfortable place.

Above all, the pastor's study should be conducive to meditation upon the things of God. The light of Heaven should be there. The minister's study should be the place of his finest labor. There he will meet God and come forth with messages to bless the people whose minister he is.

Regular Hours

The pastor needs to have *regular hours* for his study. Let the people of the congregation know what these hours are. If the people respect these hours, he will find it easier to keep them. Regular hours for study will be a great aid to the minister's efficiency. Dr. John Henry Jowett, a great pulpiteer of another generation, counseled out of his long and ripe experience that ministers should be systematic and businesslike in their work, just as systematic and businesslike as the businessman. Dr. Jowett said in one of his Yale Lectures, "Enter your study at an appointed hour, and let the hour be as early as the earliest of your business men goes to his office. I remember, in my earlier days, how I used to hear the factory operatives passing my house on the way to the mills at six o'clock. I can recall the sound of their ironclogs ringing through the street. The sound of the clogs fetched me out of bed and took me to my work. I no longer hear the Yorkshire clogs, but I can see and hear my business men as they start off early to earn their daily bread. And shall their minister be behind them in his quest of the Bread of

Life?"[1] Conditions may have changed somewhat since the days of Jowett, and the minister with so many night engagements on his calendar of duty may have to regulate his time a bit differently, but the principle is the same.

Regular hours will keep the minister from wasting time and from trifling. They will give the people of the church and community a better appreciation of the pastor's work. Dr. George Truett, late pastor of the First Baptist Church of Dallas, Texas, speaking before a large group of ministers in Washington, D.C., once said in hearing of the writer that some ministers reminded him of an elephant trying to pick up pins. The elephant was made for bigger business. Some ministers spend too much time on trifles, doing things that others can do as well or better than he, while the things that he alone is prepared and commissioned to do are neglected. [The minister is called as a leader in the most important business in the world, and he should so discipline himself that he will not squander his time on things of minor importance.]

A Study Schedule

[Moreover, the preacher ought to have a *plan* for his study program.] He ought to adopt some sort of working schedule. If the minister does not have a plan for his study hours, he is apt to waste many precious moments, yes, even hours. He needs to have his study hours so planned that a definite time will be set aside each week to prepare for sermons, Bible study classes, prayer-meeting meditations, radio talks, Sunday school classes, and the like. When the minister enters his study each day, he should know exactly what he expects to do. A commendable idea, followed by some ministers, is to make out a weekly schedule on paper, blocking out at least the morning hours of each day except Sunday and assigning particular tasks for each of these morning hours.

Of course, any schedule that the pastor may make will have to be elastic enough to allow for unavoidable hindrances or interruptions. Every minister has many of them, and ofttimes in connection with them some of his most effective ministry is accomplished. The writer will never forget a seminary chapel address to which he listened years ago on the subject, "The Ministry of Interruptions." The

[1]J. H. Jowett, *The Preacher, His Life and Work* (Garden City, New York: Doubleday, Doran & Company, Inc., 1929), p. 116.

speaker, who was a missionary on furlough, showed that often the most worthwhile ministries on the mission field were accomplished by him in connection with interruptions. God sometimes sees fit to take us away from the task we think is so important and send us to another task which at the moment may seem small by comparison. But in the end, many times the "small" task turns out to be the greater.

But, in spite of frequent interruptions, the planned schedule is essential in the minister's program. It is doubtless the best policy to set aside the morning hours, when the mind is freshest, for study purposes and to use the afternoons for pastoral visitation and other responsibilities.

Unceasing Study

Furthermore, the preacher should *never cease* his study habits. Once a pastor ceases studying, his ministry will begin to lose its luster and effectiveness. It is folly to suppose that a preacher can continue to draw upon his study of early years and the notes he gathered while in seminary to keep him going. He must continually search out new truth. Failure here has been responsible for many ministers being laid on the shelf far too soon. But, as someone has said, there is no deadline for a live man. One way for the minister to keep fresh is for him to be engaged at all times in the comprehensive study of one particular book in the Bible. If the man of God will do this continuously and persistently, he will always be coming from the mine of Scripture with precious gems to delight those who sit under his ministry. The Apostle Paul gave no age limit in his exhortation: "Study to shew thyself approved unto God, a workman that needeth not to be ashamed, rightly dividing the word of truth" (II Tim. 2:15).

Give Attention to Reading

Again, the preacher needs to *give attention to reading*. This too was a Pauline injunction to Timothy and to every other "man of God" in the ministry (I Tim. 4:13). Bacon said: "Conversation makes a ready man; reading makes a full man; and writing an exact man." The minister needs to develop all three of these faculties, but in the Scripture special emphasis seems to be laid on the importance of reading. Reading will keep the minister familiar with the things of the Lord in their many aspects and also with what is going on in the world. Reading will give him a vast fund of illustrative material and will enable him to preach more directly to the needs of the people. It will aid him greatly in the cultivation of the power of historical imagination so important in bringing life into sermons. It will tend to keep the preacher from getting into a rut in his preaching.

It is interesting to note that when Paul, the aged, was in prison and knew his execution lay in the near future he was still interested in his books (II Tim. 4:13). He wanted to read and study. Such a man will always have a ministry. Listen to John Wesley as he wrote to a minister who had neglected reading and study: "Hence your talent in preaching does not increase; it is just the same as it was seven years ago. It is lively, but not deep; there is little variety; there is no compass of thought. Reading only can supply this. You can never be a deep preacher without it, any more than a thorough Christian." Wesley exemplified his theory by his practice, spending much time reading while in the saddle riding from place to place on horseback meeting his many appointments.

Accumulate a Library

Closely related to the preacher's study habits is the need to *accumulate a well-chosen library*. Since most ministers have to watch their finances quite closely, the minister will need to adopt some regular plan for the building of his library and should seek primarily to secure source books. The subject of the pastor and his library is more fully developed in the next chapter.

Care in the matters discussed in the foregoing paragraphs will contribute toward a stronger, more effective ministry. Some giants will arise to grace our pulpits and bless the church.

RECOMMENDED READING

DYKES, J. OSWALD. *The Christian Minister and His Duties.* Edinburgh: T. & T. Clark, 1909. Chap. 5.

HOGUE, WILSON T. *A Handbook of Homiletics and Pastoral Theology.* Winona Lake, Ind.; Free Methodist Publishing House, 1946. Part II, chaps. 5-6.

²James M. Hoppin, *Pastoral Theology* (New York and London: Funk & Wagnalls Company, 1901), p. 153.

HOPPIN, JAMES M. *Pastoral Theology*. New York and London: Funk &
Wagnalls Co., 1901. Pp. 150-157.

JOHNSON, HERRICK. *The Ideal Ministry*. New York: Fleming H. Revell
Co., 1908. Part II, chap. 11.

JOWETT, J. H. *The Preacher: His Life and Work*. Garden City, N. Y.:
Doubleday, Doran & Co., Inc., 1929. Chap. 4.

LEE, MARK W. *The Minister and His Ministry*. Grand Rapids, Mich.:
Zondervan Publishing House, 1960.

MOYER, ELGIN S. *The Pastor and His Library*. Chicago: Moody Press,
1953. Chaps. 1-4.

MURPHY, THOMAS. *Pastoral Theology*. Philadelphia: Presbyterian Board
of Publication and Sabbath School Work, 1877. Chap. 3.

PLUMMER, WILLIAM S. *Hints and Helps in Pastoral Theology*. New York:
Harper and Brothers, Publishers, 1874. Chap. 8.

Chapter 3

HIS BOOKS

SOMEONE HAS SAID, "Show me the books that are your friends and I will tell you the kind of a person you are." There is a lot of truth to that. The kind of reading a person delights in is a faithful reflection of the kind of person he is. If he is surrounded with books and magazines on nature and outdoor life, you will be safe in concluding that he is a lover of the great out-of-doors. If you see in a home books and magazines on sports, the theater, and the movie world, you will be safe in judging that the occupants' interests are in the area of entertainment. On the other hand, if you see in a home books and magazines on the Christian life and the church, you can be pretty sure that the folk who live there are spiritually-minded people.

The same principle pertains to the minister. Look at the books in his library, and you can very nearly tell what kind of a preacher he is. If the majority of his books are from the pens of liberal theologians, you will probably be right in judging that he is either not theologically conservative or is theologically somewhat unstable. If most of his books are by authors known for their orthodoxy, you can be reasonably confident that the minister is an evangelical. This sort of judgment can be carried to further lengths. For instance, if the majority of the minister's books are on the subject of prophecy or on the subject of missions, you will be safe in concluding that the owner is enthusiastic about one or the other of these subjects. All of this indicates that books go a long way in showing the bent of a man's ministry and the influence they exert in his ministry.

The importance of a minister's library can scarcely be overemphasized. Books are about the most important tools of his calling, provided he knows how to use them. Without them he is helpless to go very far in a constructive ministry. W. B. Riley says, "Better go without butter on your bread than without books." Elgin S.

---

[1]W. B. Riley, *Pastoral Problems* (New York: Fleming H. Revell Company, 1936), p. 40.

Moyer, in his splendid volume, *The Pastor and His Library,* has the following to say regarding the importance of the minister's library: "A well-selected library is a storehouse of wealth for the active, growing pastor. It is a *sine qua non* for him if he is to maintain his intellectual keenness, his mental alertness, and his spiritual acumen. It will help him to keep abreast of the world's changing events. It will keep him in touch with the best thinking of his brother pastors and theologians. It will provide him with some of the best devotional literature of the past and of the present. It will clarify and purify his spiritual vision and will inspire him to greater and holier activity, and keep him in touch with the highest spiritual developments of the Christian world. It will acquaint him with the best thinking of the greatest scholars, and will challenge him to keep his eyes fixed constantly on the higher levels of devotional living and of spiritual service. It will stimulate his thinking, develop his spirituality, and keep him growing."[2]

Good books thus *contribute to an enriched ministry.* The poverty of some pastoral ministries can be easily explained by a look at the minister's library—a scanty number of books, and these poorly chosen in some cases. Lack of proper tools will do much to hinder development in a pastor's ministry. The Holy Spirit has worked through the lives of other men, and pastors ought to avail themselves of their writings, their ideas and messages. Immense spiritual profit will readily result. A good library will tend to keep a man's ministry from becoming stereotyped, monotonous, and stale. It will supply him with fresh ideas and stimuli.

Carefully selected books *will provide the minister with material for the varied types of ministry that are his to perform.* If it is commentaries he needs in his sermon preparation, he will have them. If it is material on missions that he desires, he will have that. If something on the history of the church is needed, he will have that. If help on the administration of the Sunday school is necessary, he will have pertinent material, and so on with respect to the various aspects of his work. If his library does not meet all these demands, he should not be satisfied until it does. For him the right kind of books are as indispensable as tools for the carpenter. They should be his constant companions.

Good books *enable the minister to multiply his ministry.* Many

[2]Elgin S. Moyer, *The Pastor and His Library* (Chicago: Moody Press, 1953), p. 12.

in his parish do not have access to such literature, but at times have need of it. The minister should be glad to loan his books to those who can profitably use them. The pastor should form the habit of keeping a record of the books he loans and to whom; otherwise he will surely lose some valuable volumes, as the author can testify. Or, there may be volumes which he does not need for constant reference in his personal library which he may want to loan to the church library so that they may be available for people of the church to read. In this way he will not have the personal responsibility of seeing that these books are returned to him. The regular procedure of the church library will be the means of checking on the return of his books. When he leaves his charge, his donated books may be reclaimed by him, if he desires.

Proper Selection

Of the writing of books there is no end. Fifteen thousand new books came off the presses in the United States in 1961. The minister cannot even possess a large percentage of those published in the Christian area alone. He therefore must be very selective in the acquiring of books if he is to build up a good library. Many books that come off the press are not worth space on the minister's shelves. They may not be bad books, but they do not have lasting value and the minister does not want to clutter his shelves with books which will not contribute to a fruitful ministry. He will need to discriminate between the wheat and the chaff.

Several suggestions are in point in this connection:

1. Care should be exercised to put on the minister's library shelves source books, that is, the kind that are worth referring to again and again. Some books are worth reading once, but will not be useful after that. They do not possess abiding value. The minister who influenced the writer the most in his younger days and who built up one of the largest libraries in his denomination confessed that he had too many books in his library. He said if he were beginning to build a library again, there were a lot of books he would not buy. They just took up room on his shelves and had been used but once. He stressed the importance of being more selective in the purchase of books. Most ministers do not have money to spend unwisely, and here is one place where they can conserve their funds.

2. The minister should make it his business to know what are

the best books in the various fields of his ministry. For instance, in connection with almost every good book that the minister purchases, there will be found a bibliography of comparable material. These books will have the recommendation of the author of that book. Professors in classrooms of colleges, Bible institutes, and theological seminaries give helpful bibliographies to their students from time to time in the course of their teaching. Experts on theological books, like Wilbur M. Smith, of Fuller Theological Seminary, give book lists occasionally in periodicals and books. Dr. Smith has published an excellent bibliography in his book, *Profitable Bible Study*. Bible lecturers often give the names of books of great value in connection with their series of lectures. Christian magazines from time to time present good lists of available literature. The wide-awake minister will continually be brought face to face with notices of new and old books which are available at publishing houses and bookstores. He should also make it a habit to read the book reviews which appear in such evangelical magazines as *Bibliotheca Sacra, Moody Monthly, The King's Business, Grace Journal, Christianity Today, Concordia Monthly*, and *Eternity*. *Bibliotheca Sacra* also has a review section on important articles in periodicals.

Then, too, the minister ought to see that his name is placed on the mailing list of several of the leading Christian book houses. From time to time they send out lists of available books, new and old. In this way he often may be able to procure an out-of-print book for which he has been looking a long time. And, of course, these lists call attention to the new books which are coming off the press.

3. The minister should also pay particular attention to the authors whose names bear weight in quotation, men who have been tested as to their scholarship, writing ability, and orthodoxy. He is not making the best use of his time if he spends it reading authors who are inferior and have not stood the test of time or experience when there are so many who are recognized as men of stature in the field of evangelical Christian literature. Such names as J. A. Alexander, David Baron, C. J. Ellicott, E. W. Hengstenberg, J. P. Lange, J. B. Lightfoot, F. B. Meyer, G. Campbell Morgan, H. C. G. Moule, Alfred Plummer, A. T. Robertson, Philip Schaff, James Stalker, A. H. Strong, W. H. Griffith Thomas, B. B. Warfield, B. F. Westcott, Thomas Whitelaw, and many others are recognized in evangelical circles as men who

have made distinct contributions to the literature of the Christian Church. To draw from such men is bound to enrich the ministry of any preacher, and when quotations are made from them they will carry some weight, at least among the informed. It will pay every minister to become acquainted with the best authors in the various fields of Christian endeavor. Elgin S. Moyer has performed a distinct service for ministers by reproducing in his book, *The Pastor and His Library,* the out-of-print list compiled by Wilbur M. Smith containing one hundred twenty-four authors which the latter recommended as being the best. This list originally appeared as a pamphlet of twelve pages under the title *Authors I Recommend.* This was an expansion of a list that appeared by the same author in the *Moody Student,* November 14, 1941, as an article entitled "Dr. Wilbur M. Smith Names Ninety-Seven Best Authors."

The Cost of Books

Books do cost money. But most things of a material nature which are worthwhile cost something. The fact of cost should not cause a minister to refrain from enlarging his library. He had better sacrifice some other things rather than impoverish his ministry and his own soul by failing to gather about himself a library of good books.

The cost of books is by no means prohibitive. And some of the best books may at times be obtained by a small expenditure of money. Some priceless gems may be picked up in secondhand bookstores at times. However, the better secondhand stores know their books pretty well and price them accordingly. In order to find these gems, not only must the minister do some searching but he must also know the best authors and the best titles. This knowledge is acquired through reading and study, as has been previously indicated. Then there are occasions when the libraries of elderly or deceased ministers are disposed of at very low prices. The writer knows of one occasion of this kind when a student picked up the three volumes of Peter's *Theocratic Kingdom* for twenty-five cents per copy. This valuable work was then out of print and hard to find. The writer once procured some books for which he had been looking a long time at forty cents a copy. He gladly would have paid ten times that amount for them. It is also true that some colleges carry a duplicate library of books which they are willing to sell. Through this means one of the author's students was able to obtain a complete set of Lange's commentary for ten cents a volume.

Every minister, especially a younger one, ought to have some plan whereby he steadily builds up his library. Many plans have been used. Whichever plan the minister adopts, he ought to seek the co-operation of his wife because the pastoral income is as much hers as his. Some of the plans which have been used are as follows:

1. There is the budget plan, by which a certain amount is al-located each month out of the pastoral income for books. This is a splendid plan and will yield satisfying results if adhered to faith-fully.

2. There is the book-a-month plan, which is quite similar to the plan just mentioned, although the monthly cost may vary consider-ably, depending upon the type of book acquired. To the ambitious minister this may seem like a very slow method. But he should re-member that it is not the number of books a man has that makes a good library but their character. Some incomes will not permit the purchase of many books a month. Some libraries of a hundred books are far more valuable and useful than other libraries that contain thousands of books. It may be that the minister's salary will not allow the addition of more than a book a month. But if he chooses wisely, he will witness a growing storehouse of invaluable treasure.

3. Some ministers have adopted the plan of using fees, such as wedding fees, for books. Of course it is traditional that wedding fees go to the pastor's wife for new hats! However, if the pastor can come to some happy agreement with his wife on this matter the plan may work out very well. Some pastors receive a considerable amount of money in the way of fees and gifts, but many receive very little in this way. If such pastors depended on this method to increase their libraries, they would experience a very slow growth indeed.

4. Another plan is to use a portion of the offerings the minister may receive from preaching in evangelistic meetings, Bible confer-ences and the like for buying books. In some churches the minister is allowed a specified length of time off from his pastoral duties, with pay, for the purpose of holding outside meetings. In such cases, he may find himself in possession of quite a sum of extra money. If this, or half of it, were used for the purchase of needed books, the minister could add to his library without strain on the family budget.

5. Some ministers receive payment for writing for magazines and for writing material for Sunday school quarterlies. Such income may be used to purchase books which help the owner in his writing and aid in building the minister's library.

Other methods, such as belonging to an evangelical book club, are used in order to increase the minister's library. Some methods are more productive of results than others, but it is supremely important that the minister have some plan. He owes it to himself and to his calling to pay strict attention to this matter. His library will prove to be a distinct aid to development and will help to keep him continually fresh as a minister of the Gospel.

A Balanced Library

[As the minister builds his library, he ought to give some care to the matter of balance. He should not allow his selection of books to become lopsided. He needs books of various kinds if he is to perform a well-rounded ministry.] For instance, books on prophecy are good, and the minister ought to have some, but he needs other books besides these. Books on missions are good, but not all of his books should be on this important subject. Nor should the minister be too exclusive in his choice of authors. A variety of good authors will likely add variety to a man's ministry. Then there are some libraries that are overbalanced with books of sermons. A reasonable number of books of sermons by master pulpiteers is good, but the minister will not want to rely on other men's sermons too much lest he curtail his own creative ability and become parrot-like in his preaching. He will miss the great joy of preaching if he fails to mine the Scriptures for himself.

In gathering books for his library, the minister should provide himself with the necessary reference books such as lexicons, dictionaries, encyclopedias and concordances. These are a must if he is to develop a constructive ministry. He will need to give attention to choosing the very best in the way of commentaries. He will need some general commentaries, like Ellicott's, covering the whole Bible. Then, as he preaches from particular books in the Scriptures, he should add the best available commentaries on these particular books of the Old and New Testaments. For instance, if he is preaching from John's Gospel, he will do well to provide himself with F. Godet's great work on that book. If he is preaching from the Book of

Acts, G. Campbell Morgan's monumental work on that book will be helpful. Or, if it is from an Old Testament book that he is preaching, such as the book of Leviticus, he could do no better than to procure Andrew Bonar's classic on that book. Little by little the minister will be building up a workable selection of commentaries that will become an increasing joy to him as the days pass.

Then he must be sure that he has some works on theology or doctrine, like A. H. Strong's *Systematic Theology* or William Evans' *Great Doctrines of the Bible*. He never knows when he will need to consult such works for helps on doctrinal matters even when he is engaged in the preparation of an expositional message. Then when dealing with such doctrines as justification by faith, the inspiration of the Scriptures, and the deity of Christ the average preacher will need the help of Biblical scholars who have dealt thoroughly with these subjects in their commentaries. The minister will impoverish himself and his people if he fails to avail himself of the contributions of the great men of God who have written down what God has given to them through careful study.

The minister should have in his library some good volumes on the subject of church history such as Philip Schaff's incomparable eight-volume work on the *History of the Christian Church*. If at the beginning he is unable to procure this classic, perhaps A. H. Newman's *A Manual of Church History* in two volumes will suffice for the time being or even a one-volume work such as B. K. Kuiper's *The Church in History* or Lars Qualben's *A History of the Church*. It is inconceivable that a minister in the church should be uninterested in the history of the institution with which he is so definitely affiliated. Time and again he will have occasion to refer in his sermons to the events of the past which he will find recorded in such works as we have cited. And without a knowledge of church history he will be ignorant of the present situation in Christendom.

He will also need to have available material on the subject of missions. Books on this subject are innumerable and are coming off the press in an unending stream as the work of missions is being carried forward in the various fields of the world. He can do no more than select a few choice volumes here and there, such as Thiessen's *A Survey of World Missions* which, as the title suggests, is a survey of missionary endeavor in the various fields of the world. Then some stirring missionary biographies, such as the lives of

William Carey and Henry Martyn by F. Deaville Walker and Constance Padwick in the Tyndale series of great biographies will prove stimulating and will be good books to loan to young people or mission groups in the church who need such material.

In these days when the science of Biblical archaeology is coming more and more into prominence, the minister should avail himself of at least one good general work on this subject such as Merrill F. Unger's *Archaeology and the Old Testament.* From time to time he will find in it material which will brighten his messages and make them more understandable and meaningful.

Then the minister will have need for some material on the non-Christian cults which are abroad today. One general work of this kind is Van Baalen's *The Chaos of Cults,* which every minister should possess. In addition to a volume such as this the minister may want to obtain other materials on particular cults with which his congregation may be faced from time to time. Dr. W. E. Biederwolf has written a number of very fine booklets on such false cults as Christian Science, Mormonism, Seventh-Day Adventism and Spiritism.

The subject of prophecy ought not be neglected as the minister seeks to build up his library. He may want to begin with a simple work such as W. E. Blackstone's *Jesus Is Coming,* which has long been considered a classic by students of prophecy. Then he will doubtless want to add other volumes on particular phases of prophetic study. Wilbur Smith some years ago published a booklet entitled *Fifty-five Best Books on Prophecy,* which will be useful to those who have a special interest in this subject.

These are just a few suggestions by way of explaining the meaning of a balanced library, one which will serve the minister in the various aspects of his ministry. If he has such a library, he will always have material available when it is needed, whether for sermons, Bible classes, missionary talks, young people's talks, devotional meditations, radio or television presentations, or whatever the need might be.

Opinions differ as to how much time the pastor should devote to reading newspapers and periodicals, but surely he will want to be well informed about current events and want to know what his people are reading. Andrew Blackwood tells of one pastor who made it a rule never to sit down while going through the morning newspaper and another who didn't pick up the morning paper until he went home for lunch. In addition to his denominational publications, the minister will want to subscribe to a number of periodicals, such as *Christianity Today* for general reading in the Christian field, and *Bibliotheca Sacra* for reading in the field of theology. Magazines valuable for their sections on current events of interest include *Parents' Magazine, Saturday Review of Literature, Time* or *Newsweek*.

Classification of Books

Every minister should have a plan of classifying his books if they are to be of the most service to him. Otherwise the time will inevitably come when he will not be able to find the material he needs. The minister should never allow his study to become a place of confusion. Usually the condition of his study will be a reflection of the character of his total ministry. If the minister is careless there, it will be discovered that he is careless in other phases of his ministry. What then is true regarding the orderliness of his study should also be true of his library, which is a vital part of his study. The writer once visited the study of a man of his denomination who had an earned doctor's degree and was pastor of a large church. The writer was amazed at the confusion in this man's study. His desk was a hodgepodge of confusion. Papers, books, letters, and magazines cluttered the top of his desk; apparently it would be difficult to find anything. This pastor did not remain long in his church. Furthermore, it was not long until he was out of the pastorate, doing janitor work in a public school, even though he had a doctor's degree. The general character of his ministry was pictured in his study and library.

The pastor will need to give some attention to the matter of organizing his library. Books will not arrange themselves. And the larger his library becomes, the more confusion there will be and the less efficient it will become unless there is a definite plan of classification. The time to begin this sort of thing is when the library is small. As it grows, real pleasure will be derived from its orderly arrangement and consequent usefulness.

It is not the writer's purpose to present a definite plan that ought to be followed. There are a number of plans which vary in value according to the size of the library and the desires of the owner. The minister should choose the plan that seems most practical to him and work it faithfully through the years. Doubtless the minister will find most useful a plan that arranges books by subjects. Among such systems in common usage today are the Dewey Decimal Classification system, the Library of Congress system, the system developed by Columbia University, and the system used by the Newberry Library in Chicago. Another rather complicated system is the Memory-O-Matic System.

It is the author's opinion that the Dewey Decimal Classification is the most practical for the minister. It was first worked out in 1873 when Melvil Dewey was a student at Amherst College. If interested in studying this system, the minister should get Dewey's book, *Abridged Decimal Classification and Relative Index,* Forest Press, Inc., Lake Placid Club, Essex County, New York. Elgin S. Moyer discusses this system as it pertains to the minister in a very adequate manner in his book, *The Pastor and His Library.* A minister who plans to begin using this system ought to read Moyer's book.

Not being acquainted with any of the above-mentioned methods of classification in his beginning days, the author developed a plan of his own in which he arranged his books according to subjects. He developed a plan by which his library was arranged under twelve subjects, namely, general reference; commentaries; history; missions; archaeology; practical theology, including sermons, theology, and doctrine; books about the Bible; prophecy; non-Christian religions and cults; pamphlets and miscellaneous material. This plan has had its weaknesses but the writer is usually able to find the book he wants unless he has loaned it to some student!

Some Basic Books for a Pastor's Library

It will be helpful for the minister to possess a book list or two compiled by experts in the field of evangelical literature. For example, Dr. Wilbur M. Smith some years ago published a series of articles in the *Moody Monthly* magazine under the title, "The First One Hundred Books for the Bible Student's Library". Later these articles were made part of a book entitled *Profitable Bible Study,* mentioned earlier. The list Dr. Smith presented received wide attention because of its careful selection and because he is known to be a competent student of books. He himself possesses one of the largest private libraries of Christian literature in America. Many ministers have received guidance from this list.

To give a long or detailed bibliography which a minister or prospective minister may follow is beyond the scope and limits of the size of this work. It should be useful, however, to note one or two basic books in each of some twenty divisions of a pastor's library. The works noted here are written from the conservative viewpoint almost exclusively.

Bibles. At the core of any pastor's library is his Bible. No doubt he will possess several versions. But, however numerous, they will serve two basic functions of enabling him to engage in the extensive and intensive study of the Word. For his intensive study he may wish to choose one of these old favorites: the *Dickson Analytical Bible, Nave's Study Bible, The Thompson Chain Reference Bible,* or *The Scofield Reference Bible.* He will probably also wish to have a wide-margin Bible in which to make notes as he pursues his studies. The *Oxford Wide Margin Bible* is very useful for such purposes. A Bible without notes or numerous divisions or outline in the text should be used for extensive study—the reading of many chapters at a sitting. Probably an American Standard Version (which is broken up into paragraphs like modern literature) with fairly large print will prove most satisfactory for this type of study.

Concordances. Next to his Bible a pastor will find an unabridged concordance of greatest value in his study. James Strong, Robert Young, and Alexander Cruden have all prepared concordances on the King James Version. M. C. Hazard has prepared one on the American Standard Version.

Bible Dictionaries and Atlases. No pastor's library should be without the *International Standard Bible Encyclopaedia* (5 vols.; now being revised). As to newer one-volume dictionaries, one may select *Unger's Bible Dictionary,* the *New Bible Dictionary,* or the *Pictorial Bible Dictionary. Baker's Bible Atlas* or Nelson B. Keyes' *Story of the Bible World* will provide a geographical orientation for Biblical study.

Bible Study. Help on how to study the Bible can be obtained from an increasing number of books. Among the more useful are Irving Jensen, *Independent Bible Study;* Lloyd Perry and Walden Howard, *How to Study the Bible;* Wilbur M. Smith, *Profitable Bible Study;* and Howard F. Vos, *Effective Bible Study.*

Bible Survey and Introduction. At the top of a list of Old Testament surveys should be Samuel J. Schultz' *The Old Testament*

Speaks. Merrill C. Tenney's *New Testament Survey* is outstanding in that field. Two Old Testament introductions (discussing such questions as canon, text, authorship, date, etc.) which have become widely accepted are Merrill F. Unger's *Introductory Guide to the Old Testament* and Edward J. Young's *An Introduction to the Old Testament.* Gleason Archer's new *Survey of Old Testament Introduction* is a monumental work in the field. Henry C. Thiessen's widely used *Introduction to the New Testament* will probably be replaced by Everett F. Harrison's *Introduction to the New Testament,* to be published shortly.

Commentaries. One hardly knows where to start or stop in noting books in the commentary field. Two of the most widely used older sets are the Lange series and the Jamieson, Faussett, and Brown commentary. The *New International Commentary* and the Tyndale series are finding wide acceptance today. Newer one-volume commentaries are the *New Bible Commentary* and the *Wycliffe Bible Commentary.* A poll of ministers reported in *Moody Monthly,* November, 1955, indicating that Matthew Henry's six-volume *Commentary on the Bible* was most widely used by those reporting.

Theology. A basic reference work in this area is *Baker's Dictionary of Theology.* A good survey of the divergent theological positions now current is William E. Hordern's *Layman's Guide to Protestant Theology.* Then it would probably be well to have one-volume works representing each of the three basic eschatological viewpoints. Louis Berkhof's *Systematic Theology* takes the amillennial position, A. H. Strong's *Sytematic Theology* the postmillennial position, and Henry C. Thiessen's *Systematic Theology* the premillennial position. An excellent simple treatment of Bible doctrines which the pastor may effectively use in working with laymen is *A Handbook of Christian Truth* by Harold Lindsell and Charles Woodbridge.

The Devotional Life. As is true with so many other categories of Biblical study, books in this division are legion. Among the favorite devotional authors are Andrew Murray, Alexander Maclaren, F. B. Meyer, C. H. Spurgeon, and V. R. Edman. Specific titles which rank high on polls taken among religious leaders include E. M. Bounds, *Power through Prayer* and *The Preacher and Prayer;* John Bunyan, *Pilgrim's Progress;* Andrew Murray, *The Prayer Life;* Andrew Bonar, *Memoirs of McCheyne;* F. W. Krummacher, *The Suffering Saviour;* and Marcus Rainsford, *Our Lord Prays for His Own.*

Missions and Evangelism. A good general survey of foreign mission fields is J. C. Thiessen's *A Survey of World Missions.* A survey of home missions may be found in Peter Gunther (ed.), *The Fields at Home.* An important book on preparation for missionary service is Harold Cook's *Missionary Life and Work.* David Adeney's *The Unchanging Commission* presents the challenge of missions. Howard F. Vos has edited a comprehensive work on world religions entitled *Religions in a Changing World.* J. K. Van Baalen's *Chaos of the Cults* deals with most of the major cults. J. E. Conant's *Every-Member Evangelism* discusses the evangelistic responsibility of the church. Numerous suggestions for the personal worker are provided by Robert H. Belton and J. C. Macaulay in *Personal Evangelism,* by R. A. Torrey in *How to Bring Men to Christ,* and by G. S. Dobbins in *Winning the Children.*

Christian Education. With the rapid development of the field of Christian education it becomes increasingly difficult to select a small number of basic works. A few of those which a pastor might consider are Wildon Crossland, *Better Leaders for Your Church;* Price Gwynn, *Leadership Education in the Local Church;* Gerrit Verkuyl and Harold Garner, *Enriching Teen-Age Worship;* Carol Carlson, *Young People's Program Handbook;* Nels Anderson, *Make Sunday School Interesting;* Findley B. Edge, *Teaching for Results;* James Murch, *The Sunday School Handbook;* LaVose A. Wallin, *Keys for the Sunday School Teacher;* Harold H. Ettling, *Sunday School Administration;* Ken Anderson and Morry Carlson, *Games for All Occasions;* E. O. Harbin, *The Fun Encyclopedia* and *The Recreational Leader;* Marion Jacobsen, *Good Times for God's People;* and C. B. Eavey, *History of Christian Education.*

Music. Among the more useful books on hymnology are A. E. Bailey's *The Gospel in Hymns,* E. E. Ryden's *The Story of Christian Hymnody,* and Ivan Hagedorn's *Stories of Great Hymn Writers.* Five books on the place of music in the total church program include E. L. Thomas, *Music in Christian Education;* H. G. Tovey, *Music Levels in Christian Education;* J. N. Ashton, *Music in Worship;* Carl Halter, *The Practice of Sacred Music;* and Phil Kerr, *Music in Evangelism.*

Church History. A good survey of the whole field of church history is Earle E. Cairns' *Christianity Through the Centuries.* Biographical information on individuals who have influenced the history of the church may be found in Elgin S. Moyer's *Who Was Who in Church History.* F. F. Bruce is editing a several-volume set on church history for Wm. B. Eerdmans Publishing Company under the title *The Advance of Christianity Through the Centuries.* The classic work on church history is Philip Schaff, *History of the Christian Church* (8 vols.).

Bible Archaeology. A book which relates archaeological discoveries effectively to the Biblical context is Joseph P. Free, *Archaeology and Bible History.* Merrill F. Unger has produced two volumes covering the whole field of Bible archaeology: *Archeology and the Old Testament* and *Archaeology and the New Testament.* J. A. Thompson's new *The Bible and Archaeology* is a useful survey. Jack Finegan, *Light from the Ancient Past,* integrates archaeological discoveries with the secular historical background.

Apologetics. An important text in the field of apologetics is Cornelius Van Til's *The Defense of the Faith.* Another text taking a different approach is Edward J. Carnell's *An Introduction to Christian Apologetics.* Merrill C. Tenney has edited a work that has gained significant attention in the area: *Word for This Century.* A useful new handbook, a symposium by eight Christian authorities, is *Can I Trust My Bible?,* published by Moody Press.

Biblical Languages. The student will learn about basic aids for the study of Greek and Hebrew in his language classes, but four books will prove to be especially useful in his continuing study: *Hebrew and English Lexicon of the Old Testament* by F. Brown, S. R. Driver and Charles Briggs; *Greek-English Lexicon of the New Testament,* edited by W. F. Arndt and F. W. Gingrich; *Synonyms of the Old Testament,* by R. B. Girdlestone; and *Synonyms of the New Testament,* by R. C. Trench.

Others. Numerous books on pastoral theology, homiletics, pastoral counseling, etc. appear in the bibliographies at the end of the chapters of this book. A standard work on Bible character study is Alexander Whyte's *Bible Characters* (6 vol., 2 vol., and 1 vol. eds.).

RECOMMENDED READING

ALLEN, CLARA B. "Expansion of Dewey 200," *Fuller Library Bulletin,* Numbers 7 and 8, July-December, 1950 (Pasadena, Calif.: Fuller Theological Seminary).

BISHOP, WILLIAM WARREN. *Practical Handbook of Library Cataloging.* Baltimore: Williams and Wilkins Co., ca. 1927.

COLTON, C. E. *The Minister's Mission.* Rev. ed. Grand Rapids, Mich.: Zondervan Publishing House, 1961. Chap. 18.

DEWEY, MELVIL. *Decimal Classification and Relative Index.* Lake Placid Club, Essex County, New York: Forest Press, Inc., revised in 1952.

———. *Abridged Decimal Classification and Relative Index.* 6th ed. Lake Placid Club, Essex County, New York: Forest Press, Inc., 1945.

DOUGLAS, CLARA and LEHDE, CONSTANCE. *Book Repairing—New Ideas from the Bindery.* Seattle, Washington: University of Washington, 1940.

ELLIOTT, LESLIE ROBINSON. *The Efficiency Filing System.* Nashville: Broadman Press, ca. 1951. (Rev. ed., 1959.)

MILLER, ZANA. *How to Organize a Library.* 10th ed. revised. Buffalo, N. Y.: Library Bureau, Remington Rand, Inc., 1941.

MOYER, ELGIN S. *The Pastor and His Library.* Chicago: Moody Press, 1953.

SMITH, WILBUR M. *Profitable Bible Study.* Revised ed. Boston: W. A. Wilde Co., 1951.

WARDELL, DON. *Filing and Indexing.* London, Ontario: Published by the author, 1947.

Chapter 4

HIS ETHICAL CONDUCT

ACCORDING TO THE DICTIONARY, ethics is the science of moral duty or of ideal human character. It has to do with proper practice or conduct. Ministerial ethics, then, concerns the conduct of the minister in his various relationships. It is usually taken for granted that every minister of the Gospel is a gentleman. Some, however, act more gentlemanly than others. Some give expression more fully than others to the graces which should be manifested in the life of every minister. There are some common courtesies and practices that all ministers should seek to observe. It is the purpose of this chapter to present some examples in this realm and seek to substantiate each of them.

The minister has ethical responsibilities in a number of relationships. Four of them are discussed in the paragraphs which follow: in relation to his fellow ministers, in relation to his own congregation, in relation to society, and in relation to his denominational group.

In Relation to Fellow Ministers

For the minister's own welfare and happiness, for the honor of the ministry, and for the sake of his influence, the minister needs to exercise care in his treatment of other ministers. The following matters are of importance in this regard:

1. The minister should give an interested hearing to the preaching of other ministers. Ministers are members of a fellowship, fellow servants of one Lord, engaged in the same service, and subject to the same needs. Therefore some consideration is due other ministers when they come to preach. A visiting preacher may be a bit dry and uninteresting, but the same may be true of the home pastor. Some preachers seem interested in a service only if they are doing the preaching. Here would be a good place to practice the Golden

Rule.] The author has at times been amazed to see ministers at conferences standing out under the trees visiting in sight of a brother minister who was inside the auditorium pouring out his heart in a message upon which he may have spent weeks or months of preparation. If such visiting is necessary, it should at least be done out of sight of the preacher.

Evident lack of interest in the message of a visiting minister shows disrespect and is unworthy of the man of God. By it the minister tends to create ill feeling, and he impoverishes his own soul. One of the ways in which the minister can be a good example to laymen is to give full attention when other ministers are preaching.

2. The minister should form the habit of answering mail from brother ministers promptly. This policy should be extended to include all mail insofar as it is possible. But it is especially important in relation to fellow ministers. Usually when a minister takes time to write a letter to another minister, what he is writing about is important—at least to the writer. His letter should be answered as soon as possible. Some ministers are notoriously poor correspondents. This failure is soon noised about, and the dilatory minister loses stature in the eyes of his brethren.

Failure to answer mail promptly is a careless practice. It takes no longer to respond promptly than to wait until later. It usually takes longer to answer later, because by waiting the minister has to apologize—or should—for not writing sooner, in addition to having to refresh his memory as to the content of the letter. Let the minister learn the lesson of promptness in caring for his mail. Usually the minister who fails at this point will be found to be dilatory in many other aspects of his work.

3. Let the minister follow the habit of returning borrowed books promptly. Ministers are interested in books. Most of them are not able to purchase as many as they would like. Often, therefore, they may want to borrow from brother ministers books they cannot afford to buy or which are out of print. The minister who borrows ought not take undue advantage of his privilege and keep the borrowed possessions beyond a reasonable length of time, especially if the borrowed material may likely be needed by its owner. Why not put a note on your calendar under the date when you think you may be finished with the borrowed book? This will serve as a good reminder. It is easy for borrowed books to become mixed with one's own books,

and the fact is not discovered until entirely too much time has elapsed. The author is still waiting for the return of one book borrowed by a prominent evangelist over twenty years ago. He has been told that this same individual has borrowed books from others without returning them and is also guilty of being slow in caring for his financial obligations. The borrowing habit needs to be carefully watched. Failure in this regard will hinder a man's ministry.

4. When a minister leaves a pastorate he should be careful not to meddle in the affairs of his successor. Upon leaving a pastorate, the parish should be left in the care of the succeeding pastor. It is very unwise for the former pastor to write letters to the members of the church he has left, expressing his thoughts as to how things should be run in the church. Certainly it is not good taste to discredit a pastor's work among his own members, thus creating dissatisfaction among the membership. In the medical profession, it is difficult to get doctors to criticize fellow doctors, even though they may live in different towns or cities. This is true even when there seems to be some justification for criticism. Such criticism is considered unethical. Surely Christian ministers should maintain a high standard in this regard.

Yet there have been glaring instances of violation of this ministerial ethic. One young minister told the author about the extreme difficulty he was having in his first pastorate because the former pastor, a much older man, kept writing to members of the congregation expressing his ideas as to how things ought to be run in the church. These ideas were somewhat at variance with the way the new pastor thought the work should be carried on. Both men were thoroughly evangelical. The differences were not of a fundamental character. The older man was clearly at fault in fomenting trouble.

If a pastor wishes to write to a member of a former pastorate, a good rule to follow is to write nothing he would not be willing to have the present pastor read. Perhaps he should send the latter a carbon copy of the letter. The busy pastor will have all he can do to attend to the affairs of his new charge without attempting to guide the destiny of the church which he recently left. However, get-well cards, birthday greetings, Christmas cards, cards of congratulation, and the like are always in order any place and from anyone.

5. When a pastor returns to a former pastorate, it is a matter of courtesy and due consideration for him to call on the present pastor

first before calling among the membership. Such consideration will do away with any suspicion. It will make the present pastor feel better.]

Friendships of an abiding character are often formed when a pastor is on a field for a long period of time. There is no reason why he should not call on such persons if he happens to be in the vicinity. But certainly he owes it to the pastor now on the field to inform him that he is in the community. It will be far better for the new pastor to learn of such a visit from the former pastor himself than from some of his members. This practice, which is considerate and right, will foster a happy relationship.

6. [Every pastor should make it a strict policy to refrain from speaking disparagingly of his predecessor.] Failure at this point is bound to react unfavorably on the present pastor sooner or later. No matter how adverse his opinion of the former pastor, the latter in all probability has some friends in the congregation. Why incur their enmity at the start when no possible good can result from uncomplimentary remarks? [Individuals in the office of pastor may fail at times, but the office is one of honor, and to disparage the person of one who holds it or who has held it is likely to dishonor the office.] Failure here gives evidence of lack of the fruit of the Spirit (Gal. 5:22). Criticism can easily degenerate into the evil of gossip from which the minister, of all persons, should be separate.

7. When a pastor is called back to a former field for either a funeral or a wedding, he should insist that the present pastor be invited to participate in the service. Of course, if the present pastor is ill or called out of town, this would not be possible.

In most cases the minister probably would prefer that the present pastor care for these responsibilities. But there are always some people who get very much attached to a certain man for sentimental reasons. If such folk do call for the former pastor to come back to minister on a particular occasion, he should by all means consult the present pastor and insist that, if possible, he have a part in the service. The former pastor should do all within his power to relieve any embarrassment and to show that he is seeking the present pastor's best interests.

8. When the pastor is away from his church and someone else is called in to preach for him, the pastor should make sure that the substitute is properly remunerated for his services. Some churches

are careless in such matters. Neither do they always understand what is proper. Churches vary in their policy of payment for a pulpit supply. In some cases it is the church's responsibility to care for the remuneration of the supply. In others, it is the pastor's responsibility. Whichever way it is, the visiting minister should be properly paid for his services. Though it may be the church's responsibility to care for this situation, the pastor should be sure that the matter is not neglected. And if it is the pastor's responsibility, he should care for it promptly.

9. When out of courtesy a visiting minister is called upon to preach for the pastor who is present, there is no financial responsibility. For example, a minister might be on his vacation and stop to worship in a sister church. If the pastor asks him to preach, he need not be paid. In a sense this opportunity may be a real favor to the visiting minister, inasmuch as it will enable him to become acquainted with a new congregation and it with him. Of course, the host pastor should be willing to return the ministry if asked to do so.

10. When visiting ministers come to a church, the pastor should not always feel obligated to ask them to preach. So doing might interfere with the program which has been announced. Some folk may be present expecting to hear a subject discussed which has been announced and it is not wise to disappoint them. Many churches constantly have visiting ministers in attendance. If the pastor always gave way to them, he would not be able to carry out a constructive program. A simple recognition of the visiting minister is sufficient, or the pastor may want to use the visiting brother in some way in the service, asking him to read the Scriptures or lead in prayer. There will be times, however, when the pastor will want to invite a visiting man to preach, especially if it is known in advance that he is coming. A minister should not come to the point where he thinks the people want to hear no one but himself.

11. The pastor should exercise constant vigilance lest jealousy mar his attitude. Ministers are human, and it is easy for them to covet the position or success of another. The grass often looks greener in another pastor's parish. Ministers often wonder why other men have bigger churches and larger salaries than they do or why others get places of leadership and they do not. Such wondering may easily develop into jealousy, which Shakespeare has spoken of as "a green-

eyed monster, which doth mock the meat it feeds on." [Jealousy is a vicious form of pride, and pride goes before a fall.]

With ministers in the background of his thinking, the Apostle Paul has a pertinent word to say regarding the proper attitude one should maintain toward others. In I Corinthians 4:6b-7 he exhorts "that no one of you be puffed up for one against another. For who maketh thee to differ from another? and what hast thou that thou didst not receive? now if thou didst receive it, why dost thou glory, as if thou hadst not received it?" This passage plainly teaches that every minister should be content with the position in which the Lord has placed him. God places some men in high places, others in low. Some He gives many talents, others a few. Each person will be rewarded according to the *faithfulness* he demonstrates in the place where the Lord has put him, whether that place is large or small. (See I Cor. 4:2.) This is one of the most important lessons ministers need to learn. Who among us has not at one time or another experienced the sinister working of the "green-eyed monster" in his heart? [Let us learn to rejoice with our fellow ministers in their successes and to accept the lowly place, if that be God's will for us.]

12. [The new pastor needs to beware of acting as though the congregation to which he has lately been called has never had any constructive training in the things of God before and that consequently he must begin at the foundation. He should be careful not to give the impression that the dark ages are now past and the reformation is beginning!]

The situation he faces may make him feel that way, but he will be wise to keep his feelings to himself. Those who have been his predecessors in the pastorate doubtless have some staunch friends in the congregation who will take offence at such an attitude. The failures of the past may be very evident, but to belittle the work of former pastors will only make the work of the present pastor more difficult and serve no good purpose. Let him proceed to do what needs to be done, and let the past be past, and everybody will be happier, including the pastor.

In Relation to the Congregation

In the pastor's relationship to his congregation there are some ethical standards that should be maintained. Among these are the following:

1. [He should be impartial in the treatment of his membership.] He should not show favoritism toward certain groups in the church. He is expected to be the pastor of the whole church, not just a part of it. He ought to be vitally interested in the young people, but not neglect the older people. He ought to be interested in the men of the church but he should also manifest some concern for the women's organizations. The author once knew a pastor who was exceedingly fond of children—to the extent that he geared the whole program of the church to the children, with the result that the older folk felt there was little in the services for them. There were a children's choir, children's sermons, children's programs, children's societies, children's outings, daily vacation Bible school, and so on. The program was entirely out of balance. The church tired of this type of program and the pastor had to leave. The pastor should seek to have a proper interest in every phase of the church life. Only in so doing can he be a good pastor, concerned for every member and organization of the flock.

2. He must make it a practice to keep inviolate confidences committed to him. He dare not deviate from this practice. There are some things which individuals feel led to share with him for purposes of counsel and prayer which he should not share with anyone, not even his wife. The laws of the land recognize the seriousness of such commitments. The minister cannot be compelled to tell secrets which have been told to him. [The minister needs to be tight-lipped but full of compassion.]

If it becomes known that the minister breaks the confidences which have been committed to him, his ministry will be greatly impaired. He will no longer have the privilege of helping some who sorely need his help but will not come to him because they feel they cannot trust him. That truly puts the minister in a bad light. If people cannot trust their pastor, whom can they trust?

3. [In his dealing with the members of his church, the pastor should not be dictatorial or lordly in his attitude.] The Scriptures plainly disapprove of such an attitude, and where one man succeeds with this spirit, ten find it their undoing. The pastor is called to minister to his people, to be their example, not to dictate to them. Let every pastor consider well I Peter 5:1-4, especially verses 2 and 3: "Feed

the flock of God which is among you, taking the oversight thereof, not by constraint, but willingly; not for filthy lucre, but of a ready mind; neither as being lords over God's heritage, but being ensamples to the flock." It is true that some ministers violate this principle and apparently succeed. But they succeed in spite of a domineering attitude, not because of it.

4. The minister needs always to watch his conduct towards the women and girls of his congregation. He should keep his hands off them. Many a minister has lost his influence and respect by just a little "innocent" holding of hands with members of the opposite sex, patting on the back and the like. This point is effectively made in Nolan Harmon's book, *Ministerial Ethics and Etiquette*: "Familiarity with women has got to be utterly taboo. [A minister, especially a young one, who puts his hands, however innocent-mindedly on the person of womankind, particularly young girls, is, in the mildest language I can command, an unmitigated fool.' "[1]]

The minister should refrain from riding around alone with women in his car, except in cases of emergency. The town gossips will soon get busy. He will refrain from meeting with a woman alone repeatedly, even on matters of business. There are too many instances on record where ministers were tempted and fell—due apparently to innocent meetings alone with a woman—to imagine that there is no danger in such conduct.

One of the best protections for the minister in his relation to the opposite sex is to let his congregation know frequently and in various ways that he values, admires, and loves his wife. When it becomes evident that this is not so, there are often women about who will seek to impose themselves on the pastor with tragic results.

5. [Let the pastor remember it will not be possible to rectify all the defects in his congregation in a few weeks.] Some congregations move very slowly in making changes, especially if the matters under concern are of long standing.

Patience is a virtue the pastor will need to cultivate. When a pastor goes to a new parish, he will likely see some things he will feel ought to be changed. Young and inexperienced pastors are sometimes tempted to use drastic measures to bring about quickly the desired changes. Dr. Harry Ironside called this the "hammer and

---

[1]Nolan B. Harmon, *Ministerial Ethics and Etiquette* (New York and Nashville: Abingdon-Cokesbury Press, 1928), p. 103.

tongs" method and strongly advised against it, pointing out that by using this method the pastor may do more damage than he can rectify in many years.

There is a better way. Instruct the membership over a period of time in the Word of God. Let its principles bring about the needed transformations. When the Word does this work, it will be done effectively. The writer knows of a case where a young pastor went to a new field and found conditions which he could not approve. He found worldly methods employed in that church in raising money for the church. He was grieved at what he saw. However, he was led not to take any drastic action but to spend time in teaching what the Word of God has to say on how the work of the church ought to be supported. The result was that in time the membership saw their error and made a proposal themselves to the pastor relative to a proper change. Thus without friction or trouble of any kind the difficulty was dissolved. Changes do not always come about as readily as in the case of this church. However, pastors will do well not to act too hastily in making changes. A little more time given to letting God's Word bring about changes rather than seeking to bring them about in the energy of the flesh will issue in happier results.

6. The pastor will show wisdom by refraining from undue familiarity with members of his congregation, such as calling them by their first names. Dignity ought to be maintained in the church of God, and it is far better to speak to the members of the church as Mr. Jones or Mrs. Brown than as John or Mary. (In some church groups the pastor addresses the members of his flock as Brother — and Sister —.) It is unwise to call some of the adults by their first names and others not. Sooner or later the pastor will be charged with showing favoritism. It is better to treat all his members alike. When speaking to children and young people, of course the first names are appropriate.

7. Let the minister discourage the practice of church members calling the pastor and his wife by their first names. A certain amount of reserve should be maintained by the pastor. He is more than just a first name in the congregation and the community. He holds a high office and he should seek to keep it from becoming common. He is the pastor of the flock. What better term can be used to designate him than the title "Pastor"?

The question will doubtless arise at this point about the term "reverend," used so commonly today. It may be said that "reverend" occurs but once in the Scriptures, and there it refers to God—"Holy and reverend is his name" (Ps. 111:9). Thus it can readily be seen that there is no scriptural basis for applying it to the minister of the Gospel. However, by usage the word has come to be a title applied to the minister with no irreverent meaning. Though the pastor may not like to be called "Reverend," probably it would be best for him not to make an issue of the matter. When opportunity affords, he can express his preference for the designation "Pastor."

In the May 11, 1959 issue of *Christianity Today* there appeared an interesting paragraph from William S. LaSor, professor at Fuller Theological Seminary, concerning the use of "Reverend." It is as follows:

> What really makes me grit my teeth is the use of "Reverend" as a title. If you will take the trouble to look in your dictionary, you will discover that "Reverend" is not a title (like "Doctor"), but an adjective (like "Honorable"). The use of "Reverend" before the last name ("Reverend Ladd") is as rude as using the last name alone. You might as well say, "Skinny Jones" or "Sloppy Johnson" as "Reverend Rasmussen." Several correct ways of using "Reverend" are possible: "the Reverend George Smith," "the Reverend Doctor Booth," "the Reverend Professor Harrison." It is just as correct to omit the word, and present the speaker as "Mister Jones," or "Professor Longbeard." A good method is to give the full title when first introducing the speaker ("Our guest speaker this morning is the Reverend Professor I. M. Longwinded, Ph.D."), tell where he is from, and then present him by the simplest form ("Professor [or, Doctor] Longwinded"). Above all, be sincere—whether you mean it or not!
> —In *Theology News and Notes,* October, 1958.

8. [The minister should learn to take criticism without becoming angry or sour.] Unfortunately there are some ministers who cannot take criticism from anyone without taking offence and becoming greatly irritated. Such an attitude opens the door for many unhappy hours during a man's ministry. If he would be like his Lord, the minister must assume an entirely different attitude. [If criticism is justified, he should thank God for it and profit by it. If it is not justified, let him ask God to give him grace to bear it,] remembering

Him who endured such criticism for us without becoming angry or sour (Isa. 53:7).

9. [In his preaching and teaching the pastor should always be true to his convictions, but he should learn to do it in a loving spirit.] I believe it was G. Campbell Morgan who said there was only one man whom he cared to hear preach on the subject of Hell, and that man was Dwight L. Moody. The reason given was that when Moody preached on this subject he did it with tears in his eyes. He spoke out his deep convictions in love. Too many ministers lack the compassion of Christ as they present their convictions. There is a harshness, a coldness, a sternness that needs to be melted by the love of Christ.

10. [The pastor should avoid scolding from the pulpit those who are present in the congregation for the absence or deficiencies of those who are not present.] This is not fair to those who are present and it has no effect on those who are absent. More than this, the scolding is likely to cast a gloom over the entire service, detracting from the spirit of worship, and reacting unfavorably upon the pastor's own spirit. He may feel very keenly the lack of loyalty on the part of certain members of his flock. He may be much disappointed in their conduct. But he had better forget it while directing his public services. If rebuke is necessary, let him do it in private or when the deserving folk are present.

11. [The pastor should not take advantage of those who have wronged him by whipping them from the pulpit.] Such action takes unfair advantage of those who are the objects of his anger, for they have no equal opportunity to present their side of the affair. The action is therefore cowardly and unworthy of the man of God. Let him remember the example of his Lord, of whom it was said, "He shall not cry, nor lift up, nor cause his voice to be heard in the street. A bruised reed shall he not break, and the smoking flax shall he not quench: he shall bring forth judgment unto truth" (Isa. 42:2-3).

Neither should the pastor present his invectives against sin from the sacred desk in such a way that it will be evident to everyone in the congregation that he is referring to a certain individual or individuals. This will certainly start tongues to wagging and likely will further irritate the guilty parties so that it will be more difficult to reach them. Such cases had better be dealt with privately, not from the pulpit.

12. The minister needs to be honest with his church in the use of his time. He does not have to punch a time clock, as many others do. Nor is he on an eight-hour schedule, five days a week. He is left largely on his own honor as to how he uses his time. However, he owes it to his congregation—and most of all to his Lord—to give a good account of how he spends his time. The words of Holy Scripture apply to him as well as to others, "Redeeming the time, because the days are evil" (Eph. 5:16). Most ministers, the author believes, spend more than a forty-hour week at their task. However, it has been known that some ministers have wasted much time on trivial things. Because the minister does not have to report on how he uses his time, he may be tempted to be careless in this matter. Let it be perfectly evident to everyone that the pastor is a busy man. Sooner or later it will be manifested in the pastor's ministry whether or not he is diligent in the use of his time.

13. The minister will do well to beware of putting himself under obligation to certain members of his congregation by obtaining financial loans or accepting special favors from them. Such a practice can easily place the pastor in an embarrassing situation. For example, if those from whom special favors have been received should be involved in wrongdoing, the pastor might be tempted to soft-pedal the situation. Or the pastor may find himself hampered in his preaching because he doesn't wish to offend those to whom he is obligated. If the pastor is not obligated to anyone in the congregation, he can view all his members with equality and can preach to their needs without any partiality.

14. Let the pastor refrain from talking continually about how busy he is. He may feel as though he is the busiest man in the community, and he may be. He ought to be a busy man, for he is engaged in a big business. But for him to be always telling how busy he is may sound like complaining, and some needy folk will hesitate to call on him for his services because they do not want to impose on his time. The minister ought never to be too busy to meet the needs of his congregation. Let him beware of leaving the impression that he is too busy to be concerned about the problems of even the humblest member.

15. Let the pastor be slow in taking action on complaints presented

to him by disgruntled members. Almost every church has some mal-
contents. A disgruntled member is likely to see everything through
blue glasses and his judgment should not be trusted apart from a
thorough investigation. The facts in the case would likely reveal that
the main trouble is with the person who brought the complaint. The
challenge the pastor faces in such a case is to get the complainer
in a right relationship with the Lord. If the pastor is successful,
usually the complaints will dissolve in short order.

16. The pastor and the membership committee will do well to
investigate disqualified members of another church carefully before
they are admitted into membership. Otherwise the church may be
inviting trouble similar to that which caused their withdrawal from
the church which disqualified them. These applicants should demonstrate a proper Christian attitude before they are admitted. Only
Christians who are right with the Lord should be admitted into
church membership.

In His Social Relationships

Apart from his deportment among ministers and in the church,
there are certain practices that should characterize the pastor in relation to the community.

The pastor should be diligent in keeping all his appointments,
both private and public. Our Lord made appointments with men
and kept them. For example, there is reference in Matthew 28:16
to an appointment He made with His disciples. The verses immediately following show the remarkable consequences connected
with the keeping of that appointment, namely, the giving of the
Great Commission. He has some future appointments which He
will surely keep (see Heb. 9:27-28). Certainly His undershepherds
ought to follow the example of their Leader in this regard. The
minister ought to be prompt in keeping his business appointments
lest he lose the confidence of those among whom He should develop
confidence. He ought to be prompt in discharging his responsibility
in connection with interviews, which will be such an important part
of his ministry. Then there are various church meetings, committee
meetings, and social engagements at which the pastor should arrive
on time, or he may acquire the opprobrious title of "the late pastor
John Smith"! The Scripture admonishes all of God's children to
be "not slothful in business" (Rom. 12:11). Instead, he ought to

be "diligent in . . . business" (Prov. 22:29). The pastor should set a good example for his flock in this matter.

The minister needs to exercise care not to proselyte among the membership of another church. In other words, he should not be guilty of "stealing sheep." Such a course of action will result in unfavorable reaction to the pastor and his church. When situations arise involving members of other churches, the pastors concerned should be consulted, even though the situation pertains to the transfer of a membership for one reason or another. Failure in such matters is likely to cause an unwholesome rivalry in the community and will do the church no good. This is an ideal opportunity to apply the Golden Rule.

Let the pastor beware of developing a critical spirit. Such a spirit will make his profession unattractive and warp his own soul. Some pastors have allowed this attitude to develop to such an extent that the impression is given that nobody is right but themselves. They are critical of other pastors, of the denomination, of the ministerium, of the church boards, of the schools that train the leadership, and even of some of the leaders in their own pastorate. Criticism is a malady that can ruin a man's ministry, to say nothing of his digestion! Ulcers are common among such ministers. A close examination of this attitude will undoubtedly reveal a great deal of selfishness and jealousy. From these the minister ought to divorce himself.

It is not suitable for a minister to act like a clown much of the time. It is good for a pastor to be able to have a good time with his people at certain times, to tell a humorous story, and to have a wholesome sense of humor, but the church did not hire him to be a jester. Incessant wisecracking, pun-making and the like can detract from his ministry. Folks with serious burdens are likely to hesitate to take them to such a minister lest he make light of them.

The minister should not give the impression that because he is a minister he is a privileged character in society. It is true that many privileges are granted to ministers. They are usually treated with a great deal of respect. Honors and gratuities are bestowed upon them. Railroads give them a discount. Some stores grant reductions to ministers. They are given season tickets to baseball games and other events. But the minister should not abuse his privileges or seek them. He is called like his Master to minister, not to be ministered unto. Take the matter of hospital rules. In practically all hospitals ministers are not bound by the regulations that govern ordinary visitors. They can visit morning, noon, or night. But ministers ought not to take advantage of these privileges and haughtily disregard closed doors and such precautions as are arranged for the welfare of the patients. Proper deference ought to be shown to those in charge. Some ministers have made themselves obnoxious by their intrusions.

In relation to traffic laws, discounts, and so on the minister should consider himself on an equality with others. The minister ought to be an example to the community in the matter of obeying the speed laws instead of being notorious for disobeying them. When discounts are offered, there is no wrong in accepting them, gratefully. But it will be wise for him not to *ask* for them. In business matters let him be on the same basis as his members.

The minister and his family should determine that they will live within their income. This is necessary if they are to maintain a good reputation in the community and bear a good testimony for the church. Failure at this point has resulted in the ruination of many a good preacher. In order to live within his income, a preacher may have to reduce his budget and adhere to a lower standard of living than is desired—but better far this situation than the bringing of the cause of Christ into disrepute. In some cases it may be necessary for the minister to be gainfully occupied in some work outside the ministry in order to supplement what the church pays him. This is not ideal, but it has been done many times. Even the Apostle Paul made tents to pay expenses in order that he might not be chargeable to anyone.

In Relation to His Denominational Group

The minister also has an ethical responsibility toward the denominational group with which he is affiliated.

The minister ought to maintain a vital interest in the work of the denomination with which he is associated. The underlying theological basis for this is the fact that the Church is the Body of Christ. This implies close fellowship in work as well as in worship. Surely the leaders in a church fellowship ought to work together in close harmony. If possible, a minister ought to be in a denominational group that is true to the Word of God. Then he ought to support it to the best of his ability. This includes attending its conferences, keeping informed about its boards and officers, knowing as much as possible about its missionary program, its schools, and other departments of its organization, sending delegates to the district and national conferences and instructing the local church officers to send in their offerings promptly to the proper denominational agencies. The pastor should also know when the various phases of the denomination's work should be emphasized in his church and see that proper financial support is given during this time. By taking an active and prayerful interest in the denomination to which he belongs, he will be an influence in making it what it ought to be.

In conclusion, and most important of all, the minister ought to remember always and everywhere that he is a man of God, a representative of the Lord Jesus Christ, and should seek to do the thing that Christ would have him do. By so doing, he will be a Christian gentleman in the truest sense of the word.

RECOMMENDED READING

BARNETTE, HENLEE H. *Introducing Christian Ethics.* Nashville, Tenn.: The Broadman Press, 1961.

HARMON, NOLAN B., JR. *Ministerial Ethics and Etiquette.* Rev. ed. New York and Nashville: Cokesbury Press, 1956.

HENRY, CARL F. H. *Christian Personal Ethics.* Grand Rapids: William B. Eerdmans Publishing Co., 1957.

LEACH, WILLIAM H. *Handbook of Church Management.* Englewood Cliffs, N. J.: Prentice-Hall, Inc., 1958. Chapters 18-21.

———. *The Making of the Minister.* Nashville: Cokesbury Press, 1928.

McAFEE, CLELAND B. *Ministerial Practices.* New York: Harper and Brothers, 1928.

POST, EMILY. *Etiquette.* 10th rev. ed. New York and London: Funk and Wagnalls, 1950.

RILEY, MARIE ACOMB (Mrs. W. B.). *Handbook of Christian Etiquette.* 11th ed. Minneapolis, Minn.: Northwestern Theological Seminary, 1956.

SCHUETTE, WALTER E. *The Minister's Personal Guide.* New York: Harper and Brothers, 1953.

SHEDD, WILLIAM G. T. *Homiletics and Pastoral Theology.* New York: Charles Scribner's Sons, 1895. Pp. 371-388.

SMYTH, NEWMAN. *Christian Ethics.* New York: Charles Scribner's Sons, 1892.

SPANN, J. RICHARD (ed.). *The Ministry*. New York and Nashville: Abingdon-Cokesbury Press, 1949. Chapter, "His Ethics," by Nolan B. Harmon, pp. 146-156.

TURNBULL, RALPH G. *A Minister's Obstacles*. New York: Fleming H. Revell Co., 1946. Chapters 4, 5, and 9. (Paperback ed., 1959.)

VANDERBILT, AMY. *New Complete Book of Etiquette*. New York: Doubleday & Company, 1963.

Chapter 5

THE PASTOR'S WIFE

ONE CANNOT READ the New Testament qualifications for the Christian minister (elder, bishop) without being impressed with the fact that for him the married state is set forth. As he reads I Timothy 3:1-5 and Titus 1:5-9 he finds that the bishop is to be "the husband of one wife." Moreover, he is to be "one that ruleth well his own house," and his children are to be faithful and obedient. Then, too, the matter of hospitality is mentioned in both of the above passages. This grace can be much more easily manifested with the help of a good wife in the parsonage. It takes a woman's touch to glorify this virtue.

It is clear then that the married state is taught as the proper state for ministers in the Scriptures. The Roman Catholic viewpoint differs from this teaching of Scripture. But it is better to follow the Word of God than human tradition. The Protestant Church from its beginning has exalted the marriage relationship for its clergymen. Martin Luther set a worthy example in this regard when he left the celibate state and married an ex-nun, much to the amazement of many in his day. The result, however, was a happy home life, and Katherina Von Bora exemplified those characteristics in a preacher's wife which many have manifested since her time. Others among the reformers followed Luther's example and took unto themselves wives who proved a blessing to their ministries. Ulrich Zwingli married Anna Reinhart. John Calvin took as his wife Idelette de Buren, and John Knox married Marjorie Bowes. Since Reformation days Protestant ministers, in the vast majority of instances, have not hesitated to enter the married state.

There are many advantages in the married state for the minister. The unmarried minister may live a very lonely life. When he marries, a good wife can provide him with companionship, encouragement, and understanding, as well as make him an attractive home. The minister's wife should indeed be a helpmeet for him, one fitted to answer his need for a happy homelife and to assist him in many ways in his work as a minister of the Gospel. With her help and encouragement, he will be a better man and do a better work as a preacher.

Then the married state with the blessing of children can readily provide an example of ideal Christian homelife in the community. This sort of thing is sorely needed everywhere.

The preacher who is unmarried faces special problems. He will be prey to the attentions of women who would like to become the object of his affections and to marry him. Fond mothers of unmarried daughters will invite him to dinner at their homes. While seeking to offend no one, he will need to maintain the greatest watchfulness in his relations with women. He faces a situation where jealousy and envy may be the stimulus to gossip. It might be easier for him if his social engagements are with young women outside his congregation. Of course, one cannot lay down hard and set rules for affairs of the heart. However, when he is seeking God's will as to who shall be his life companion, he will do well to keep in mind that she, too, should be a Christian with a sincere desire to serve the Lord. Many a minister's wife fails or is unhappy in her role because she hasn't received a call from the Lord. If she knows that she is called of the Lord, then she can rely on the Lord to be her help, wisdom, and strength as she stands by the side of her husband in serving the Lord in the pastorate.

It is difficult to estimate the importance of the pastor's wife. She can contribute to the success of his ministry if she is a dedicated servant of God, or she can detract from his ministry if she is not what she ought to be. In other words, she can either make or break his ministry.

What then are some of the characteristics and responsibilities of a good pastor's wife?

1. Her first responsibility is to her home. She should be the queen of the parsonage. The pastor's home is distinctive. Folk in the community know where the preacher lives. His home is marked, whether the pastor desires it to be so or not. Something extra is expected from the home where the pastor and his family live. This being so, it should be a model home, an ideal for others to imitate. If it is to be all of this, the help of a faithful wife is needed.

The pastor should recognize the importance of his wife in this respect and not allow too many outside responsibilities and duties to be heaped upon her which will make it impossible for her to be her best as a homemaker. Order, hospitality, neatness, happiness and attractiveness in the parsonage is the responsibility of the pastor's wife. Some well-meaning wives have failed in some of these qualities, spending so much time in church and community activities that they have not had time to make the pastor's home all that it should be. This is a mistake and is bound to lessen the influence of the pastor's total ministry.

2. The pastor's wife should not seek to fill too many positions in the church. Since hers is a unique ministry as queen of the parsonage, she has a responsibility there that will require much of her time and attention. She will fail in this responsibility if she is loaded down with too many tasks in the church.

In most cases, there is no reason why the pastor's wife should be the pianist, choir director, president of the women's missionary society, superintendent of the primary department, a Sunday school teacher and, possibly, chairman of a committee or two in the church. In assuming many positions she is likely to deprive someone else of an opportunity to serve. Furthermore, she runs the risk of the criticism that she is trying to run the church, to say nothing of the time it all takes—some of which at least she ought to devote to her home! She may also make it difficult for her successor, who may not have the talent, the health, or the conviction that she ought to do all the things her predecessors did.

But on the other hand, the preacher's wife ought to do something in the church, thus setting a good example for the other women of the congregation. When first coming to a'new charge, the pastor's wife will show wisdom in not taking positions of service too quickly. Let her wait a little while until she has time to see where her services are most urgently needed. A Sunday school class may need a teacher. A position in the women's missionary society may need to be filled. Or she may be needed most as counselor to one of the young people's societies. Having accepted a position, she should fulfill it with all diligence. It's far better to serve well in one position, in addition to her home duties, than to endeavor to fill many positions in a mediocre way.

3. The pastor's wife can be of service in the matter of certain calls that need to be made. This question is often asked in connection with pastoral calling: Should the pastor's wife always accompany her husband when he calls? Two extreme attitudes have been taken. There are people who say that she should always accompany him when he calls. Others say she should never accompany him.

It is the conviction of this writer that both of these positions are wrong. If the pastor's wife must *always* accompany her husband when he calls, much calling will never be done. The average pastor has a family. And with family responsibilities, keeping the parsonage neat, and so on, the pastor's wife cannot spend a great amount of time in calling. If she does, her home will be neglected and this will bring reproach upon the pastor's ministry. The viewpoint that the pastor's wife must always go with her husband in his calling ministry seems to have grown out of the idea that the pastor needs protection against evil temptation and advances. And it implies that because a few pastors—comparatively—have become prey to traps set for them by the opposite sex, all pastors are liable to fall into sin if they call alone. This is a reproach upon the ministry, and pastors should seek to live it down.

Then there is the viewpoint that the pastor should never take his wife with him when he calls. According to this view a third person in the call will make it more difficult for the pastor to accomplish the ministry that needs to be done. Folks will not open their hearts in the presence of a third party. It is also insisted that the wife's presence is liable to convert the call into a social visit, with the talk centered on children, the home, school, and related topics. Surely there are times, and they are probably in the majority, when it will not be wise to take the wife along. When an urgent hospital call needs to be made, or when a definite ministry of personal evangelism must be accomplished, or when there is some definite problem to deal with, the pastor had better go alone.

However, there are times when it will be wise for the pastor to have his wife with him when he calls. When calling upon single women or women of questionable character, the pastor may save himself some criticism if he is accompanied by his wife. Then there are the calls that have as their purpose a better acquaintance between certain families and the pastor and his wife. By her presence on such occasions, folks in the church, especially the women and teen-age girls, will come to know her as one with whom they can counsel in time of need. Thus the pastor's wife will do well to be ready at times to go with her husband in his calling. It will be an aid to him and it will set her forth as one who is interested in the church flock.

4. The pastor's wife can be of great help to her husband in connection with certain personal problems with which he will be faced. In this realm she can be a real helpmeet for him.

Take the times when the pastor's morale gets low. Almost all pastors have their "juniper tree" experiences when everything seems to go wrong. The carefully prepared sermons fail to hit the mark. The attendance falls below average. Plans go awry. Somebody makes a cutting remark or fails to do his job. At times like these the pastor is inclined to see everything through blue glasses. Then a good wife can come to the rescue—unless she gets under the "juniper tree" at the same time, which is a most unfortunate situation!

She can help by being cheerful and exercising the faith which God has given her. It was during the trying times of the Reformation that Martin Luther got very low in his spirits. When he came down to breakfast one morning looking exceptionally glum, his wife solemnly said, "Martin, God is dead." Luther was taken aback by this statement and reprimanded her for it. She responded, "But, Martin, you act as though He were." He got the point and faced up to his responsibilities again. Katherina set a good example for all her sisters of the manse in this little incident. God is able for every situation no matter how difficult it appears. Moreover the pastor's wife at such times can direct the conversation away from the vexing things of the day and thus help to clear the atmosphere. Maybe the most helpful thing she can do at such a time is to provide an extra good meal, bake a cake or make something that will delight his palate. It is amazing what a good meal can do to raise the sunken spirits of a man!

Then ministers unknowingly are liable to develop mannerisms in the pulpit offensive to those who sit in the pew. One minister known to the writer developed certain facial contortions when he preached. They developed to the point that they appeared ludicrous to those who heard him for the first time. If he had corrected the mannerism in its early stages, doubtless it would never have developed into the grotesque thing that it became. But probably no one told him of it, not even his wife. Members of the church are slow to tell the pastor of his faults. They only tell him the good things about his preaching. In like manner ministers can get into a rut by using certain expressions repeatedly until they become monotonous to the audience. Ministers can even be guilty of grammatical errors of which they are not conscious. Again, their members will not have the boldness in most cases to tell them of these weaknesses. A good wife can be of great help in such matters. She should be the pastor's most faithful critic. But if she is to be helpful in these matters she will need to have the willing cooperation of her husband. Some men in the ministry resent criticism of any sort. This is one of the marks of a small man. By such an attitude a minister will deprive himself of the privilege of improvement and growth. He will likely carry his defects to the end of his ministry. When the pastor's wife criticizes her husband, she should always do it in a kindly and constructive spirit. Moreover, she ought to pick out the right time to do this sort of thing. This will not be when he is down!

Consider also the matter of finances. Some preachers are very poor financiers. They readily allow themselves to get into debt. They are unwilling to live within their budget. Debts have ruined many preachers. The pastor's influence in the community will be ruined if it becomes known that he is careless in money matters. And, alas, some preachers' wives have contributed to this sort of thing by their uncontrolled desires for material things and by failing to be willing to live within the family income.

But the preacher's wife can be of great help in seeing to it that the the home is run within the limits of the family income. In most cases this will involve some problems. Ministerial salaries are usually not large, though they are increasing as churches realize more and more that the minister must pay his bills as well as all others in the congregation.

The wife should encourage her husband to work out a family budget so that the income may be wisely distributed to the various areas of living. Moreover, she should do all she can to see that the family budget is adhered to. She ought to insist that her pastor husband take something from the budget for books and magazines. If she does, she will be able to listen to better sermons week after week! It will help to keep him fresh in his ministry. By the same token the pastor's wife should not be forgotten in the way of items which will minister to her cultural well-being.

5. The pastor's wife may exercise a very precious ministry among the women and girls of the congregation. By her consistent walk she can be an example or an ideal of true Christian womanhood. She may have a very wholesome and valuable ministry in counseling with women and girls of the church and community who have problems. A wise pastor will send certain women to her for this sort of ministry. In order for her to perform a helpful ministry of this kind, she should acquaint herself with the problems that face modern woman. She should read some helpful books on the pastor's wife as *The Shepherdess* by Arthur Wentworth Hewitt, *The Pastor's Wife* by Carolyn Blackwood, *The Parson Takes a Wife* by Maria Sheerin. These will enlighten her as to her responsibilities and privileges.

She will need to learn to listen without being shocked to all sorts of stories from burdened and broken women. She must know how to sympathize with such as these in their misery and need without compromising her convictions. She ought to be able to point them to the Word of God and, in some cases, to psychiatric or medical help. Hers ought to be a ministry of prayer, bearing up into God's presence the burdens which are shared with her.

In these and other ways the pastor's wife can be an angel of light and mercy to many women, girls, and children of the congregation and community.

6. The pastor's wife must learn to be tight-lipped. This is true also of her husband. People often unburden themselves to the pastor and his wife about things which they cannot or will not tell to members of their own families. They have confidence in the pastor and his wife, looking upon them as spiritual leaders. And if they cannot help in matters of the soul and in the complex problems that vex them, who can? There will be times when women of the congregation will want to speak to the pastor's wife in a confidential way, seeking spiritual help and encouragement. Perhaps they feel there is no one else to whom they can turn. There will be times when the pastor will share with his wife some confidence that has been committed to him, wanting her advice and prayers. This should be done only with the consent of the one who has committed the matter to the pastor. To betray such confidence is despicable. And when it becomes known that matters committed to the pastor and his wife in confidence are likely to be broadcast, the influence of the latter will be greatly diminished.

If the pastor's wife is guilty of betraying confidences and talking when she should keep silent, the pastor will have a difficult hurdle to overcome. Some preacher's wives have talked their husbands right out of pastorates. According to St. James in his Epistle the tongue is a fire which, if it gets out of control, can cause untold damage in many ways. On the other hand, the tongue can prove of inestimable blessing if used properly. Let the pastor's wife learn from the Word of God how to guard her tongue against its evils and to use it as an instrument for God's glory.

7. The pastor's wife ought to give all diligence toward the training of her children so that they will be a credit and not a hindrance in the work of the church. In this she deserves the wholehearted support of her husband. Whether the minister's children like it or not, they are always in the public eye. What they do is observed far more than what other children do. This may be unfair to the children but it is true. Thus their deportment is an extremely important matter.

The pastor's wife must not be so interested and involved in the affairs of the church that she neglects her own children. In the majority of cases it is evident that she does give adequate time to their training, for the children of the parsonage by and large have given a good account of themselves. The list of illustrious men and women who have come from ministers' homes is long. But there are the exceptional cases which sometimes bring the parsonage into reproach. Such cases can lead to very sad results, even to the forcing of the pastor to leave his charge. The pastor's children should be under control at home and in the church. They should not be allowed to manifest an attitude of special privilege in the church because they come from the manse. They should not be allowed to run up and down the aisles of the church or to walk on the pews. Neither should they be permitted to go in and out of the services continually. Let them be taught specific manners to be practiced in and out of the church. Well-trained and well-mannered children are a credit to any parsonage and to any congregation. The minister's wife has much of the responsibility in this important matter.

These are a few of the things that should characterize the wife of the pastor. Above all, she should love people, for her work consists in being with people outside the home as well as within. As she works and prays with them, laughing and weeping with them, loving them for their own sakes and for the Lord's sake, she will in turn receive their devotion. If she is faithful as a wife and mother and if she grows spiritually along with her husband, it will be said of the queen of the parsonage, "Her price is above rubies." The pastor's wife should always remember she can lend an influence for God and the church that will make the work of the pastor much easier and more effective.

RECOMMENDED READING

BADER, GOLDA MAUDE (ELAM) (ed.). *I Married a Minister*. New York and Nashville: Abingdon-Cokesbury Press, 1942.

BLACKWOOD, ANDREW W. *Pastoral Work*. Philadelphia: The Westminster Press, 1945. Chap. 6.

BLACKWOOD, CAROLYN. *The Pastor's Wife*. Philadelphia: Westminster Press, 1951.

DODS, ELIZABETH (as told to John Kord Lagemann). "What Are You Doing to Your Minister's Wife?", *Good Housekeeping*, June, 1959.

ERDMAN, CHARLES R. *The Work of the Pastor*. Philadelphia: The Westminster Press, 1924. Chap. 2, Sec. 5.

GUFFIN, GILBERT L. *Called of God*. Westwood, N. J.: Fleming H. Revell Co., 1951. Chap. 8.

HEWITT, ARTHUR WENTWORTH. *The Shepherdess*. Chicago and New York: Willett, Clark and Co., 1943.

HOPPIN, J. M. *Pastoral Theology*. New York and London: Funk and Wagnalls, 1909 (5th ed.).

JOHNSON, ANNA FRENCH. *The Making of a Minister's Wife*. New York and London: D. Appleton-Century Co., 1939.

LEACH, WILLIAM H. *Handbook of Church Management*. Englewood Cliffs, N. J.: Prentice-Hall, 1958. Chap. 19.

SHEERIN, MARIA WILLIAMS. *The Parson Takes a Wife*. New York: The Macmillan Co., 1948.

"Preach the word; be instant in season, out of season; reprove, rebuke, exhort with all longsuffering and doctrine" (II Timothy 4:2).

Part II

THE PASTOR AND HIS PUBLIC MINISTRY

Chapter 6

THE SUNDAY MORNING WORSHIP
SERVICE

THE SUNDAY MORNING WORSHIP SERVICE is the major service of the
week in the church. It is designed specifically for the purpose of the
worship of God. Nothing is so important as this. Man is not fit
to serve God until he has first worshiped Him. Worship is man's
first duty. Jesus answered the scribe who came to Him with the
question, "Which is the first commandment of all?", by saying, "The
first of all the commandments is, Hear, O Israel; The Lord our God
is one Lord: and thou shalt love the Lord thy God with all thy
heart, and with all thy soul, and with all thy mind, and with all thy
strength: this the first commandment" (Mark 12:28-30). Implied in
this commandment is the idea of worship. And worship is no less
incumbent upon believers today than upon those under the Mosaic
economy. When we worship God, we revere and honor Him, we
praise and adore Him, we offer ourselves and our gifts to Him, for
He is worthy.

More people normally attend the Sunday morning service than
any other. This in itself provides unusual opportunity in the ministry of the Word. The ministry of the Word should be such that God
is exalted and magnified, so that in turn the hearts of the people
are stimulated to love, thanksgiving, praise, and surrender of life.
The Sunday morning service should not be, week after week, a
harangue, scolding the people for their shortcoming and failures.
While there is a place in the pastor's total ministry for rebuke, a
pastor should remember that he is to "feed the sheep," not to "beat
the sheep." In a definite sense the worship service prepares God's
people for the other services. At this time inspiration is generated
for the Sunday evening service and for the midweek prayer service,
as well as for the other services within the program of the church.

But inspiration is to be thought of not only in connection with the services of the church. The believer who attends should be inspired for everyday Christian living in the office, the factory, the home, the marketplace, and the school. The non-Christian who attends should be made to feel something like this: "These Christians have something I want. I want to know their God. I need Him!" For these reasons and others the pastor can afford to devote major attention to the Sunday morning service in order to make it worthy of the God we worship and serve.

Characteristics of the Worship Service

As the pastor plans the Sunday morning worship service, there are several characteristics that he should keep in mind. Let us note them.

1. *It should be unified.* That is, there ought to be harmony between the various parts of the service. For example, if the sermon subject is prayer, the other parts of the service, such as the Scripture reading, the hymns, the special music and, to a certain extent, even the prayers, should be made to harmonize with the pastor's subject. This will not result in monotony if done properly. Unity and continuity will serve to leave a more lasting impression upon the worshipers than a service which is not unified.

2. *It should be cooperative.* The service should be so conducted that the whole congregation will take part in it. Those who sit in the pew should not be just silent listeners. They have a responsibility to worship God along with the man behind the pulpit and those who sing in the choir. Worship should be a corporate act. Everything possible therefore should be done to gain total participation in this human obligation.

3. *It should be animated.* We worship a living God. He is the dispenser of life that is life indeed. Therefore the worship service should never be allowed to become dreary, dull, or perfunctory. Every part should be vibrant and meaningful, contributing to the spiritual benefit of those in attendance.

The animation referred to is not necessarily that of action or noisy demonstration. This is not desirable. But the service ought to reflect life, movement toward God, and provide a sense of His presence. As an aid in keeping the service animated, punctuality should be observed in beginning the service. There should be a direct passing from one part of the service to another. The pastor should never have to search for notes or places in the Bible or the hymn book. There should be no long Scripture lessons, prayers, or anthems. The pastor's sermon should be of a reasonable length; the excellence of a sermon is not determined by its length. A sluggish tempo for the congregational singing should not be tolerated. The attitude of the minister should be one of vigor and enthusiasm, reflecting the joy of the Lord.

4. *It should be dignified.* This does not mean that it should be unduly formal or stilted. But nothing cheap, grotesque, flippant, or offensive should have a part in this service which is to honor God. The minister should always have an attitude of reverence, remembering that he is the leader of the service of God. The word *dignity* comes from the Latin *dignus,* which means worthy, with distinction, elevation, honor, excellence, or stateliness. The Sunday morning worship service should contain those elements that are worthy of being associated with God's high and holy character. A quality of excellence should pervade the service.

5. *It should be edifying.* It should be of such character as to build up the saints of God in their faith. The singing, praying, reading of Scripture, and the preaching should all be intelligible with the intention of lifting the worshipers into the presence of God. At the conclusion of the hour of worship, the members of the congregation should be more conscious of God than when the service began. They should be stronger in the faith. When Moses was with God upon the mountain, some of the divine glory was reflected upon his countenance and lingered there. A congregation that truly worships God will have a sense of His glory.

The Pastor's Preparation

Since the Sunday morning worship service is so important, it hardly needs to be emphasized that the pastor should enter into it at his best, ready for his task of leadership.

He should be fully prepared for his responsibilities before Sunday morning arrives. Lack of preparation will make it difficult for him to enter wholeheartedly into the spirit of the occasion and to contribute to this spirit. His sermon should be well in hand, the order of the service ready, and the announcements carefully worded. He should make sure that the information on the hymn boards is correct.

To have last Sunday's hymns announced on the boards can be very disconcerting!

By proper preparation the minister will be able to exhibit much more composure when he comes to the pulpit. Only thus will he be able to worship heartily with his people as he ought to do.

Let the pastor retire early enough on Saturday night so that he will be refreshed for his Sunday tasks. He should never leave arduous preparation until Saturday night. If he does, his sermons are likely to suffer from immaturity. "Sleep as soundly as possible all [Saturday] night if you want to keep your congregation awake on Sunday"[1] was Theodore Cuyler's admonition to ministers, and it makes good sense. A congregation deserves something better than a baggy-eyed minister in the pulpit on Sunday.

The pastor should have prayer with his choir before going into the service. This will help both the preacher and the choir. It will tend to create an atmosphere of reverence and seriousness for both the pastor and the choir as they assume the tasks for which they are responsible.

Last, and of great importance, the pastor and the choir should always be ready to begin their ministries at the proper time. It produces a deadening effect and sets a bad example for the leadership of the worship services to be late in beginning their responsibilities. The pastor will need to discipline himself and instruct his choir as to the importance of punctuality. It will mean much to the successful operation of the services of God's House.

The Operation of the Sunday Morning Service

The order of service in the Sunday morning worship service varies from church to church. Some churches have gone to an extreme in formalism. Others have gone to the opposite extreme and make their service very informal. Both extremes are objectionable. The service of the Lord should be carried on with dignity, "decently and in order." On the other hand, it should not be so formal as to be cold and meaningless. Each part of the service should have a purpose which can be readily grasped by the humblest soul present.

A suggested content for a Sunday morning service is presented here with brief remarks on the various parts. This content, of course,

---

[1]Theodore L. Cuyler, *How to Be a Pastor* (New York: The Baker and Taylor Co., 1890), p. 56.

allows for considerable variation to suit the situation. But the writer believes that there is good reason for each of the items suggested.

1. Organ or piano prelude. This lets the congregation know that the service is about to begin. It helps to create a worshipful atmosphere. It is the signal for everyone to get in his place, thus preparing for an auspicious and dignified beginning to the service. This prelude should last about five minutes and should merge into the main service.

2. The choir entrance. It is very fitting for the choir, after entering, to remain standing and sing prayerfully, "The Lord is in His holy temple. Let all the earth keep silence before Him," or a similar refrain. Some churches use a processional, during which the choir sings a devotional hymn as it marches to its place in the chancel.

3. The doxology by the congregation. When the choir is in its place and has finished its entering hymn or refrain, it is well for the congregation to stand and join with the choir in singing the doxology. Some churches prefer to use the doxology at the time of the receiving of the offering. Where this is done, the congregation may sing "Glory be to the Father" or some such tribute to God at the beginning of the service. Such a beginning tends to set the tone or atmosphere for the entire service. It expresses the fact that this service is dedicated to the purpose of worship.

4. The pastor's invocation. This should be carefully worded and should be what the word implies, an invoking of God's blessing upon the service. Care should be exercised by the pastor not to include too much in this prayer lest there be a duplication in the regular pastoral prayer. In the main, the invocation should be limited to the matter already suggested, leaving other matters to the pastoral prayer.

Some pastors like to use a call to worship in the form of pertinent Scripture just before the invocation. Such passages as Psalms 95:1-3, 96:8-9 or 100:1-5 are often used for this purpose. This can be done with good effect providing the portion of Scripture is not too long and is carefully chosen. The passage used should direct the congregation to the privilege and responsibility of worship.

5. Congregational singing. There should be no substitute for the singing of the people who sit in the pew. Special music by the choir and by various groups and individuals has its place, but it should never be allowed to displace singing by the whole congregation.

God's people are exhorted to sing—not part of them, but all of them. This is a part of their worship. It is an audible expression of their attitude toward God and holy things. In view of this, the people of God should be instructed as to their responsibility and privilege to sing God's praises and His message. Many souls have found salvation, rest, and comfort through the singing of God's people in the church. Therefore, from time to time the pastor ought to stress the importance of congregational singing. It goes without saying that care should be exercised in the choice of the hymns the congregation is asked to sing. These hymns ought to be in harmony with the main emphasis of the service, which is worship. If this is kept in mind, songs which are sentimental, centered mainly on the individual's experience, will be eliminated. Hymns should be chosen for correct doctrine, good poetry, and good music. This music should be singable so that the congregation will enjoy singing.

6. Responsive Reading. Practice and opinion differ as to the use of responsive readings in the worship service. It has been estimated that about half of the Protestant churches use responsive readings. The writer likes the practice. This is one way to gain participation of the whole congregation in the experience of worship. Many folks seldom read the Word of God at other times. It is good for them to read it aloud at least in the church service. In order to be done well, the congregation needs some instruction in reading of the Scriptures. The pastor himself should set the pace in a proper responsive effort. Such reading should not be too fast or too slow. There should be a proper observance of commas, colons, semicolons, question marks, and periods. Selections for responsive readings may be chosen either from the back of the hymnal or from the Scripture itself. They should not be too long. If the pastor desires to read from the Scriptures for responsive readings week by week, worshipers ought to carry their Bibles, and Bibles should be available in the pew racks for visitors.

7. The Scripture lesson. By this is meant that portion of the Scripture which includes the text of the sermon. Since the Scripture should be so well read that the reading becomes an interpretation of the passage, the pastor should practice reading the passage so that it will be done most effectively. It is a shame for a minister to stumble over big words or to mispronounce names. It is an evidence that he has not spent the necessary time with the Scripture passage before coming to

the pulpit. It is suggested that every pastor will benefit from a careful consideration of the contents of A. T. Pierson's classic work entitled *How to Read the Word of God Effectively*. It is worth going to church just to hear some ministers read the Scriptures. Alas, it is not always so!

8. The Pastoral Prayer. This prayer usually follows the reading of the Scripture lesson, the message of which somewhat directs the content of the prayer. The importance of this pastoral function is incalculable. "The most sacred function of the Christian ministry is praying," said Henry Ward Beecher. "Never in the study, in the most absorbed moments; . . . never in any company, where friends are sweetest and dearest,—never in any circumstances in life is there anything that is to me so touching as when I stand, in ordinary good health, before my great congregation to pray for them. Hundreds and thousands of times, as I rose to pray and glanced at the congregation, I could not keep back the tears. . . . there is no time when Jesus is so crowned with glory as then! . . . it seems as if God permitted me to lay my hand on the very Tree of Life, and to shake down from it both leaves and fruit for the healing of my people."[2]

This prayer should be carefully considered in advance. It should contain the elements of thanksgiving, praise, confession, and petition and present to the Lord the pressing needs and burdens of the congregation. For this reason the pastor himself should usually offer this prayer. Only in exceptional instances should others be called upon for this responsibility. The pastor knows more about the needs of his congregation than anyone else.

It is the writer's conviction that most pastors would do well to give a great deal more thought to the content and structure of their public prayers. Andrew Blackwood calls attention to six weaknesses often to be observed in public prayer. They are: (1) Lack of the note of reality, (2) lack of proper purpose, (3) lack of proper subject matter, (4) weakness of structure, (5) unfortunate style, and (6) undue familiarity in the use of the Lord's titles.[3] Let the pastor study his public praying to see how he can improve this ministry. When he stands to voice the supplications for the whole congregation, he has no right to do it in a haphazard manner.

---

[2]Henry Ward Beecher, *Yale Lectures on Preaching*, Second Series (New York: J. B. Ford & Co., 1873), pp. 46-47.
[3]Andrew W. Blackwood, *The Fine Art of Public Worship* (Nashville: Cokesbury Press, 1939), pp. 164-168.

9. Announcement time. Doubtless it will always be necessary to make certain announcements from the pulpit. However, unnecessary ones should be eliminated. Let the church bulletin carry those announcements that pertain only to certain groups in the church. The time of the entire congregation should not be taken up by presenting matters that concern just a few people. Those announcements which are made should be well in hand. The pastor should instruct folks who have announcements that should be publicly made to get them to him in writing before the service begins. It detracts from the dignity and reverence of the service to have an usher or some other individual rushing down the aisle to hand the pastor a belated announcement.

The announcement time should be kept as brief as possible lest attention be diverted from the main purpose of the service. Ten or fifteen minutes *is too long for announcements*. If the pastor will train his congregation to read the bulletin carefully, he will rarely need to make public announcements.

10. The Ministry of Giving. This part of the service should be considered a definite part of the total worship experience. Apologies should never be offered for receiving an offering. We read in the Scripture, "Give unto the Lord the glory due unto his name: bring an offering, and come into his courts" (Ps. 96:8). The offering should be received in a dignified manner, attended by a fitting offertory played on the organ or piano. Prayer for God's blessing upon the offering may be made either before or after it is taken, as best suits the individual pastor or congregation.

11. Special Music. This is a matter of importance and one that needs careful direction. It is better to have no so-called "special" music than music which does not fit or which is poorly rendered. Messages in song by the choir, a quartet, a duet, or individuals can be very effective just before the sermon or at other places in the program. The one who selects the special music should see that it is in keeping with the sermon to be preached. Otherwise the music will not minister to the effectiveness of the service and had better be eliminated. A pertinent congregational hymn will be better. Special care needs to be exerted in the choice of anthems. Some anthems minister real blessing, others become extremely boring. A good anthem is marked not only by good music but a message which is true to the Scriptures. Needless to say, the choir should so sing that the

words are understood by the congregation. This is necessary if the congregation is to worship with the choir.

12. The Sermon. Preaching has been the strongest asset of the Protestant church. The central place should continue to be occupied by the pulpit. In spite of the present-day tendency to discount the importance of preaching, the evangelical church should stress the preached Word. The apostolical admonition to "preach the word" has not been revoked. Men are still saved by preaching (I Cor. 1:21). By it they are built up in the Christian life and challenged to devoted service.

The sermon should not be too long. Nor should it be so short as to merit being called a sermonette. Usually, about thirty minutes is a good length for the regular Sunday morning sermon. The minister can say what needs to be said in that length of time if he is well prepared. People can concentrate for only a limited period on one particular trend of thought. If the minister wishes to hold his congregation week after week, he had better not preach too long. One able pastor, well known to the writer, often preached over an hour on Sunday morning to the delight of some of his older members. But he lost the younger people in his congregation, those whom he especially needed to hold. In this fast-moving day with restriced time on radio and television, pastors need to adjust their ministry accordingly.

13. The closing moments. The moments following the sermon are exceedingly important. Then is when the impressions of the entire service are brought together. Decisions ought to be made. Souls often stand in the balance. The pastor should aim to make these moments fruitful. Usually an appeal is made for responses to the message that has been delivered. These responses need not always be in the form of people coming forward in an open confession. Ofttimes decisions may be made in the pew with no outward manifestation. But decisions of one kind or another should be made. At this time an invitation or consecration hymn is sung as an aid to a proper climax to the service.

Following this time of invitation and dedication, the benediction is pronounced while the congregation remains standing. Immediately following the benediction, it is good for the congregation to remain standing with bowed heads while the pastor makes his way to the door to greet people as they leave the church. The pastor should not miss this opportunity, for he may then make some contacts that will prove of inestimable value. The organ or piano should continue playing for a short time following the benediction. This will tend to allay the confusion too often witnessed at the conclusion of worship services and to continue the worshipful atmosphere.

The congregation should leave the church assured that it has been in the presence of God. A holy hush should have settled down upon the people during the service and ought not to be allowed to depart too quickly. God's people should go forth better fortified to meet the varied experiences that life brings from day to day.

RECOMMENDED READING

BLACKWOOD, ANDREW W. *The Fine Art of Public Worship*. Nashville, Tenn.: Cokesbury Press, 1939.

———. *Leading in Public Prayer*. Nashville, Tenn.: Abingdon Press, 1958.

DAVIS, HORTON. *Christian Worship, Its History and Meaning*. Nashville, Tenn.: Abingdon Press, 1958.

DOBBINS, GAINES S. *The Church at Worship*. Nashville, Tenn.: The Broadman Press, 1962.

ERDMAN, CHARLES R. *The Work of the Pastor*. Philadelphia, Pa.: The Westminster Press, 1924. Chap. 5.

EVANS, GEORGE. *The True Spirit of Worship*. Wheaton, Ill.: Van Kampen Press, 1941.

GEFEN, ROGER (ed.). *The Handbook of Public Prayer*. New York: The Macmillan Company, 1963.

LITTLE, GERTRUDE. *Together We Worship*. Anderson, Ind.: The Warner Press, 1948.

PIERSON, ARTHUR T. *How To Read the Word of God Effectively*. Chicago: Moody Press, 1925. (A pamphlet.)

RILEY, W. B. *Pastoral Problems*. New York: Fleming H. Revell Co., 1936. Chapter 5.

SPURGEON, CHARLES H. *Spurgeon's Lectures to His Students*. Grand Rapids, Mich.: Zondervan Publishing House, 1955. Chapter 4.

URANG, GUNNAR. *Church Music for the Glory of God*. Moline, Ill.: Christian Service Foundation, 1956.

Chapter 7

THE SUNDAY EVENING SERVICE

EVER SINCE that first Easter Sunday evening in Jerusalem when Jesus met with His disciples behind closed doors, Sunday evening services have had a special significance. Upon that first occasion wonderful things took place. The risen Lord in His body of glory suddenly appeared in the midst of the disciples. He spoke peace to their fearful hearts. He showed them the scars of His recent sufferings to impress upon them that He was truly the One who had died upon Calvary but had risen from the dead "as he said." Gladness filled their hearts when they saw the Lord. When hearts are receptive to Him it is always a glad experience to see the Lord.

Then the disciples listened to their Lord as He commissioned them to a great task—"As my Father hath sent me, even so send I you." They also experienced His enablement for the task He had given them.

In countless Sunday evening services since that memorable occasion, the Lord has been revealed to men through His Word, peace has come to troubled hearts, and souls have caught a vision of the privilege of living for Christ.

In many places today the Sunday evening service has been abandoned. This is a great loss to the Church. The world has not abandoned its allurements on Sunday evening. The Church ought to have its Gospel meetings to counteract in a measure at least these evil influences and to bear witness to the victory Christians have in the risen Christ. This service ought to be radiant, like that first service, bright with Christ's presence and power. The evening service should be distinctive in character, pointing men and women to the living Christ, who is able and willing to give real meaning and purpose to life.

89

It Should Be Different from the Morning Service

It will be a mistake to make the Sunday evening service just like the morning service. God delights in variety, and His creatures enjoy it too. For the sake of attractiveness and interest, in addition to the merit of variety, the Sunday evening service ought to be different.

It should be less formal than the Sunday morning service. Those who do not care for formality will find special delight in this service. And those who like formality will probably enjoy the contrast the less formal evening service offers. Thus practically everyone will find satisfaction in the diversity. Both services will make for an increased appeal in the total Sunday program of the church.

More time should be given to congregational singing in this service. At the close of the day the mind and body tend to be a bit weary. Good, spirited Gospel singing will have the effect of stimulating the congregation and putting it in readiness for the rest of the service. Then, this is one way in which all can join in praising the Lord. More than this, it is a way in which the whole church can participate in an evangelistic ministry. The man who established the work of foreign missions of the writer's denomination in central Africa was won to the Lord through the lively singing of the First Brethren Church in Philadelphia. James Gribble was a streetcar conductor. He often passed by this church and was attracted by the joyous singing he heard as he rode by on his itinerary. He determined that when he had an opportunity he would attend that church. He did, and at the first service he confessed Christ. Soon after he was on his way to Africa. This sort of experience has been duplicated many times. Who can estimate the value of spiritual singing in the ministry of the church?

More emphasis may be placed upon evangelism at the evening service than in the morning service. One cannot be too dogmatic, however, at this point. It has been true in a good many places that it is easier to get the unsaved to attend a service on Sunday evening than on Sunday morning. This situation calls for a definite emphasis upon evangelism. There are other places where this is not true. The plan which has been followed by many evangelical churches and pastors in the past is to preach to the saints on Sunday morning, building them up in the nurture and admonition of the Lord, and to the unsaved in the evening. This plan cannot work perfectly in every case due to the economic situation. Some saints cannot attend the morning service and they need building up in the faith, and it is true that often there are unsaved people in the Sunday morning service who need to be evangelized. The best that pastors can do therefore is to evaluate their particular situation and employ the method that will prove most effective for their church. They may feel it to be the part of wisdom to divide their times of preaching to the saints between the morning and the evening and do the same with respect to their efforts to win the lost. But surely there will be a place for some evangelistic preaching in the evening.

Suggestions for Increased Appeal

Along with observing the differences in the Sunday morning and evening services which have been mentioned, the pastor should consider some items which may be used in the Sunday evening service to make it attractive and to provide variety. The main ideas of worship and the presentation of the Word of God should never be set aside, but in order to increase interest in these vital factors, some means may be employed.

1. Special features may be used in order to attract more people to the evening service. If these features are wisely chosen, they can result in spiritual profit for those who attend the service. The pastor should make sure that these special features are of high order. Nothing cheap or trivial should be allowed at any time and certainly not in the Sunday evening service. Let everything exhibit the same high spiritual tone that pervaded that first Sunday evening service long ago!

Among these special features may be musical attractions such as quartets, duets, choral groups, the singing of favorite hymns, and the telling of hymn stories, possibly through the use of the projector.

Some pastors have made good use of the question box devoting ten or fifteen minutes in the opening part of the service to answering questions which the church constituency has been invited to place in the question box. This plan gives the pastor the opportunity of speaking on some subjects that otherwise might be untouched in his preaching, and serves also to alert him to what the people are thinking and to the cults and false doctrines that may be infiltrating the community.

Using different groups at various times to conduct the opening part of the service has stimulated interest in some churches. Careful supervision needs to be exercised if this plan is followed so that what is presented is of a high caliber. The young people may have charge of the opening part of the program on certain occasions. They often do a splendid job. Or the men's group may present an attractive opening service. Other groups may be used with good success, and they will receive a blessing from such service as well as provide a blessing for the church.

Some pastors have used the flannelgraph to present the evening message. If this is done, much care needs to be given to make the flannelgraph attractive and to make sure that a spiritual message is presented and that it is conducted on an adult level. The writer once had a minister in his church who presented such a sermon on the two ways, the broad way and the narrow way. He graphically portrayed in an unforgettable manner these two ways, the people who took them, and the ends of those ways. The audience did not soon forget that message. It made a double impression upon them. They *heard* it and they *saw* it. It is good if the pastor is able to vary his program in this way occasionally.

Once in a while it will be beneficial for a church to invite a good Gospel team from an evangelical college or seminary to conduct the Sunday evening service. These young people, by their music and testimonies, will inspire the congregation and will also attract the young people of the congregation toward definite Christian service.

Missionary speakers also prove a blessing to a church. Ofttimes they come with pictures of their field of service which add interest and meaning to their presentation. The presence of missionaries in the pulpit is an object lesson in dedication which is of tremendous value, and something which every congregation needs from time to time.

2. Special nights can be used effectively to add interest to the Sunday evening program occasionally. Not only will they serve to create interest and increase attendance but they also can provide an opportunity to emphasize some very important matters. Some special nights which have been tried and found to be successful are Bible Night, Sunday School Night, Young People's Night, Old Hymns Night, Dads and Daughters Night, Moms and Sons Night, Family Night and Neighbors Night. Dolloff in his unique book, *Sunday Night Services Can Be Successful,* has many other suggestions

along this line. It can readily be seen that such services commend themselves from the standpoint of human interest. They also give the pastor an opportunity to stress some particular aspects of life that need emphasis.

3. An attractive series of sermons may serve to increase interest in the Sunday evening service. The pastor might present a series on the various aspects of prophecy. Or he might give a series on some of the anti-Christian cults which confront the people of God in these days. In such a series the pastor can fortify his people against the error these cults promote. Or he might deliver a biographical series dealing with some of the outstanding Biblical characters in a connected way. Dr. Andrew W. Blackwood has an interesting chapter in his book, *Preaching from the Bible,* entitled, "The Biographical Series" (Chapter IV), in which he gives some good illustrations. For instance, he suggests a series bearing the general title, "Six Dramatic Scenes in the Life of Elijah." He also suggests four sermons on Abraham, Isaac, Jacob, and Joseph, naming the sermons as follows: "Abraham—the Faith of a Godly Father"; "Isaac—the God of the Average Man"; "Jacob—the God of the Wicked Man"; and "Joseph—the God of the Normal Man." A series on night scenes of the Bible was suggested by one minister. Another minister preached a series of Sunday evening messages on courtship, marriage, divorce, the home, and related matters.

In any series that is presented there ought to be a unifying thought and purpose. The sermons should not be completely isolated from each other. If they are, they are not really a series.

When a series is decided upon, there should be careful advertising of the sermons in the newspapers, by printed cards, and in the church bulletin. The series should be talked about from the pulpit so that the people will see that these sermons are to be something special— something they cannot afford to miss.

The need of the people should largely determine the nature of the series the pastor will use. The pastor may feel that a particular book in the Bible has the message that his people need at a given time. One pastor felt that First Corinthians was the book his people needed at a certain period in his pastorate, and so he presented a series on that book to the great blessing of his people. This pastor was wise in not going into too much detail as he preached on this

comparatively long book; he used selected portions for his exposi-
tions.

Aids to a Successful Sunday Evening Service

In working for the operation of a successful Sunday evening service, there are several things the pastor should seek to do:

1. Maintain a high spiritual standard at all times. The pastor
should use every legitimate means to attract people to these services,
but he must make sure that the people get something worthwhile
when they come. Never should the means employed be allowed to
displace the main purpose of the service, namely, to preach the Word
of God and to win people to the Lord Jesus Christ and build them
up in Him.

2. Impress upon the membership of the church its responsibility
for the success of this service. This is increasingly important in
these last days. With the radio, the television, sports events and
drive-in theatres bidding for attention, it becomes more and more
difficult to get folk to come to the house of God on Sunday evening.
Even some professed Christians feel if they have attended church in
the morning they are relieved of responsibility to attend in the evening.

Therefore, the pastor needs to lay before his members their duty
of cooperation in connection with the Sunday evening service. If
the pastor cannot count on his own members to be loyal to this service by their attendance and prayers, it is not likely that outsiders will
be attracted. But with a membership that is enthusiastic about this
service, it is sure to be successful. Enthusiasm is contagious, and folk
will begin to see that attendance on Sunday evening is worthwhile.

Many churches do have a well-attended Sunday evening service
from week to week, which proves that this is not an impossibility.
People are bound to do something on Sunday evening. They need
to be challenged to do something worthwhile. Being in a church
where the glorified Lord manifests Himself in His Word is the best
possible place for Christians to be at that time. Think how much
Thomas missed by not being in "church" that first Sunday evening!

3. Enlist the support of the young people in the Sunday evening
service. Young people are attractive. Their presence will do something for the service. Young people are energetic, and they will do
something on Sunday evening. The church ought to seek to capture

this energy for a worthwhile purpose. This will not only add attractiveness to the Sunday evening service but will doubtless save some young people from moral and spiritual shipwreck.

The pastor can enlist the support of his young people by visiting their meetings and challenging them to support the evening service. He can use them in the service from time to time. He can encourage a young people's choir. He may arrange for singspirations following the regular service. Such a gathering may be held in the church or in the homes of the young people. The pastor can also gear some of his sermons to the problems and challenges of young people. This will tend to attract them to the services.

Many pastors are finding that young people go beyond the adults in loyalty and willingness to support the work of the church, including the Sunday evening service as well as other phases of Christian service. The young people need this service, and this service needs the young people. Therefore every effort should be made to see that the two are brought together.

4. Keep the Sunday evening service within a reasonable time limit. Many folk have to rise early on Monday morning to begin a new week's work. Children and young people have to go to school. The children can get home in time for a full night's rest if the service is closed early; thus the parents will be more likely to attend this service and bring their children. Moreover the older young people will be able to have a singspiration after the regular service without being kept up too late. Therefore the pastor will do well to keep his Sunday evening service from becoming too long.

RECOMMENDED READING

DOLLOFF, EUGENE D. *Sunday Night Services Can Be Successful.* New York: Fleming H. Revell Co., 1943.

BLACKWOOD, ANDREW W. *Preaching from the Bible.* Nashville: Abingdon-Cokesbury Press, 1941.

Chapter 8

THE MIDWEEK PRAYER MEETING

THE MIDWEEK PRAYER SERVICE has often been called the barometer which shows whether the spiritual life of the church is up or down. The pastor who does not emphasize prayer and the prayer meeting will not develop a spiritual church. His careful attention to building up this service will pay rich dividends. He should be persuaded that it is the most important service of the week apart from the Sunday services. The great need of developing the prayer meeting is apparent when it is observed that many churches have no such service at all and many others who do have one have a very small attendance. The neglect of prayer services in the Protestant church is appalling.

One authority on statistics has come forth with the sobering figures showing that whereas 40 percent of the Protestant church membership attend the Sunday morning worship service and 15 percent the evening service, only 5 percent attend the midweek prayer service of the respective churches.[1] The writer is glad to report that the denominational group to which he belongs (The Brethren Church) has a somewhat better record than this, namely, 80 percent attendance at the Sunday morning service, 49 percent at the Sunday evening service and 26 percent at the midweek prayer service.[2] But even the best statistics are not flattering and doubtless reflect one of the reasons for the church's spiritual impotency.

The development of the prayer service is bound to deepen the spiritual life of the church. It will teach believers to pray, cultivate Christian fellowship, and unite the church in seeking God's blessing upon the great enterprises of the church.

Different names have been given to this service by different pastors

[1]E. P. Alldredge, quoted by John E. Huss in *The Hour of Power* (Grand Rapids: Zondervan Publishing House, 1945), p. 30.
[2]*The Brethren Annual* (Winona Lake, Ind.: Brethren Missionary Herald Co., 1957), p. 16.

and churches. It has been called The Hour of Power, The Hour of Prayer, The Fellowship Service, The Mountaintop Hour, The King's Business Hour, The Church Night Service, The Family Night, The Sanctuary Service, as well as others. More often it is simply called The Prayer Service or The Midweek Prayer Service, but whatever the designation, the same objectives ought to be observed in this meeting.

Characteristics of the Midweek Service

Let us now turn our attention to some of the characteristics of a good prayer meeting.

It should be informal. Some have made the mistake of making this service just another preaching service, and prayer is given a very insignificant place. Others have made the midweek service a Bible study period, and again prayer is relegated to the background. This is unfortunate and minimizes the conception of prayer presented in the Scriptures.

Let the midweek service be an informal gathering of the saints of God for the purpose of taking seriously the promises of God about prayer. All who attend should be encouraged to take part. By such participation, they will grow in grace and receive a sense of really belonging to the family of God. Participation can be in the form of audible prayer, the quoting of a Scripture passage, the giving of a testimony, or the sharing of a thought gathered from reading a chapter of the Bible which has been assigned in advance for special consideration. Or, all who are present may quote in unison a familar passage from the Word of God or read responsively a section from it.

A spirit of friendliness and brotherly interest should pervade the service, for those who meet to pray are members of the family of God.

It should be a radiant service. Brightness and the joy of the Lord ought to pervade it. Much should be made of the song service. Sing the songs the people love to sing. Usually these are the old songs of the faith which emphasize prayer, devotion, and the varied character of Christ in whose name all true prayer is offered. This service of song is sure to help in brushing away some of the clouds which may have been hovering low over some during the busy weekdays of toil and trial. The songs will lighten the hearts and make it easier to pray and praise. A person may come to the prayer service depressed in spirit and a bit discouraged, but the melody of spiritual song and the pleading of the promises of God can send that same person away uplifted and encouraged.

It is a long step from Sunday to Sunday without this spiritual retreat. And the prayer meeting should be just this—a spiritual retreat filled with hope, assurance, joy, strength, and inspiration. Christians should leave the service knowing they have had an audience with God and are fortified to meet the difficulties of the way.

It should be a purposeful service. Because it is, first of all, a *prayer* meeting, prayer should be very prominent in it. And the praying ought to have an end in view, some purpose. Some praying is so indefinite that an answer would not be recognized if it came.

Definite matters for which to pray should be suggested. The pastor, who is in closer touch with the needs of the church than anybody else, will bring some of these things to the attention of the meeting. He should also give opportunity for others to present requests. Just as the marksman will not hit the target without careful aim, so aimless praying will not bring definite results.

The Bible meditation, too, should have a definite purpose. The Bible study should lead the group to better praying. It should also contribute to better praising of the Lord in testimony.

The Prayer Service should be fourfold in its content. The four elements which make up a well-rounded, complete service may be used in different ways and with varying order. There may be times when it will seem wise to dispense with one or another of them. But surely each of the following has a vital contribution to make to a good prayer service.

Praise. In this connection we are thinking of praise as it expresses itself in song. Let us teach our people the obligation and privilege of praising the Lord in song. We are taught to sing God's praises in the Word. "Serve the Lord with gladness: come before His presence with singing" (Ps. 100:2). After the redemption experience in Egypt, Israel sang a song on the banks of the Red Sea (Exod. 15). The Apostle Paul speaks about praising the Lord with "psalms and hymns and spiritual songs, singing and making melody in your heart to the Lord" (Eph. 5:19. See also Col. 3:16).

It is a wrong idea that some have that singing is just a nice way to pass the time until all the people arrive, and after that the service can really begin. Instead of this, the singing should be considered a vital part of the service.

John Huss says, "Music supplies the sparks in The Hour of Power."[3] Dolloff, quoting Auerbach, says, "Music washes away from the soul the dust of everyday life."[4] In Christian worship music has a unique place and can be used by the Holy Spirit to create a spiritual atmosphere.

Bible Meditation. Through the Bible God speaks to man. Surely man needs to hear God's voice before he goes to Him in prayer. It is well to think of the Bible meditation at the prayer meeting as a preparation for the prayer period. The Bible meditation should so warm the hearts of the listeners that they will find it easy to pray.

The midweek prayer service should not be made a Bible class but there should be time in it for a brief message of a devotional type. In this part of the service the pastor may choose to consider from week to week some of the great prayers of the Bible, or some of the aspects of prayer as presented in the Scriptures. He may want to go through one of the books of the Bible, usually one of the shorter ones, calling attention to a few of the major teachings of each chapter. Some pastors have used a series of Bible character studies. One pastor following this plan began with Abraham and concluded with Zacchaeus, finding a character to answer to each letter of the alphabet. Sometimes it is a blessing to receive the Scripture lesson from the audience, preferably along some particular line of thought. One leader of the writer's acquaintance once led a very interesting meeting of this kind, asking the people present to quote or read as many verses as possible having to do with the blood of Christ. After the verses were given, he then proceeded to base his remarks upon the ideas suggested by these verses. There are many other ways to present the Word of God in an attractive manner. The message from the Word should provide a good basis for the season of prayer which should follow.

Prayer. The element of prayer should never be eliminated from the midweek service. This is the main reason for gathering. When the pastor comes to the meeting, he should have carefully considered the matters that ought to be prayed for. Let him present these matters to the congregation. Let him also ask the congregation to present their requests. As the requests are presented, it is well to ask individuals to volunteer to pray for specific requests. This makes cer-

[3]Huss, *op. cit.*, p. 84.
[4]Dolloff, Eugene D., *It Can Happen Between Sundays* (Philadelphia: Judson Press, 1942), p. 34.

tain that no requests will be overlooked. Doubtless there will be times when the pastor will want to leave the taking of the requests on a purely voluntary basis. It is good to vary the procedure.

Public prayer should be more definite and concise than prayer in one's personal devotions. In order for many people to participate in the prayer session, two rules should be observed: (1) be brief, (2) be specific. If one person prays for twenty minutes, remembering all the church missionaries around the world and all the sick and bereaved at home, not many requests remain for others to remember—and not much time!

Prayer at the prayer meeting should concern the needs of the local church program (which would include the pastor, staff, officers, and various organizations of the church) the church's missionaries, the sick, the mourning, the unsaved, the church members as witnesses in their daily contacts, and so on.

If the congregation is sufficiently large, it is good to divide the group into several smaller groups. More individuals can and will participate in prayer in this way. In such a division the adult men usually form one division, the adult women another, the high school group another (others divide these to avoid the dating experience in the prayer meeting), the junior boys and girls still another, and possibly others. There are some pastors who have found it good to divide the assembly into twos—two men together, two women together, and in suitable age combinations—so that everyone can participate in the prayer experience. At times groups of four may engage in the prayer experience.

Let the pastor choose the plan which he thinks will best suit his situation. Better still, let him vary the methods he uses. This will help to keep the meetings from becoming monotonous.

Testimony. "Let the redeemed of the Lord say so" is a pertinent Scriptural exhortation from the Psalmist (Ps. 107:2). Believers from time to time ought to be given opportunity to testify about the goodness of the Lord in their lives. The point at which the period of testimony is conducted may vary. Sometimes it may seem best to have it before the season of prayer. At other times, the response will be better after it. At still other times the testimonies may be called for during the song service.

In some places it is difficult to get people to testify, since they have not been accustomed to it. In such a case, the pastor will need to develop them along this line. Some such aids as the following may be found helpful in getting a good response: (1) Suggest that each one present tell one thing for which he is thankful. (2) Have them tell of some answer to prayer they have experienced. (3) Have them give their favorite verse of Scripture and tell the reason why. (4) Read a chapter from the Word and ask those present to remark on their favorite verse in the chapter. (5) Start off with some such statement as "I love the Bible because . . . . . ." or "I love Jesus because . . . . . ." or "I am glad I am a Christian because . . . . . ." and ask them to finish the statement. (6) Ask the Christians to tell how old they are spiritually, relating also some of the experiences connected with their new birth. (7) Have a witnessing period around the subject, "Lives that have helped me most and why." (8) Have a season of testimony in which the testimonies are limited to three words, such as "I love Jesus," "Jesus is mine," or "Prayer changes things." There are many other such means which can be skillfully used to get people started in experiencing the privilege of giving a testimony. The use of such aids helps to vary the testimonies from time to time and tends to make them more interesting.

The prayer service should also be diversified. It should not be allowed to become monotonous. The main objectives of praise, prayer, meditation in the Word, and testimony should always be the same, but different methods may be used to gain those ends. Dolloff has very well sized up the situation in this regard when he says, "No person can relish the same food served in the same way every day in the year. Uniformity dampens the keenest enthusiasm after a brief time. If every instrument in the orchestra were a violin, we would soon weary of the music. If every flower in the world were a rose— though it were an American Beauty—our appreciation of flowers would eventually reach the zero point. This is true with regard to any church service, but especially so concerning the midweek gathering. If you want to eliminate the meeting, just do the same thing in the same way at the same time every week. Variety is the spiritual spice of an effective week-night service."[5] How may this variety be achieved? Consider the following suggestions:

(1) Vary the leadership occasionally. Usually it will be best for the pastor to be in charge of the service. This tends to give dignity to it and emphasizes its importance. However, upon occasion the

[5]Dolloff, *op cit.*, p. 31.

pastor may call upon the Sunday school superintendent, the chairman of one of the church boards, the missionary committee, the young people, or some other person or group to take the leadership. Calling upon others at times to lead the meeting not only provides the quality of change but also contributes to the upbuilding of those who provide the leadership. For instance, calling upon the young people to lead a meeting will give them a taste of definite Christian service and will show them they have a definite place in the prayer meeting. It is a misconception to think of this service as only for adults. There are splendid churches where the young people contribute more than their share to the attendance and, when given opportunity, do an excellent job of leading the prayer service.

(2) Use a missionary speaker in place of the regular Bible study. Missionaries do a lot for a church, and their appeal ofttimes aids greatly in leading the people to prayer. Pastors will be wise to have many missionaries speak in their services. They can be used effectively on prayer meeting night.

(3) Have a precious promise meeting from time to time. Before such a meeting the pastor should ask each individual to come to the meeting with a precious promise from the Word. When these are presented he should list them on a chalkboard for effect. The pastor then can make a brief talk on the promises of God.

(4) Give assignments to some individuals before they come to the service. This may be to read a particular chapter from the Word and pick out the most precious verse in it and be prepared to tell why, to present brief devotional thoughts, to lead the singing, and to present the prayer requests of the church's missionaries, perhaps reading a missionary letter.

(5) Make the service before Communion Sunday a preparatory service. At such a time it will be well to sing hymns that center in the Cross and have to do with dedication of life to Christ. The pastor may use a passage of Scripture bearing upon the Communion, explaining the meaning of the ordinances of the church. The prayer season should be directed along the line of self-examination. There should be petitions for a renewed appreciation of the meaning that lies behind the elements of the Communion.

(6) Some pastors have successfully used the question box in the midweek service. When this is done, usually about ten minutes is used in answering questions that members have placed in the box.

This plan has the advantage of showing the pastor what things are disturbing the minds of his constituency. He may learn, for instance, that some anti-Christian cult is making inroads among his flock. The pastor then can show from the Scriptures the solution to the problem at hand. The question box may also give him an opportunity of speaking concerning some things that would not ordinarily be dealt with from the pulpit. If conducted properly and over a limited period of time, the question box can produce constructive results and prove very interesting.

(7) Variety is also achieved in the prayer service by observing the season of prayer in different ways. Sometimes it is well to have the prayer season with the whole group together. At other times it is good to divide the group, as previously suggested. This latter method enables more people to take part in prayer, and some who would feel too timid to pray in a large meeting will not feel that way in smaller group. At still other times the pastor may divide the assembly into two or more groups irrespective of sex or age.

There are many ways to diversify the prayer meeting, but we have suggested only a few. The wide-awake pastor will use all the ingenuity the Lord has given him to make the midweek service interesting and contributory to the spiritual welfare of his church.

Concluding Considerations

In bringing to a conclusion our discussion of the midweek prayer service, there are several items which should not be overlooked if the service is to continue to be a vital factor in the life of the church.

1. Careful announcements need to be made about the service from week to week from the pulpit and in the church bulletin. It does not pay to rebuke those who do not come. Make the announcements so appealing that people will want to come. Cause them to see that they are missing something by not attending. It is reported that Spurgeon once said to his young preachers, "You will always catch more flies with sugar than with vinegar." Some pastors get into the reprehensible habit of scolding their members, but it is much better to make the service worthwhile and publicize it attractively.

John Huss offers three suggestions for interesting pulpit announcements about the prayer service: (1) feature the topic for the next meeting, (2) give a picture of what happened at Pentecost as the result of the preceding prayers in the Upper Room, and (3) call .

attention to the many people who would be enriched if the church would come to pray at the Hour of Power.[6]

2. Each meeting should be carefully planned. If nothing is done in the way of preparation for the prayer service except to select a few hymns and a Scripture passage, the pastor need not be surprised if the meeting tends to fall flat. This service is worthy of more attention than is ofttimes given it. Prayerfully plan the service, and use the plan that has been prepared unless the Spirit of God definitely seems to direct otherwise.

3. Begin the service on time, and by the same token close the service on time. Carelessness in the matter of commencing the meeting will lead the people to become careless in coming on time. It is just as easy to begin the service on time as ten or fifteen minutes late and if people learn that the time announced for the beginning of the meeting is the actual time the service will begin, they will come on time. Then the pastor ought to be fair with his people and close on time. Some of them have to rise early to go to work. Then there are children who must go to school. Commence the service on time, keep it within an hour's length, and close it on time. In the long run, this care will yield rich dividends.

4. Let the pastor persevere in the face of all discouragements. Such perseverance will usually issue in satisfying results. There is no place in the ministry for the pastor who grows weary in well-doing. Helen Keller defied every suggestion of defeat, even in the face of almost insurmountable difficulties, with amazing results. Abraham Lincoln sustained at least eight major political defeats before emerging upon his victorious career. What about the pastor and his struggle to develop a radiant prayer meeting? Success awaits him if he will put some real effort into it.

RECOMMENDED READING

BANKS, LOUIS ALBERT. *Illustrative Prayer Meeting Talks.* New York: Fleming H. Revell Co., 1901.

DOLLOFF, EUGENE D. *It Can Happen Between Sundays.* Philadelphia: Judson Press, 1942.

ERDMAN, CHARLES R. *The Work of the Pastor.* Philadelphia: Westminster Press, 1924. Pp. 102-105.

[6]Huss, *op. cit.,* pp. 51-52.

HUSS, JOHN ERVIN. *The Hour of Power*. Grand Rapids: Zondervan Publishing House, 1945.

LUCCOCK, HALFORD E. and COOK, WARREN F. *The Midweek Service*. New York: The Methodist Book Concern, 1916.

SELL, HENRY T. *Prayer Meeting Talks*. New York: Fleming H. Revell Co., 1931.

Chapter 9

THE EVANGELISTIC MEETING

EVERY TRUE GOSPEL CHURCH should be evangelistic at all times. Decisions for Christ ought not to be limited to special times when extra pressure is brought to bear. It should not be an uncommon thing for persons to confess Christ as Saviour and Lord at any service of the church. There are no "closed seasons" for the winning of souls. The "accepted time" for receiving Christ as Saviour is the immediate present which means that a Gospel-preaching church ought to have an outreach for decisions for Christ 365 days of the year.

But there are some distinct advantages in having special series of meetings when intensive efforts are put forth to win the lost and to revive the saved. Sometimes these meetings are called evangelistic meetings. At other times they are called revivals. Strictly speaking, there is a distinct difference between the two. The first has to do only with the effort to save the lost while the second has to do with quickening those who are already saved. However, the term "evangelistic meeting" will be used in this present treatment.

The Importance of Evangelistic Meetings

A consideration of the importance of such special efforts will likely induce the pastor and his church to give more attention to them. If they are not important, it is not worth the time and effort which they entail. The writer is convinced that they are important for a number of reasons.

They are scriptural. Numerous instances may be observed to show that in Bible times great spiritual blessing was brought to God's cause through special meetings. This is true both in the Old and in the New Testaments. There was the meeting on Mount Carmel when all Israel was called together in a time of great spiritual need in the nation and Israel turned back to God (I Kings 18). There was the meeting at Mizpeh in the days of Samuel when Israel came together

106

for the judgment of their sin and a new dedication unto the Lord (I Sam. 7). There was a great meeting at Samaria in New Testament times, with Philip as the evangelist. Many found Christ upon that occasion "and there was great joy in that city" as a result of this effort (Acts 8:5-8). A protracted meeting was held in Ephesus under the leadership of the Apostle Paul where first he preached in the synagogue for three months and then for the space of three years in the school of one Tyrannus. So successful was this evangelistic effort that the record says that "all they which dwelt in Asia heard the word of the Lord Jesus" (Acts 19:8-10).

The fact that God has called some to be "evangelists" in the church is a clear indication that there must be certain times when their ministry can be employed for the building up of the body of Christ (Eph. 4:11-12).

Evangelistic meetings produce results of lasting character. History reveals that such meetings have been owned and blessed of God. The efforts of such men as John and Charles Wesley, George Whitefield, Charles G. Finney, J. Wilbur Chapman, Reuben A. Torrey, Dwight L. Moody, William A. Sunday, and lately of Billy Graham demonstrate the moving of God in such meetings. A test made in almost any congregation will reveal that a large proportion of those who are Christians came to Christ in evangelistic meetings.

Moreover, such meetings tend to stimulate unusual interest and earnestness in prayer. In connection with them, special prayer meetings often are held. The Christians concentrate in praying for the salvation of certain individuals. When answers begin to come, those who pray are encouraged to further praying. Such a situation has a wholesome effect upon the church.

These meetings also incite special efforts for the salvation of the lost. Usually a personal workers' band is organized to aid in the meeting. Instruction is given in the art of soul-winning. These efforts have a good effect during the meetings and also tend to prepare the church to do the thing that it ought to be doing all the while.

Evangelistic meetings often stir up an unusual interest in the subject of religion in the community. People get to talking about the evangelist, the church, the pastor, and related subjects, and this interest is likely to influence some to come to the church to see what is going on, with the final result that some of them will obtain saving faith.

Therefore, because of these and other reasons that might be named, the pastor should not underestimate the value of such meetings.

Preparation for the Meetings

Assuming that the pastor is persuaded of the importance and possibilities of the evangelistic effort, what can he do to get ready for the meetings in his church once the decision has been made to conduct them? It is not sufficient simply to announce to the congregation that the meetings are about to begin. The average person today is so busy with so many activities that unless he is convinced of the importance of this project and made to see that it deserves a place of precedence in his program, he is not likely to give much attention to it. Proper preparation for an evangelistic effort should be in progress weeks ahead of the actual meeting. Following are some of the essential elements connected with a successful meeting:

1. The ministry of prayer needs to be emphasized. It is doubtful if there ever was a really effective evangelistic effort which was not preceded by prayer. There have been great results in the salvation of souls apart from great preaching, but not apart from earnest praying. It is still true, as it was in the early church, that the winning of the lost and the edification of God's people are connected with the prayers of the saints (Acts 2:42; 4:31). Every pastor ought to realize that a true demonstration of God's power cannot be worked up; it must be prayed down. The pastor will find that to get his people's earnest, continued prayer support is often the most difficult part of the meetings.

In looking toward a soul-winning effort, the following suggestions may prove helpful in utilizing the possibilities of prayer:

(1) *Begin praying for the meetings as soon as the decision concerning them is made, even though it be a year in advance.* Besides presenting a definite plea to God for His blessing in the forthcoming effort, prayer will help to awaken the people to the importance of the meetings. The repetition of this plea will deepen the impression.

(2) *Several weeks in advance of the meetings, there should be, in every service, increased emphasis on the need of fervency in praying for the meetings.* Not only should this emphasis be made in the Sunday services but also in the midweek prayer service and in the organizational meetings of the church.

(3) *About three weeks in advance of the evangelistic meetings,*

begin cottage prayer meetings in convenient sections of the church community. The number of these will depend on the size of the church and the geographical distribution of the members. Cottage prayer meetings have the advantage of focusing attention on the prayer ministry and of getting more people definitely engaged in the business of praying.

(4) The pastor will do well to help his membership in *the formulation of prayer lists.* He may provide them with small blank sheets with the wording at the top, "My Prayer List," with room below for the names and addresses of several persons. At the bottom of the list a place for the name of the one submitting the list should be provided. Encourage the membership to fill these out in duplicate, one copy to be kept by the person filling it out and the other to be given to the pastor. From these lists the pastor can add names to his prospect list. In most instances, the members of the church already have some contact with these people, and thus they are in a definite way the church's responsibility.

(5) *A definite room should be set apart for prayer during the progress of the meetings.* Individuals and groups should be urged to use this prayer room at any time of the day. A period for prayer just before each evening service may prove very helpful.

Additional plans to encourage people to pray include the setting of a certain time each day when all will covenant to pray unitedly for the meetings, the division of the membership into prayer partnerships with each partnership agreeing to pray together at definite times of their own choosing for the meetings, and the arrangement of a "prayer chain" around the clock so that a continuous volume of prayer ascends to the throne of grace while the meetings are in progress.

Some pastors have appointed a prayer chairman to organize the prayer ministry for the meetings. This is a good plan if the right person is available.

2. Then there is the matter of prospects. Before the meetings begin, a carefully prepared list of prospects should be available. The evangelist who comes is likely to ask for this. He will want to know that the church is definitely interested in reaching the lost and the unchurched. A list of prospects that the pastor can show him will encourage him and will make the task easier.

Where will the pastor get this list? From a number of sources:

(1) From the prayer lists he has received from his members.

(2) From observation of those who have been coming to any of the services of the church who have made no profession of faith or who belong to no church. In almost every church there are those who come from time to time to the Sunday school, the worship services, the young people's meetings or some other meeting of the church who are not affiliated with the church. Such are good prospects. The church already has a point of contact with them, and they may very readily be approached in the interests of the special meetings.

(3) From the Sunday school teachers. In many classes there are those who have not made a profession of faith, but they are already in contact with the church through attendance in one of its important departments. These people should be considered excellent prospects, because of the fact that the largest proportion of those who come into membership of the Protestant church come through the Sunday school.

(4) From the young people's societies. These young people are at a very impressionable age and can often be reached for Christ in an evangelistic meeting.

(5) From the pastor's calling ministry, in which he is constantly brought in contact with people who have spiritual need. Such names ought to be added to the prospect list and contacted during the meetings.

(6) From a canvass of the community surrounding the church for the purpose of seeing just what the field for evangelism actually is. This is especially true if the church is located in a large city or in a growing community. Such a canvass will provide many names for the prospect list.

A good prospect list will not only prove valuable in the time of the evangelistic meetings but, it will be of great service after the meeting is over as efforts to evangelize the community are continued.

3. Prior to the meetings the pastor will want to give some definite attention to the matter of *personal work*. He can preach on this subject with profit, emphasizing the responsibility of all believers to witness for Christ. Such a text as John 1:42, "And he brought him to Jesus," may be used for this purpose. This text sets forth the thrilling account of Andrew's bringing his brother Peter to Christ. Or he may use the story of the paralytic, as found in the second chapter of Mark. This unfortunate man was brought to Christ

by his four friends. Personal soul-winning on the part of its members should characterize every church.

In this connection, the pastor may want to urge some of his leaders to read some such book as James Conant's *Every-Member Evangelism,* in which the author shows how the idea suggested by the title really works.

Some pastors have found it successful before an evangelistic effort to give a series of lessons on how to win the unsaved to Christ. This can be done in connection with the midweek prayer service or at some more convenient time.

Before the meetings begin the pastor should have a band of personal workers who will be ready during the progress of the campaign. Quite likely the evangelist will ask to meet with this group and will urge them to make definite contacts for the meetings. The pastor should be ready to make assignments at this time. There is a principle in fishing that operates also in the work of the church. If we are to catch fish, we must go where they are. The personal contact, the invitation, and definite manifestation of concern for those in spiritual need are essential if the unconverted are to be brought under the sound of the Gospel.

4. *Publicity.* "It pays to advertise" is a slogan well known in the business world. The church is engaged in the most important business in the world. When a special effort for the salvation of men and the edification of the church is planned, the church ought to let the world know about it. People cannot be expected to come to meetings they know nothing about.

There are numerous ways to publicize an evangelistic effort. The pastor ought to select those means which seem most practical for his situation. Some of them are: attractive cards (postcard size) mailed and scattered throughout the community; window posters placed in public locations, such as business houses; the use of the radio with frequent spot announcements, and a telephone brigade to invite people to the meetings. One of the most effective means of advertising, of course, is the newspaper. News items and paid ads will yield results. Every pastor ought to cultivate a friendly relationship with the editor of the local paper as well as with the reporters. Furthermore, he ought to develop skill in writing interesting and terse articles for the newspaper. News items should adhere to the four *w's*: who? what? where? when?

If there are in the church the right kind of men for an advertising committee, the pastor will relieve himself of a lot of responsibility by appointing such a committee. Otherwise he had better see to this matter himself. Carl F. H. Henry's book, *Successful Church Publicity* is replete with suggestions on how to publicize the work of the church. Either the pastor or the committee he appoints will do well to consult Dr. Henry's book for fresh ideas.

In summary at this point, the church ought to use every legitimate means available to let the community know that something worthwhile is going on at the church. Good news ought to be told.

5. The music ministry of an evangelistic campaign should be given careful attention. Obtain the best song leader available, one who will be well qualified to select songs and special music conducive to evangelism. Impress upon the choir the importance of its ministry to the effectiveness of the meetings, and urge the choir members to be faithful throughout the meetings. It is important that there be plenty of good songbooks on hand. If the ones the church has been using are old and worn, this may be a good time to introduce a new book. Sometimes an abridged, paper-covered songbook is purchased for use during an evangelistic campaign. Since good singing can be a tremendous contribution to the meetings, careful planning for the music aspect of the endeavor is very worthwhile.

6. The conduct of an evangelistic meeting is so important and so increasingly difficult in these days that the pastor should seek the enlistment of the entire church before the effort is undertaken. All departments ought to cooperate enthusiastically. He will surely want the wholehearted support of the Sunday school in this endeavor. He will confer with the superintendent and gain his assistance and, if possible, appear before the Sunday school cabinet or Christian Education Council to tell the teachers and officers of his need of their help in this venture. Then the pastor will want to enlist the help of the young people's societies, the ushers, the deacons, and deaconesses, and all other active groups in the church. The ushers have a great responsibility in welcoming and seating strangers. Ofttimes the first impression newcomers get of a church is through the ushers. The pastor will make special effort to impress this corps of men with the need of faithfulness on their part. The pastor will also want to make sure that the sexton is on hand to be helpful during the meetings.

If the pastor can get his people to work with him in the evangelistic effort, he has gone a long way toward success. Perhaps one of the chief causes of failure among pastors is their inability to get people to work with them.

Before a special project of this kind begins, very likely the pastor will want to send out a pastoral letter outlining the plans for the meetings and requesting the earnest support of the membership. In this connection, some pastors have made very effective use of an "I WILL HELP" sheet listing ways members of the church can help in the evangelistic effort. A small square is placed beside each item, and the individual member is asked to check what items he will be able to care for during the meetings. Included in the list may be such matters as a promise to attend all of the meetings, agreeing to invite someone each day to the meetings, offering to use one's car to bring prospects to the meetings, helping in the entertainment of the visiting evangelist, distributing announcements, singing in the choir if requested, using the telephone in the interests of the meetings, and setting aside a definite time each day to pray for definite decisions for Christ.

The "I WILL HELP" sheet is helpful in showing the different ways people can serve. And usually when people definitely commit themselves to do certain things, they will do them.

7. The pastor ought also to see that there is a good selection of *tracts* available for the personal workers. It is a good thing to have in the vestibule of the church a well-filled tract rack with attractive tracts available for interested persons. Many evangelical churches have tract racks which make good Gospel messages in tract form constantly available. The tract rack can be of special service during evangelistic services.

8. The element of *special features* can be used effectively in such services, adding attractiveness and interest to the effort and often serving to bring to the services people who otherwise would not attend. Special features need to be carefully planned. They should contribute to the main purpose of the meetings and not be simply an end in themselves. Pastors and evangelists have used the Family Night, Young People's Night, Neighbors' Night, Father and Son Night, Mother and Daughter Night, Old Hymn Night, and other special designations to emphasize some vital phase of life and to increase attendance. One evangelist makes use of a Bible Night in his campaigns. He urges people to bring any interesting Bibles they

may have, big or small, in various languages, and puts them on display on a long table in the front of the church. He makes some remarks about them, invites the people to examine the Bibles at the conclusion of the service, and then proceeds to preach on "The Wonderful Word."

Children's meetings may be used with good results. They are usually held in the afternoons just after school. Not only do such meetings interest the children but through the children ofttimes parents become interested, and thus new homes are opened for the church.

In these and other ways special features may be employed, but only such features should be used as will definitely contribute to the main purpose of the meetings.

9. If during the evangelistic series, there is to be a *Sunday School decision service* it needs to be very carefully planned well in advance. The officers and teachers of the school need to be called together and inpressed with their responsibility in the undertaking. The teachers are the key persons. They should be urged to contact their pupils who have not made decisions so that there will be reasonable assurance that some will be ready to make decisions when the time of the service arrives. Usually such a service is held on one of the Sunday mornings during the campaign, preferably not the first. At this time the evangelist usually gives a short message to the Sunday school and asks for decisions. On a good many occasions the Sunday school decision service is one of the highlights of the meetings.

10. Of major importance in any evangelistic effort is the choice of the evangelist. The matter of *preaching* should be given first place in this effort. Who should the evangelist be? Sometimes he may be the pastor, with good results. Some pastors have the gift of evangelism to a marked degree. The Apostle Paul exhorted the young pastor, Timothy, to "do the work of an evangelist" (II Tim. 4:5), and there is no good reason why other pastors cannot be effective evangelists in their own churches.

In most situations, however, it seems best to engage an outside evangelist. There is a certain attraction about a new face and a new voice. Then, too, an outside man can get at certain difficulties in the church without seeming to be personal. It is apparent from the New Testament that God has called some men to be evangelists and not pastors (Eph. 4:11). Quite evidently the Lord intended for these men to be used in the church, in addition to the regular pastors, for the upbuilding of God's people. If an outside man is called to conduct an evangelistic series, the church will do well to make sure that he is a winner of souls, a sound preacher of the Word, and sane in his financial demands.

Some evangelists are strongly liked or disliked by some people in the congregation. The church should only invite an evangelist with whom the entire congregation will cooperate.

11. In preparing for an evangelistic meeting, careful consideration needs to be given as to how to care for those who come forward in response to the evangelist's invitation. Some evangelists have used the *inquiry room* to real advantage. This provision was an important factor in the evangelistic work of such men as Torrey, Chapman, Moody, Sunday, and—in modern days—of Billy Graham. The inquiry room method works well in the large campaigns, but it can also be adapted to the smaller ones. It has several advantages: (1) those who come forward are less likely to be embarrassed, (2) the personal worker is able to deal with the particular need of the inquirer and to establish new converts in their newfound faith, and (3) inquirers who may not have had the courage to make a decision in the public service are given an opportunity to talk with a spiritual leader. With the latter possibility in mind, it will be well to announce that if any are interested in talking about spiritual matters they are invited to come to the inquiry room at the close of the service.

The Revival In Progress

We have been considering what the pastor may do to get ready for a campaign. All such preparation, however, will not insure success. We must rely upon the Spirit of God, or all our planning and preparation will be of little value. Only the Spirit of God can bring a time of spiritual refreshing to the church.

Thus when the meetings begin, it should be the prayer of the pastor that the Holy Spirit will take every means at hand and use them for the quickening of the saints and the regenerating of sinners. It may be that the Spirit of God will work in His own marvelous way, setting aside some of the plans which have been made, to produce a work of grace in the church. This should be cause for rejoicing, but this does not mean that earnest preparation should not be made for evangelistic efforts. When prayerful preparation has been made, it is good then to stand by and see what God will do.

Through the faithful preaching of the Word, through the Spirit-directed praying of the church members and their earnest witnessing for the Lord Jesus Christ, the desired results will come. Let the fact be ever remembered in this sort of work that the victory comes "not by might, nor by power, but by my Spirit, saith the Lord" (Zech. 4:6). Since this is true, there are times when the Spirit of God brings a season of revival in a church without any human planning at all. Dr. Theodore L. Cuyler tells that in his own great church in Brooklyn, N.Y., gracious revival experiences most often came when he was preaching God's Word in his usual way and when the church was in an "average" condition. How blessed are such experiences!

The Follow-Up Work

After the meetings are over, a time of special responsibility confronts the pastor. It is no time to let down. Ofttimes such meetings reveal opportunities for a larger ministry. There are times when a special series of meetings does not realize many outward results. But usually they open doors of opportunity which, if entered, will produce results in days to come. Failure to conserve the efforts of a series of meetings can mean serious loss to the church and bring to naught much of the energy expended during the meetings.

In relation to the follow-up work, the following responsibilities are important:

1. Effort should be made to establish the new converts in the faith. The pastor should see that they get placed in the proper groups in the church, such as the right Sunday school class or the suitable young people's society. He should urge them to start right in the Christian life by faithful church attendance, definite Christian service, consistent reading of the Word of God, and prayer and attendance at the new converts' class if one is available. Some pastors have successfully used the Big Brother and Big Sister idea, in accordance with which each new convert is assigned to a mature Christian for a definite period of time, thus providing spiritual oversight and instruction. If more of this sort of thing were done, doubtless fewer converts would be lost to the church.

2. Instruction about *baptism* needs to be given to the new converts. The pastor should show them that this is the Lord's will for

a believer, that this is one of the first ways in which they can manifest their obedience to the Lord and give witness for Him. Baptism is a picture of the believer's identification with Christ in His death, burial, and resurrection, and every time the rite is observed the Gospel is preached to those who observe it. It is, therefore, the pastor's responsibility and privilege properly to instruct the new convert as to the significance of this sacred ordinance. Those who don't believe in immersion believe baptism is a symbol of purification.

3. Evangelistic preaching should be continued by the pastor following the meetings. He should seek to reach those who have not made a decision during the meetings but who were definitely under conviction. There is a type of individual who will respond more readily to the invitation of a faithful pastor than to that of a professional evangelist. At any rate, the pastor will do well to keep on drawing the net for an additional spiritual ingathering.

4. Attention should be given to conservation of the zeal for personal evangelism which was manifest during the meetings. Now may be the best time for the organization of a regular personal workers' band if one is not already in operation in the church. There will be further consideration of such an organization in chapter 20. Zeal for this sort of work, which has been stirred up during the meetings, should not be lost.

5. Some sermons on how to grow in the Christian life should be preached by the pastor. Such sermons will be helpful to the new converts, who are "babes in Christ" and know little of the Christian life. These sermons will also benefit the older Christians, some of whom may not have been taking advantage of the means of grace as they should. Such a text as II Peter 3:18, in which the believer is definitely exhorted to "grow in grace, and in the knowledge of our Lord and Saviour Jesus Christ, may be used with great blessing." Growth is normal for the Christian, and God's supply of the means to this end needs to be emphasized by the pastor again and again. Furthermore, the pastor needs to expose some of the hindrances to growth in grace which the Word of God points out. Such Scriptures as II Corinthians 5:20, Luke 19:13, Acts 1:8, the parable of the sower in Matthew 13, and countless other passages may be used by the faithful pastor to the profit of his people.

Realizing what a real heaven-sent revival can do for a church, the burden of the true pastor's heart will echo the requests expressed in olden times by the Psalmist and the Prophet: "Wilt thou not revive us again, that thy people may rejoice in thee?" (Ps. 85:6) and "O Lord, revive thy work in the midst of the years" (Hab. 3:2).

RECOMMENDED READING

CONANT, J. E. *Every-Member Evangelism.* Philadelphia: The Sunday School Times Co., 1926.

CUYLER, THEODORE L. *How To Be a Pastor.* New York: The Baker and Taylor Co., 1890. Chap. 9.

EVANS, WILLIAM. *Personal Soul Winning.* Chicago: Moody Press, 1910.

HARRISON, EUGENE MYERS. *How To Win Souls.* Wheaton, Ill.: Van Kampen Press, 1952.

HENRY, CARL F. H. *Successful Church Publicity.* Grand Rapids: Zondervan Publishing House, 1943.

LEAVELL, ROLAND Q. *Evangelism: Christ's Imperative Commission.* Nashville: Broadman Press, 1951.

PECK, JONAS ORAMEL. *The Revival and the Pastor.* New York: Hunt and Eaton Publishers, 1894.

RICE, JOHN R. *We Can Have Revival Now.* Wheaton, Ill.: Sword of the Lord Publishers, 1950.

RILEY, W. B. *Pastoral Problems.* New York: Fleming H. Revell Co., 1936. Chap. 15.

TORREY, REUBEN A. *How to Promote and Conduct a Successful Revival.* New York: Fleming H. Revell Co., 1901.

Chapter 10

THE PUBLIC INVITATION

THE PASTOR should always be preaching for a verdict. He should expect decisions as a result of the preaching of the Word of God. There are many different kinds of decisions that people need to make, but it is indeed a poor sermon that does not lead to decisions of some kind. Some people need to decide to accept the Lord Jesus Christ as Saviour. Some ought to decide to dedicate their lives to Him. Others will need to trust Him more fully. Some will need to forsake a particular sin. There will be those who feel the need of praying more, reading the Bible more, witnessing more, being more faithful to the services of God's house, being more generous in their offerings to the Lord's work, and so on.

The type of sermon will determine to a large extent the nature of the decisions to be expected. But, when the Word of God is proclaimed faithfully and in the power of the Holy Spirit, decisions will be made. The pastor therefore should expect them. Not all of them need to be public decisions, though many of them should be. Let the pastor be persuaded as to the importance of giving invitations and proceed to give them in the most effective way possible.

Why Give Invitations?

Why should the pastor give public invitations at the conclusions of his sermons? There are four good reasons:

1. Invitations are Scriptural. Many examples can be shown that men of God in both Old and New Testament times gave invitations in their preaching. Moses stood in the gate of the camp of Israel and challenged the people in these words: "Who is on the Lord's side? let him come unto me" (Exodus 32:26). Listen to Joshua as he gave his last charge to his people before his death: "Choose you this day whom ye will serve; whether the gods which your fathers served that were on the other side of the flood, or the gods of the Amorites,

in whose land ye dwell: but as for me and my house, we will serve the Lord" (Josh. 24:15). After King Josiah of Judah had read the Word of God to the people, "he caused all the people in Jerusalem and Benjamin to stand to it" (II Chron. 34:32), that is, he exhorted them to be true to the words which he had read.

Coming to the New Testament, we find Jesus again and again challenging his hearers to make decisions. He said to the two brothers, Andrew and Peter, on one occasion, "Follow me, and I will make you fishers of men" (Matt. 4:19). In words of tenderness and beauty, He said to the multitude, "Come unto me, all ye that labor and are heavy laden, and I will give you rest" (Matt. 11:28). In concluding the record of Peter's great sermon on the day of Pentecost, the Scripture says, "With many other words did he testify and *exhort,* saying, Save yourselves from this untoward generation" (Acts 2:40). When Paul preached in the synagogue at Ephesus for three months, he *persuaded* the things concerning the kingdom of God (Acts 19:8). When Paul ministered to the Jews while a prisoner in Rome, "he expounded and testified the kingdom of God, *persuading* them concerning Jesus" (Acts 28:23).

It should not be overlooked that the closing chapter of the Bible contains an invitation of tremendous power: "And the Spirit and the bride say, Come. And let him that heareth say, Come. And let him that is athirst come. And whosover will, let him take the water of life freely" (Rev. 22:17).

The pastor, therefore, has good precedent from the Scriptures for giving invitations.

2. Invitations are reasonable. The purpose of preaching is to get men and women to receive Christ as Saviour and to get them established in the Christian faith. The invitation aims to get people to act on what has been proclaimed as a responsibility and a privilege. It is quite logical to urge them to do the thing that has been set forth in the Word. It would be a poor salesman who would describe in glowing and attractive terms the product he is supposed to sell but would do nothing to get his prospect to purchase the product.

So it is in spiritual matters. People need to be exhorted, persuaded, and invited to do the thing that has been set before them. Sometimes just a little urging, just a little persuading, is all that is needed to get folks to make a great decision. It is a tragedy, then, not to supply this need!

3. The giving of an invitation at the conclusion of a sermon is supported by good modern psychology. Emotions aroused and desires stirred soon pass away unless they are acted upon at once. Good impulses are harder to generate the second time. Therefore, pastors ought to "strike while the iron is hot" and take advantage of the good work which has been accomplished by the preaching of God's Word. It seems like a spiritual crime to fail to get people to do what they know they ought to do upon the basis of the Word.

4. Finally, the giving of public invitations is practical. They work. They produce results. This has been proved by evangelists and soul-winning pastors and churches. Many are the individuals who, feeling that the evangelist's or pastor's invitation was the call of God to their hearts, responded and found life and satisfaction in the Lord Jesus Christ.

Methods of Giving an Invitation

There are many different ways of giving an invitation. It will be a good thing for the pastor to study carefully different methods of discharging this part of his responsibility lest he get into a rut and prove less effective than he could be. Dr. F. D. Whitesell has written a very interesting and helpful book entitled *Sixty-five Ways to Give an Evangelistic Invitation*. Not all of the invitations that the pastor will give will be of the distinctly evangelistic type, yet Dr. Whitesell's book will provide good suggestions as to how to vary his procedure in this phase of his work. Some hints are offered in the succeeding paragraphs on methods of giving an invitation.

Give it upon the basis of the sermon which has just been preached. It should not be difficult to give an effective invitation if the sermon leads up to it. At least it should be much easier. This method will tend to prevent monotony and give greater effectiveness in presenting the invitation, for people then can easily see the purpose of it. There is also a psychological principle here. It is easier to continue the same train of thought than to break into something entirely new. In the invitation the preacher should not want to break the train of thinking his message has developed. Rather he should capitalize upon it and get his listeners to do something about the message of God which has been proclaimed. The import of the invitation should be: "God has spoken to your heart; now what are you going to do about it? You ought to receive God's message wholeheartedly."

If the pastor has been preaching on Christ's stilling the storm on Galilee, let him appeal to his hearers to let Christ still the storm in their hearts, the storm that sin has brought. Or, if his sermon has been on Christ, the Good Shepherd, he should appeal to his hearers to make this Shepherd their own. He is the one who willingly laid down His life that they might have life. Or if the sermon is on the woman at the well, let the preacher appeal to his listeners to drink of the water of life which only can satisfy the thirst of the soul. In this way it will be easy to introduce a bit of variety into the invitations, tending to make them more effective.

Sometimes the invitation may be given immediately at the conclusion of the sermon without singing a hymn. There is no rule that demands the singing of a hymn when the invitation is given. There will doubtless be times when the invitation will be more effective without a hymn. This method harmonizes with the psychological principle which recognizes that the interests aroused are likely to linger for some time. Why, then, break into the advantage which has been attained by a forceful message? The pastor must allow himself to be led by the Spirit of God whether to use a hymn or to omit it. Very effective invitations have been extended immediately following the close of the sermon by challenging those who wish to accept Christ to come forward or to stand to their feet.

It is often well to announce a hymn appropriate to the sermon at its close and ask people to respond in the way suggested by the sermon. Recognizing the truth of what was said in the preceding consideration, we know, on the other hand, that there are some distinct advantages to the use of a hymn in the invitation. For one thing, a good invitation hymn possesses an emotional appeal that is helpful. Then again, it aids in removing embarrassment for those who wish to take a stand for Christ. When the audience is singing, their attention will be partially, at least, concentrated upon their singing and not entirely upon those who may be responding to the invitation. This may be a condescension to human frailty, but it is a factor none the less. Some persons are extremely sensitive to the gaze of a congregation. Let the pastor be considerate in these matters and use every legitimate means to get individuals to make the decision they ought to make.

The pastor may well offer a few remarks between the verses of the invitation hymn, urging decisions for Christ. The words of the hymn may suggest these remarks, or some thought in the sermon may be reemphasized. But the pastor should guard against the habit of prolonging his invitations unduly. He should not add extra points to his sermon, just a few pertinent words of appeal. If the practice of prolonging the invitation becomes a regular thing, the main purpose will be defeated in the end. If the Spirit of God has done His work in the preaching of the Word, undue urging will be unnecessary.

Some pastors and evangelists find it effective to call for the bowing of all heads when the invitation is given. They then ask if there are those present who will indicate by the raised hand their desire to accept Christ. In other cases, they may ask how many there are who will indicate by the raised hand their desire to be prayed for. Then, if there are responses, these are urged to come forward for public confession or further consultation. When this method is used, the preacher should make sure that he keeps faith with those who raised their hands for prayer and pray for them whether or not they come forward. The pastor should avoid all trickery in the giving of the invitation.

It is important for the preacher to make clear the exact nature of his invitation. Some invitations are altogether too general. If individuals responded, they would not know why they responded. Sometimes it is well to emphasize one plea; for instance, to confess Christ as Saviour. Or the plea might be for rededication of life. Or the preacher might feel led to make a special appeal for commitment of lives for definite Christian service. At other times he may feel led to make a twofold or even a threefold invitation. But however he does it, he ought to make perfectly clear just what the invitation is. This is no time for the preacher and the congregation to be in a fog.

There will doubtless be times when the pastor will feel led not to give the regular invitation but to invite any who would like to speak to him on spiritual matters to meet at the close of the service. Some sermons do not lend themselves very readily to the extending of an invitation at the close.

Then there will be other times when the minister will feel led to ask everyone to make a decision without any public manifestation. The type of sermon preached will determine this. He might be preaching on the subject of prayer. After challenging his people to be more faithful in this ministry, he might feel it best to ask each one, where he is, to covenant with God to set aside some time each day for prayer. It is doubtful that a public manifestation would be wise in this situation.

No matter what the invitation may be, it should always be given in great love and tenderness. "Come unto me," said Jesus. People cannot be driven or scolded into the kingdom of God. And it is doubtful if much real success is derived from trying to scare people into making a decision. In this part of his ministry the pastor needs the filling of the Holy Spirit so that he will manifest the compassion of Christ and be guided to say the right words. He needs to remember how often God says "come" in the Scriptures. From the time when God said to Noah, "Come thou and all thy house into the ark" until the last chapter of the Book of Revelation, God has been inviting man to "come" to Him for His salvation and for all that man needs for his welfare. God's ministers need the love and the power to say it like He says it, in some degree at least. This fact impressed itself upon the writer's mind in an unforgettable manner one time during an evangelistic meeting in his church. The evangelist was drawing the net in a Sunday school decision service. Apparently everything was in readiness for a good response. The teachers had worked faithfully. Some of their class members had indicated that they were ready to make a public confession at this service. But the evangelist appeared a bit sophisticated. He was gruff in his manner. He took it for granted that many would come forward when he gave the invitation. But no one came. Everyone stood motionless. Finally, in disgust the evangelist gave up and walked off the platform into a side room to cool his ire.

The Sunday school superintendent sensed the situation and took charge. He gave the invitation in his quiet, earnest manner, and while the evangelist was sulking in the side room, about twelve young people gave their hearts to the Lord! Let the love of Christ permeate the invitation. It will pay rich dividends.

The Frequency of Invitations

Should an invitation be given at every service? Pastors differ considerably as to this matter. Situations differ also. The writer feels that usually some sort of an invitation should be given for response to the message which has been delivered. This is especially true in a congregation where an evangelistic type of ministry is practiced.

It is also true in churches where there are many visitors. In some churches, where a static situation prevails and all of those who attend the services are members of the church, it may be futile to give an invitation at every service.

In this matter, however, the pastor should not trust his feelings altogether. The time when he feels the least like giving an invitation may be just the time when someone is ready. The best policy to follow is to preach the Word of God faithfully at all times and let the Holy Spirit be the guide as to when the invitation should be given.

RECOMMENDED READING

WHITESELL, FARIS D. *Sixty-five Ways to Give Evangelistic Invitations.* Grand Rapids: Zondervan Publishing House, 1945.

Chapter 11

THE TAKING OF CONFESSIONS IN
THE PUBLIC SERVICE

THE NORMAL, HEALTHY CONDITION in a church is for individuals to be coming to the Lord all through the year. Too often decisions are only made at particular times, such as Easter, Christmas, or during evangelistic meetings. But a much better spiritual condition is manifested if confessions of faith in Christ, as well as other commitments to Him, are made all through the year. Of the early church we read, "The Lord added to the church daily such as should be saved" (Acts 2:47). In those days there were no closed seasons on confessions of faith.

The Word of God stresses the importance of making public confession of faith. Its virtue is evident in the following four ways:

1. It is obedience to very plain statements of God's Word, such as Matthew 10:32-33 and Romans 10:9-10.

2. It is a witness to the world that the individual has taken a definite stand for Christ. The Scriptures exhort believers to be separate from unbelievers. The testimony of believers should give forth no uncertain sound. Their light should not be hidden under a bushel. A declaration in the public service of their faith is a definite step in this direction and is to be encouraged. See II Corinthians 6:17 and Acts 1:8.

3. It enlists the prayers of God's saints on behalf of those who make confessions. The spiritually-minded folk in the church will be apt to pray for those who have made a public declaration of their faith with the result that they will be more likely to become established in their newfound faith.

4. Finally, it stimulates courage and boldness on the part of the new convert, aiding him to get off to a good start in his Christian experience.

126

A public confession of faith is not to be mistaken for personal, heart acceptance of Christ as Saviour. The latter is outwardly expressed and affirmed by a confession of faith. The pastor needs to make sure as far as possible that those who respond to an invitation in the public service have had a vital experience with the Lord. Coming forward in a church service can never be a substitute for that. But folk who have made definite decisions for Christ should be willing openly to announce the fact to the world. "Whosover therefore shall confess me before men, him will I confess also before my Father which is in heaven" (Matt. 10:32).

Let us now consider the different types of confessions which are made by individuals who come forward in the public service and how they should be dealt with by the pastor.

I. *How to Take the Confession of One Who Comes Forward to Confess Christ as Saviour.*

1. There should be no awkwardness at such a time. The pastor should know just what to do and should indicate what the one coming forward is to do until the pastor is ready to take the confession. He should tell him where to stand or sit until the pastor has finished giving the invitation or until the singing of the final hymn is completed, thus preventing awkwardness as much as possible.

2. Quietly question the one who has come forward as to his desires, unless they are perfectly clear already. In many cases, those who come forward have done so by previous arrangement with the pastor as a result of personal dealing or counseling. In such cases, the action is understood and there is no need of questioning in the public service.

3. It is well to have the congregation remain standing while the purpose of the stand which the person has made is stated and while the confession is taken. This tends to relieve embarrassment and is a mark of respect.

4. The pastor may then question the confessor somewhat as follows, taking him by the hand:

(1) "Mr. Doe [or, my friend or brother], do you believe that the Bible is the Word of God?" This is a good place to begin the questioning, for unless there is a realization that God has spoken in the Bible, there is not much of a foundation upon which to build.

(2) "Do you believe what the Bible has to say with respect to the Lord Jesus Christ as God's only begotten Son?"

(3) "Do you believe that when He died upon the Cross He died for the sins of the whole world and for your sins in particular and arose for your justification?"

(4) "Do you now definitely accept Him (or confess Him) to be your own personal Saviour?"

When the pastor has received affirmative answers to these questions he will give the new convert some words of assurance such as, "The Bible says, 'As many as received Him, to them gave he power to become the sons of God, even to them that believe on his name.' You have *received* Him. You have *believed* on His name. Therefore you may be sure that you are a child of God and have eternal life." See also Romans 10:9-10, John 5:24, and John 3:36, which may be used in this connection.

5. Then let the pastor follow by saying, "May the Lord bless you abundantly for the confession you have made and help you to walk in the way He shall lead." Prayer should follow immediately, with the releasing of the hands.

6. The congregation should be encouraged to show a special interest in those who come forward by expressing their joy to them. Such folk need comfort and encouragement at this time. They should never be left unnoticed at the close of the service. Such instruction of the congregation had better be given at some time other than when individuals come forward. It may be well to give such instruction at the midweek prayer service or at the church business meeting. In addition, it is a good thing for certain individuals to be assigned the responsibility of greeting the new converts. This responsibility may be given to the deacon board or to the personal workers' band.

7. It should be understood that in all cases where individuals are making profession of faith or entering the membership of the church that the church clerk will get the names and addresses of such persons.

8. Finally, but not least important, the pastor should arrange for the baptism of new converts and attend to the necessary follow-up work. This is of extreme importance in order that the new folk

THE TAKING OF CONFESSIONS IN THE PUBLIC SERVICE 129

shall become established in the church and not lost to it as has too often been the case because of neglect at this point.

II. *How to Take the Confession of One Who Comes Forward for Rededication of the Life.*

1. In such cases the pastor will follow the same preliminary steps as indicated in the case of those coming forward to confess Christ as Saviour. See points 1-3 under previous consideration.

2. A statement then should be made to the congregation as to why the individual has come forward. It may be something after this fashion: "This brother [or sister] comes to confess that he has not been living as close to the Lord as he should, that he has wandered from the path of His will and desires to get back into His fellowship and service."

3. The confessor then should be questioned somewhat as follows:

(1) "Brother, do you reaffirm your faith in the Lord Jesus Christ as your Saviour and Lord?"

(2) "Do you confess that you have walked apart from His will and that it is your desire to be restored to fellowship with Him?

"The Bible says, 'If we confess our sins, he is faithful and just to forgive us our sins, and to cleanse us from all unrighteousness.' It also says, 'I will heal their backsliding, I will love them freely' (I John 1:9; Hosea 14:4).

"Inasmuch as you come with sincerity of heart you may claim these promises for yourself just now.

"In order that you may keep close to Him in all the days which are ahead, let Christ be the Lord of your life, read His word every day, pray to Him often, do not neglect the worship of His house, and seek to be guided by His Spirit into some service for Him every day."

3. There should then be a prayer of rededication seeking strength from the Lord for this person, asking God to give him complete victory in his life.

4. The saints of God should come forward after the service is dismissed and rejoice with the restored one in his victory.

III. *How to Take Care of a Life-Service Commitment.*

1. Preliminary steps similar to the former cases should be followed.
2. Then the pastor should make a public statement somewhat as

follows: "This young man has come this morning in response to the call of the Lord to give his life for definite service, as the Lord may lead. Surely this is a joyous occasion for all of us. Romans 12:1 says, 'I beseech you therefore by the mercies of God that ye present your bodies a living sacrifice, holy, acceptable unto God, which is your reasonable service.' This one has come today in answer to this exhortation to give himself completely into the hands of the Lord. It is a decision that is pleasing unto the Lord."

3. The individual then should be questioned somewhat as follows:

"Is it your purpose to offer your life for full-time service as the Lord may lead?

"Are you willing to be guided by the Spirit of God as to the nature of this service and in the preparation for it?"

4. If there are other life-service folk in the congregation it will be a splendid thing to have them also come forward and join hands in a prayer of dedication and, possibly, the singing of a consecration hymn such as "Oh Jesus, I Have Promised" or "Take My Life, and Let it Be." Such an expression is a good object lesson for the congregation. It can easily result in the dedication of other lives to the Lord's service.

5. Some words should then be directed to the one (or ones) who has presented himself to the Lord in this definite way, assuring him that the Lord will guide him in the matter of the choice of a field of service, the preparation for it, and related matters. The words of Psalm 37:23 will be found to be true in his case, "The steps of a good man are ordered by the Lord: and he delighteth in his way."

6. There should be a prayer of dedication and of seeking direction for the person who has so dedicated himself. It pays to be very personal in such cases. A lasting impression likely will be made.

7. The members of the congregation ought to express at the close of the service their joy in the commitment which has been made.

8. The pastor will not neglect to follow up such decisions with counsel and encouragement. He will want to take an interest in the young person's schooling, in his companions, in his spiritual habits, and in his reading. He will want to guard him against relapses. If there are several young people in the congregation who have dedicated themselves to the Lord's service, it will be well for him to form them into a Life Volunteer (or Service) Band for purposes of prayer, counsel, and encouragement.

IV. *How to Read a Church Letter and Receive Iindividuals into the Church.*

1. During the time of invitation the pastor may announce that he has received the church letters of the individuals he will name and that if they will come forward during the singing of the closing hymn he will be glad to read the letters and receive them into the membership of the church. In some churches such letters are previously acted upon by the official board, which recommends the reception of these people into the fellowship of the church. But in any case, the writer feels that it is good to dignify these letters by reading them before the congregation.

Some pastors prefer to have an understanding before the service begins with the parties whose letters are to be read so that they will come forward without any word from the pulpit at the time of the invitation. The writer prefers the former method because it avoids misunderstanding.

2. Upon coming forward, the candidates for membership should be greeted and directed where to stand until it is time for their reception into the membership. Some churches receive new members whenever they present themselves. Others prefer to set definite times during the year and to precede these occasions with training sessions for prospective members. The latter has the advantage of preparing individuals for more intelligent decisions and more adequate participation in the life of the church.

3. When the invitation has been completed or the closing hymn finished, with the congregation remaining in a standing position, the letter or letters should be read in their entirety, as before indicated. This procedure may be modified somewhat if there are several members of one family with a definite similarity in the letters. In such a case, the first one should be read with the indication that the others are similar.

4. Following the reading of the letter or letters, the pastor will take the prospective member by the hand and say, "My brother [or sister, or first name in case of children], it gives me great pleasure as pastor of this church to extend to you the right hand of fellowship and to welcome you as a member of this congregation. We pray that your coming among us may prove of genuine blessing to your soul and that you in turn may be a blessing to the church. May God bless

and use you." On this occasion the minister may ask the chairman of the official board to stand with him and to extend the right hand of fellowship.

5. The pastor then offers prayer for the newly received member or members, asking God to bless abundantly this new relationship.

6. The pastor will encourage his members to greet the new members and make them feel welcome in the church family. If the time of reception has been set long enough in advance, a reception for new members may be held after the service and accompanied by refreshments.

V. *How to Deal with Those Who Come Forward Looking Toward Church Membership in the Near Future.*

Those in this category may include some who have not yet had their church membership transferred, or who have not been baptized according to the practice of the church, or who have suddenly come to the persuasion that they would like to join the church they are now attending.

1. The same preliminary steps should be used as in the first type previously considered.

2. The pastor should then state the situation to the congregation clearly and announce that when baptism has taken place or church letters have been received or any other necessary requirements are fulfilled these folk will be received into the church.

3. This statement may well be followed by questioning the one who has come forward in the following manner:

"In coming forward today for church membership, do you reaffirm your faith in the Lord Jesus Christ as your personal Saviour?

"Is it your desire in coming into the church that your spiritual life shall be deepened and that your walk with God shall be closer than ever before?

"Is it your purpose to make the Bible your rule of faith and practice from day to day?"

4. Following an affirmative answer to each of the above questions, an assuring statement such as this may be made: "May the Lord bless you for the step you have taken, and may your coming into the fellowship of this church cause you to grow in grace and in the knowledge of the Lord Jesus Christ."

5. The experience may be closed with a prayer which looks to-

ward the near future when the applicant or applicants shall be received into the membership of the church.

In conclusion, it needs to be emphasized that in dealing with the several classes of individuals as they come forward in public meetings, the pastor will be in the place of special privilege. In each case, with rare exceptions, individuals come forward in response to some sort of a spiritual decision. Their hearts are tender toward the things of God and the church. They are reaching for higher attainment in the Christian realm. This is the pastor's opportunity to be of great spiritual help. By a faithful ministry at such times, he will be able to exert an influence that will mean much in the way of spiritual development in future days. Let the pastor be at his best at such times!

Chapter 12

ADMINISTERING BAPTISM
AND COMMUNION

THE IMPORTANCE of the ordinances of baptism and communion should be evident to every pastor. Practically every denomination practices at least these two ordinances. Their importance is further suggested by their prominence in the New Testament. They symbolize truths that relate to the very heart of the Gospel.

Baptism was approved by Christ when at the beginning of His public ministry he insisted that the rite be performed upon Himself at the hands of John the Baptist. Then at the close of His earthly ministry as He gave the great commission He commanded baptism to be observed until the end of the age (Matt. 28:19-20).

As for the communion, it was instituted by our Lord on the night before He was betrayed. He asked that it should be observed "in remembrance of Me" (I Cor. 11:24) and added in connection with one phase of the service, "If ye know these things happy are ye if ye do them" (John 13:17). Their observance is essential not to salvation, as many have thought and argued, but to obedience. The Captain of our salvation has asked His followers to observe them, and no good reason can be assigned for setting them aside.

It is not the purpose of this chapter to discuss the doctrinal aspects of baptism and communion but to consider their administration. Incidentally, of course, doctrinal implications will be suggested. The services should be made as impressive as possible, in keeping with the great truths which they symbolize. No little care is needed to make them so. Proper administration of these rites will contribute much toward the impression they will make upon their recipients.

BAPTISM

Thinking first of the baptism service, let us note the preparations that need to be made for it.

1. Proper instruction of the candidates is necessary. The importance and meaning of the rite should be explained to candidates so that they will enter into it with an appreciation of its significance. The pastor can care for this by individual or group instruction, depending upon the number to be baptized. It is unfortunate when baptism is thought of simply as a form to be observed in order to gain membership in the church. It should be made clear to the candidates that baptism has nothing to do with obtaining one's salvation. Salvation comes solely through faith in the finished work of the Lord Jesus Christ. Baptism is a picture of the salvation which has already been received and is one of the first acts of obedience in which the redeemed soul should engage. The true believer enjoys profound happiness in obeying his Lord. What has just been said excludes the idea of baptismal regeneration, which tends to make salvation consist in what man does rather than in what God has done. The concept that there are mystical powers in the baptismal waters which somehow wash away man's sins should be repudiated. Let the candidate be sure of the meaning of the rite in which he is to participate.

2. The baptismal service should be announced in at least two worship services in advance. It should be stressed in the weekly bulletin and included in the monthly calendar of services and meetings. The rite is worthy of being witnessed by a large group. There is a wonderful sermon in it. The whole work of the Lord Jesus Christ for the believer may be seen in the observance. Immersionists, of whom the writer is one, commonly believe that baptism pictures the identification of the believer with Christ in His death, burial and resurrection. It sets forth death to sin and the burial of the old life. It portrays the new birth of the believer, who rises with Christ into a new experience of blessedness. Further, immersionists commonly hold the view that the Apostle Paul had this ordinance in mind when he wrote, "We are buried with him by baptism into death: that like as Christ was raised up from the dead by the glory of the Father, even so we also should walk in newness of life. For if we have been planted together in the likeness of his death, we shall be also in the likeness of his resurrection" (Rom. 6:4-5). Non-immersionists, on the other hand, usually view baptism as a symbol of the Holy

Spirit's work in coming upon the believer for cleansing and power. They point out that in the baptizing work of the Holy Spirit at Pentecost He came upon each of the assembled throng in cloven tongues like as of fire (Acts 2:3; cf. Acts 2:16-18). Non-immersionists also believe that baptism is a sign and seal of ingrafting into Christ.

Since baptism pictures such important spiritual truth, the pastor should do what he can to see that the rite is witnessed by as many folk as possible.

3. The deacons should be contacted about the service so that they will have the facilities in readiness. Usually the deacons and deaconesses are charged with the responsibility of caring for the physical aspects of the service. They need to see that the baptismal garments are ready when a service of immersion is to be performed. Not all churches use baptismal robes but when they are used it is important that the right number and right sizes be in readiness. In any event, towels should be provided for the use of the candidates. The rooms to be used by them should be ready with clothes hangers, receptacles for wet garments, and chairs.

The candidates should be contacted as to what, if anything, they should bring in the way of clothing in order to be ready for the baptismal service. The deacons should contact the men in this regard and the deaconesses, the women. The deacons and deaconesses will handle all these matters well in most cases and will find joy in doing them, but the pastor should make sure that they know when the ceremony is to be observed. In preparation for services where immersion is not practiced, deacons merely need to prepare the baptismal font.

4. Last, instructions to the sexton are very important. He usually is the one responsible for seeing that the baptistry is filled to the proper depth and that the water is at a comfortable temperature by the time the service is to begin. Water too warm tends to produce a smothering effect on the candidate, while water too cool can cause chilling and shivering, especially in cases where there is nervous tension. If only children are to be baptized, the water will not need to be as deep as for adults. In cases where both children and adults are being baptized, it may be necessary to baptize the adults first and then reduce the depth of the water for the children. This problem may be met by providing a weighted platform in the bottom of the pool. If the pool is not large enough to leave the platform in place, how to get it into place after the adult baptisms needs to be

considered. The problem is greatly minimized if a small metal stool is used when children are baptized. In order to avoid adverse effects on the administration of the baptismal service, it is highly important that the sexton know his responsibility.

The Time for the Service

Just when should a baptismal service be held? There is no fixed rule. However, it seems best to hold it at a time when it is likely to be observed by the largest number of people. It does not deserve to be relegated to an unimportant time. The pastor can help to emphasize its significance by scheduling the service for a choice time.

It may be administred at the close of a regular Sunday service, morning or evening. It should, in this case, be made a part of the regular service. The congregation should not be dismissed. Dismissal tends to minimize the importance of the rite and to decrease the number who will be present to receive the testimony which baptism bears.

Sometimes it may be more convenient to have the ceremony before the Sunday evening service. In this case, the opening part of the service can be shortened and the rite of baptism can be fitted nicely into the total evening meeting. In some cases baptism is performed shortly before the regular time for the opening of the regular evening service and merges into it. Let the pastor employ the method that seems most practical, at the same time seeking to preserve the importance of the ceremony.

In some instances it may seem best to have the service in connection with the midweek prayer service, either before or after the time for prayer and praise.

When a large number of people are baptized, it may be well to have a special service just for this purpose. At this time the pastor will present a brief message on the subject of baptism, followed immediately by the administering of the rite.

In any event, this rite is of such importance as to merit a time when it can be observed by numerous witnesses.

The Place for the Service

In former decades those who practiced immersion as the form of baptism almost universally used outdoor streams and lakes for that purpose. Some congregations still do, since they have no indoor facilities. In fact, some groups have felt that since Jesus was baptized in the out-of-doors and in running water this method should still be followed. Most denominational groups now feel, however, that the place is immaterial. The service may he held outdoors or indoors, in running water or still, with equal significance. Most important is the meaning behind the rite. However, when the service is held in the church, a conspicuous place ought to be provided for it. It hardly seems appropriate to relegate this sacred rite to the basement, unless absolutely necessary.

Most churches now provide baptistries in the main auditorium. They are usually in the front of the church or to one side and closed off with attractive drapes when not in use. Good lighting is installed, and a painting or verse of Scripture beautifies the wall behind the pool. Attractive, adequate facilities tend to make the service more appealing and to set forth the importance of the ordinance. Salvation is a wonderful and glorious thing. Why not make its symbolism as attractive as possible?

The pastor who has anything to do with the building of a church should insist upon a careful consideration of the baptistry. He should see that it is well placed, well lighted, well made, and of the proper size. Good construction is of special importance. A leaky baptistry is an abomination that can produce no end of aggravation. He will do well to insist that the latest developments in waterproof baptistries are investigated before the building project gets under way. Proper facilities should be installed so that the baptistry can be filled with warm water in a minimum of time. In the total matter of providing baptismal equipment for the church, it would be well to consult some such book as that by W. A. Harrell entitled *Planning Better Church Buildings* (Broadman Press, Nashville, Tenn.) . Non-immersionists almost always conduct the baptismal service at the front of the sanctuary. Since no elaborate equipment is necessary, on occasion they perform it in homes.

The Service Itself

In the majority of cases where immersion is practiced baptismal services are held at the conclusion of a regular Sunday service. In such instances there should be no intermission between the regular service and the baptismal service. An intermission only invites people to leave and tends to minimize the importance of baptism. The pastor may well give a few remarks as to the purpose and meaning of the rite, or he may omit these. While the closing hymn is being sung the candidates should go with their attendants, if any, to the proper rooms to prepare themselves for the service. About the same time the pastor should retire to make himself ready for the administration. The song director or someone else appointed to the task should care for the congregation in the absence of the pastor. And the deacons will make any changes that need to be made, such as moving the pulpit to one side or rearranging chairs so that everyone will be able to observe the ceremony easily.

If the pastor is provided with a waterproof baptismal suit and a matching robe, he will be enabled to prepare much more quickly for the service and to dress quickly after the ceremony and be among the people at the close of the service to greet them.

The writer also thinks it wise for the church to provide baptismal robes for those to be baptized, with the possible exception of small children. Otherwise folk are apt to provide themselves with attire unbecoming such a service. Women candidates are known to have chosen garments which caused embarrassment at the time of baptism, both to the candidate and to the audience. Proper baptismal robes, similar in appearance to choir robes, are the solution to this problem.

The procedure in the pool varies, depending upon whether the candidate stands and is immersed backward or whether he kneels and is baptized forward. In either case, the full name of the candidate should be pronounced in connection with the rite somewhat as follows: "John Adams Brown, upon your profession of faith in the Lord Jesus Christ, I now baptize you in the name of the Father, and of the Son, and of the Holy Spirit." Immediately before the actual immersion takes place, it is well for the pastor to take time to assure the candidate and to allay as much of his nervousness as possible. In fact the writer has found it good to take time, previous to entering the baptismal waters, to explain exactly what is to be done in the pool.

The minister himself needs to be relaxed in the baptistry. He can by his own tenseness or unskilled manner destroy the effectiveness of the ceremony. As he immerses the candidate he should do it deliberately so as not to splash water out of the pool. Says Dr. Riley, "Don't slap people into the water, sloshing it by the vigorous and sudden dip."[1] Neither should he give the appearance of strangling

[1]W. B. Riley, *Pastoral Problems* (New York: Fleming H. Revell Company, 1936).

the candidate by undue gripping of the nostrils. In order to avoid this, the writer followed the plan of asking the candidate to cover his nostrils and face with his own hands. The baptizer then laid his left hand over their hands and provided the forward motion into the water with his right hand which was placed at the back of the candidate's head. In this manner, according to the practice of his church, he immersed the candidate three times forward in the name of each person of the trinity.

The baptismal service may conclude with prayer as hands are laid on the head of the one baptized. This is symbolic of the filling of the Holy Spirit for a life of victory. Some pastors follow this by receiving the baptized person into the membership of the church. Others prefer to care for the reception into membership at a later service. Yet others receive members into the church after profession of faith, on promise of baptism.

There are two definite things which the pastor ought to do following the ceremony. First, he should see that each person receives a baptismal certificate, which is often treasured in memory of a precious event in the person's life. Very attractive certificates are now available at most Christian supply houses. Second, the pastor should be sure to record the date of the person's baptism. He may need this information at some future time.

In churches where immersion is not practiced as the form of baptism, the preparations are much simpler. However, many of the principles involved in the immersion type of baptism and set forth in the preceding paragraphs pertain when sprinkling or pouring is the method used. Where the latter method is used the minister should follow the practice of his church, exercising all possible care to make the service impressive and meaningful. An easily accessible form for conducting a baptismal service in which sprinkling is the mode, may be found in the *Book of Common Worship* of the United Presbyterian Church in the United States of America.

THE HOLY COMMUNION

"This do in remembrance of me," said Jesus as He originated the service of Communion. There need be no other reason for observing the ordinance than obedience to our Lord and Saviour. He left no marble shaft by which to remember Him. Nor did He dedicate any building to commemorate His ministry. But the memorial of the bread and the cup is far more meaningful than any monument in stone. The bread pictures His body which was wounded for us. The cup speaks of the blood which He shed for our salvation. By these elements His followers are to be constantly reminded of the price of their redemption. In the presence of these elements we are graphically reminded that "He was wounded for our transgressions, he was bruised for our iniquities: the chastisement of our peace was upon him; and with his stripes we are healed" (Isa. 53:5). Then there are some, among whom the writer is included, who believe that the service of the washing of the saints' feet (cf. John 13) and the Love Feast, or *Agape* observed in connection with the bread and the cup, also speak of definite aspects of the believer's salvation. Such as these count it a privilege to observe a threefold communion in order to commemorate the three aspects of our salvation, namely, the past, present, and future aspects.

The Time for Communion

When should this service be held? In answer to this question, at least three things deserve to be said: (1) It should be held at regular intervals. A definite time should be established for its observance. Folk will then be able to plan accordingly. (2) It should be held with a reasonable degree of frequency, not too often, lest it become common and a mere matter of form, and not too infrequently lest God's intended blessing be missed and people lose sight of the importance of the Communion. (3) It ought to be held at the most convenient time. That is, it should be held when the most of the membership can attend. The value of the service merits the participation of the largest possible congregation.

Getting Ready for the Service

In anticipation of the Communion there are several things which the pastor may do in order to make the service meaningful and to insure the best possible attendance.

1. The service should be announced well in advance of the scheduled time. We live in complex days and unless such services are stressed they are likely to be forgotten. These announcements should be made from the pulpit, in the church bulletin, in the newspaper, and at times at least through a pastoral letter to the members of his congregation.

2. The pastor needs to preach on the significance of the Communion periodically. An uninstructed congregation is likely not to sense the importance of this observance. The whole Gospel is wrapped up in the Communion. It provides the pastor with a splendid opportuity to declare anew the blessed truths of the Cross and to challenge his people again to loyalty to Him who said, "This do in remembrance of me."

3. The pastor may well devote one special service to preparation for Communion, dwelling on the meaning of the symbols and exhorting his people to examine themselves lest they partake of these symbols in an unworthy manner. Such a service should also give time for earnest prayer which seeks the Lord's blessing in the forthcoming service. This preparation can well be cared for at the midweek prayer service. Sometimes it may be well to have a week of special services in which the deeper life is emphasized, the series concluding with the Communion.

4. The pastor should make sure that the deacons and deaconesses or elders have everything in readiness so that the service will progress smoothly. In this connection he will want to know that the equipment is adequate. The latter is especially important where the threefold Communion is observed. But it is important in any case. This is no time to run short on supplies.

5. The pastor should confer well in advance of the service with the elders and deacons who will be assisting him. He will assign such duties as reading the Scriptures, praying, making comments, and passing the elements. Careful preparation will do much toward a well-ordered and effective service so that the attention of those who attend will not become focused on confusion but on the service.

6. Finally, but not least important, is the heart preparation that the minister himself needs to make. He should never allow past preparations to suffice for the present occasion. Before each service he ought to contemplate anew the Calvary experiences and to realize again the preciousness of these events in relation to his own life. These ordinances should never be administered in a perfunctory manner!

The Direction of the Service

Insofar as possible, the minister should seek to help the congregation to relive the solemnity and significance of the night when this sacred rite was instituted. This can be done by a careful selection of hymns centering in the Cross, by reading Scripture passages that set forth the experiences of our Lord's last hours before His crucifixion, by prayer that has in it a burden for the realization of the significance of the Lord's Passion, and by brief remarks on the meaning of the elements. Reverence will permeate the assembly if the people recognize that the bread of which they partake is a type of the broken body of Christ and the cup is a symbol of the shed blood of the Lamb of God. And for those who practice the threefold Communion, if they realize that the water in the basin is the symbol of the Word of God which cleanses the believer's walk and that the meal upon the table is typical of the Marriage Supper of the Lamb to be enjoyed by the saints of God at the Lord's Coming, God's holy presence will be felt and a profound appreciation of the price of our redemption will prevail.

There is no better way to close the Communion service than to do as they did on the memorable night when it was instituted. "And when they had sung an hymn they went out. . . ." (Matt. 26:30). It is not known what hymn was sung then, but we may be sure that it was pertinent to the occasion. The Spirit of God gives liberty to His servants today in this matter. But His direction should be sought in the choice of the parting hymn.

RECOMMENDED READING

BLACKWOOD, ANDREW W. *The Fine Art of Public Worship.* Nashville: Cokesbury Press, 1939. Chap. 12.

Book of Common Worship. Philadelphia: Board of Christian Education of the United Presbyterian Church in the United States of America, 1946.

DAVIES, HORTON. *Christian Worship, Its History and Meaning.* New York and Nashville: Abingdon Press, 1956. Chap. 13.

EVANS, GEORGE. *The True Spirit of Worship.* Chicago: The Bible Institute Colportage Association, 1941. Chap. 12.

HEICHER, M. K. (compiler and editor). *The Minister's Manual.* New York: Harper and Brothers, 1959. Pp. 41-49.

McAFEE, CLELAND B. *The Communion Service.* Philadelphia: Board of Christian Education of the Presbyterian Church in the U. S. A., 1937.

McCLAIN, ALVA J. *The Threefold Ministry of Christ and Its Appropriate Symbols.* Winona Lake, Ind.: The Brethren Missionary Herald Co., n.d. (A pamphlet.)

PHILLIPS, J. B. *Appointment With God.* New York: The Macmillan Co., 1956.

RILEY, W. B. *Pastoral Problems.* New York: Fleming H. Revell Co., 1936. Chap. 6.

Chapter 13

THE DEDICATION OF INFANTS

ANTIPEDOBAPTIST CHURCHES, of course, do not believe in infant baptism. Many of them, however, do practice the public dedication of infants and very small children to the Lord. It is a beautiful expression on the part of godly parents of their desire to give their children unto the Lord at the very beginning of their lives. The experience can be of tremendous blessing both to the parents who from time to time remember the promises which they made in connection with the dedication and to the child himself who later in life will often be reminded of the fact that he was given to the Lord in infancy. This is likely to produce a sanctifying influence upon him.

When certain parents indicate a desire for a dedication service for their child, the pastor should be willing and ready to perform such a service at the earliest convenient time. The response which he should make to this request is outlined in the following paragraphs:

1. The pastor should have a conference with the parents to make clear the purpose of the service. There is likely to be a bit of confusion or misunderstanding in the minds of some about its true nature. The pastor will make clear that this is not a baptismal service. In antipedobaptist churches baptism does not take place until an individual is old enough to make his own profession of faith. Baptism follows faith and is the symbol of the believer's identification with Christ in His death, burial, and resurrection. Baptism is also the sign of the new birth. The infant dedication service is, therefore, not in any way to be confused with the baptismal rite.

Neither is infant dedication to be thought of as a christening service whereby when water is applied the infant in some mystical manner becomes a Christian. In some churches quite an elaborate ceremony is used in connection with the so-called christening of infants. In it there is a godfather and a godmother who become responsible for the child in case the parents die or find themselves unable to discharge their parental responsibilities. Sometimes the infant is given an additional name at this occasion. The dedication service, or the blessing of infants, as the service has sometimes been incorrectly called, must not be confused with the christening rite. The real significance must be made clear.

Neither should the dedication service be considered as for the infant only. It is as definitely for the parents as for the infant, in some respects more for the parents than for the child. No mystical influence is brought into the child's life at such a time. The memory of such an act performed in his behalf will be of spiritual profit to the child as he grows older. But nothing happens in this service as far as the child is concerned. It does not assure him an entrance into Heaven. As far as the parents are concerned, they should feel a deep sense of their responsibilities. Thus it can readily be seen what part they have in the service.

Moreover, this is not a service for unbelieving parents. God is not pleased to receive gifts from those who reject His Son. If the parents are not Christians, here is the pastor's opportunity to win them for Christ. The heart of a parent is apt to be very receptive at such a time. And who more needs the help of the Lord than parents, with their tremendous responsibilities in rearing their children? Where one or the other parent is not a Christian, that one should either become one or have no part in the service. A dedication service may be observed with only one parent taking part. It is sad when such must be the case, but the one believing parent should not be deprived of the privilege of dedicating the child. In some such cases a believing mother, sister, or some other relative may attend the believing parent in the service.

The pastor's conference with the parents at such times can do much toward getting them to see the great responsibility that is theirs, with the likelihood that they will give themselves faithfully to discharging it.

In connection with such a conference, the time for the dedication will be arranged. It may be held in conjunction with almost any public service, preferably a Sunday morning worship service. The ceremony does not take long and can be included at a time convenient for the parents. The Sunday morning hour is usually considered the best time, for then the infant is less likely to be fussy, and parents like their progeny to show off to good advantage! Some churches have the custom of emphasizing dedication of infants on Mother's Day or Easter Sunday but this is altogether a matter of choice. As the minister plans with the parents for the occasion, it will be well for him to outline the procedure of the service. This will tend to allay nervousness and enable them to concentrate more on the meaning of the service.

2. When the time arrives for the service the pastor should announce to the congregation that there are parents (naming them) who wish to dedicate their infant (s) or child (ren) to the Lord.

In this connection, it is well to state the practice of the church in this matter, namely, that the church does not baptize those under the age of accountability but dedicates them at this tender age to the Lord with the prayer that when they come to the proper age they will of their own free will and choice accept the Lord Jesus Christ as Saviour and enter into the membership of the church.

It may be noted that in the Old Testament we have the record of Hannah bringing Samuel to the house of the Lord to dedicate him to His service there. We read of mothers in the New Testament bringing their little children (small enough to be held in His arms) to Jesus for His blessing. Joseph and Mary brought the infant Jesus to Jerusalem to present Him to the Lord shortly after His birth (Luke 2:22).

Godly parents believe that their children are among God's very best gifts to them. Therefore it is fitting for them to give their children into His hands in a definite way. It is incumbent upon the parents to give themselves anew to God for their added responsibility.

3. Having stated to the congregation the practice of the church, the pastor should invite those who have infants to be dedicated to bring them forward for the service. The parents will stand directly in front of the pastor. Although it is immaterial who holds the infant, more often the father does. But if the mother can better care for the child, she should hold it. Parents usually are very eager that there be as little disturbance as possible. Mothers often have a way that fathers do not of quieting little ones who become upset. The plan that will work best should be used in each individual case.

4. The pastor may then read a brief portion of Scripture suitable to the occasion. Some pastors prefer to quote Scripture at this time rather than to read it. Portions of the Word which are fitting in-

clude I Samuel 1:20-28, Psalm 103:17-18, Matthew 19:13-15, Mark 10:13-16, and Luke 18:15-17.

5. Following the Scripture reading, the pastor should say something like this: "Brother and Sister (or Mr. and Mrs.) John W. Doe (giving full names) present their child, Susie Marie, for dedication."

It is important that the pastor obtain the infant's correct and full name before the service commences. It is equally important that he is sure of the sex. It is embarrassing for a pastor to discover that he has used words indicating dedication of a boy, when in reality it was a girl!

6. The parents may be questioned somewhat as follows:

"Dearly beloved, do you in presenting this child for dedication renew your own solemn pledge to your Lord to follow Him closely, and do you promise by word of mouth and the holy walk of your daily life to lead your child in the way of the Lord? If so, answer, 'We will.'

"Will you seek earnestly and prayerfully to bring this child when he [she] grows to a suitable age to an acceptance of Christ as Saviour and Lord and to seek membership in the church? If so, answer, 'We will.' "

7. The pastor will then take the child in his arms or place his hand gently on the infant as the following words are spoken:

"We dedicate this child to the Lord to be nurtured by these parents in the fear of God, and to be instructed by them in all the ways of the Lord, that at the proper age he [she] may willingly choose Christ as Saviour. We do this in the name of the Lord. Amen."

Whether or not the pastor takes the child in his arms is entirely up to the pastor. Some pastors do this sort of thing very naturally and easily, and it is greatly appreciated by the parents. In other cases, the pastor feels he would be awkward in handling infants. In such cases, it is probably better if the pastor does not hold the child. The success of the service does not depend upon the pastor's holding the child, but the heart attitude of the parents is of supreme importance.

(Sometimes 7 is omitted and the idea is incorporated in the prayer discussed under 8).

8. The prayer of dedication is then offered. This prayer should incorporate within it thanksgiving to God for the gift of this child, petition that its life will always be lived in conformity to the divine will, and a request that the parents may be given special wisdom and direction in discharging their responsibility of parenthood.

It can be very effective to have the choir sing prayerfully at the conclusion of the pastor's prayer such a hymn as, "Saviour, Like a Shepherd Lead Us." With this the dedication service ends and the parents return to their places in the congregation.

9. It will be well for the pastor to give the parents an infant dedication certificate soon after the service. It will be greatly appreciated and will serve as a constant reminder of that which has been done. Publishing houses now provide very attractive certificates of this sort upon which the full name of the child can be inscribed, the date, and place of dedication, as well as the name of the minister who performed the ceremony. The writer has discovered that parents often have these certificates framed and hung in the child's room, or they place them in a special book they may be compiling which records the early life of the child.

Surely the pastor will want to file a record of this important event. The child who has been dedicated is a prospective member of the future church. Furthermore, he will want to make sure that this child is a member of the cradle roll in the Sunday school. The minister will maintain a special interest in the child's growth and development and will look forward to the day when there will be a fulfillment of the purpose of the dedication.

Chapter 14

THE WEDDING CEREMONY

As Jesus and his disciples long ago were called to the marriage in Cana of Galilee, so ministers today are often called upon to minister in joining men and women in the bonds of holy matrimony. This very pleasant duty brings the minister into vital association with people in one of the happiest experiences of their lives, at a time when their life lies before them in happy prospect.

At the same time, it is a very serious duty, for he speaks the mystic words that are meant to bind two individuals together for life—two individuals who by deliberate choice have decided to become "one flesh." It is God Himself Who has ordained marriage for the happiness and blessing of man. When the minister performs the ceremony which publicly proclaims the fulfillment of God's plan for two persons, he becomes God's servant in a very special sense. Therefore he needs to enter into this ministry reverently and with the best possible preparation, remembering each time he performs a wedding ceremony that true marriage is a beautiful type of the relation of Christ to His Church. His attitude and bearing on such an occasion are important in view of the loose and frivolous ideas concerning marriage which are so prevalent in the world today.

The minister's part in the wedding ceremony offers definite opportunity for Christian influence. Usually young people who call upon a certain minister to marry them will continue to feel an attachment for him. They will likely heed his ministry and become co-laborers with him in his work. They will listen to his counsel.

Because of the importance of the institution of marriage and because of the far-reaching effects his part in the ceremony may have, the minister should seek to serve faithfully and well each time he is asked to officiate at a wedding.

Preparation for the Wedding

The pastor should not consider that his responsibility for a wedding is discharged if he has on hand a good ceremony and performs the ritual on the occasion of the wedding. Much more than this is involved. Adequate preparation for such occasions includes some things in the realm of long range preparation and other things in the category of immediate attention.

1. The pastor's ministry ought to include proper teaching on marriage, the home, and related subjects. Institutions so vitally important to the welfare and happiness of his constituency as these should not be neglected in his pulpit ministry. The pastor will save himself some embarrassing situations and others a lot of heartbreak if he will preach on these matters. People have a right to know what the Bible has to say on such vital subjects. In these days of loose thinking on the relation between the sexes and subsequent marital laxity, the need along this line is more urgent than ever.

Every pastor will do well to preach periodically a series of sermons on such related subjects as courtship, marriage, the home, divorce, the blessing of children and the family altar. It is a sad thing when folk come to the pastor after some tragic marriage situation and say that they never had any teaching from the Bible on these matters. Every pastor should be faithful to his congregation by opening up the Scriptures on these vital things.

2. He ought to be acquainted with the laws of the state regarding marriage. He should know about such matters as age requirements, health demands, the number of days' notice required for those intending to get married, whether or not the minister must have a license in the state where he is ministering to perform ceremonies, and the grounds for divorce. In every particular, the minister should fully comply with the law. A book like *The Pastor's Legal Advisor* by Norton F. Brand and Verner M. Ingram will be found helpful for consultation in pertinent legal matters.

3. If possible, the pastor ought to have a conference with the prospective marriage partners. This, of course, has to do with his immediate preparation for a wedding near at hand. He will want to find out if either the man or the woman has been previously married. Has either one been divorced? If so, upon what grounds? He will then act in accordance with his convictions and denominational regulations in the matter of marrying divorcees. Some ministers ap-

parently are not bothered by this problem and will marry any couple who applies to them for the service. Other ministers will marry no divorced persons except those who have been divorced upon Biblical grounds, fornication, or adultery. There are still other clergymen who follow an absolutist position and will marry no divorced persons whatsoever. Those who hold this view say that it is difficult to be sure who is innocent and who is guilty in divorce proceedings. Thus, to save themselves a lot of trouble and in order to uphold the high standard of marriage which is set forth in the Scriptures, they refuse to marry all divorcees. The writer himself came to adopt the latter policy, feeling that it is the most practical way to deal with a difficult problem. But whatever policy the pastor adopts, he ought to make his position known and consistently follow it. Otherwise, he may find himself in some very embarrassing situations.

In a conference with prospective marriage partners, the pastor will also seek to discourage wrong marriages, as between a believer and an unbeliever. Such an alliance is definitely contrary to the Word of God, which speaks plainly against Christians being "unequally yoked together with unbelievers" (II Cor. 6:14). Face to face with such a situation, the pastor has a splendid opportunity to endeavor to win the unsaved one to Christ. But failing in this effort, the pastor ought not have any part in doing something that is definitely contrary to God's will. He will also do his best to discourage marriages between Protestants and Catholics, showing how a divided loyalty mitigates against the building of a happy Christian home. He will also discourage marriages between those of different races because of the problems arising out of different social backgrounds and the obstacle that public opinion too often erects. He should have no part in secret marriages. A useful book on the subject of mixed marriages is James A. Pike's *If You Marry Outside Your Faith*.

When it is evident that a couple is worthy of his services, the pastor should take time to counsel with them concerning the responsibilities of marriage. He will do his best to show them how to make theirs a happy and successful marriage. He may also find it very worthwhile to place in their hands some helpful reading along the line of marriage and related subjects, such as *For Better Not For Worse* by Walter A. Maier, *Home: Courtship, Marriage, and Children* by John R. Rice, *Make Yours a Happy Marriage* by O. A. Geiseman, and *The*

Problem of Marriage, a pamphlet containing articles from *His* magazine.

As a particular wedding is being planned, the pastor will want to make sure of the exact time when the wedding will occur and note it upon his calendar. The place where the wedding will be held must also be determined and the proper contacts made, especially if it is to take place in the church. If the wedding is to be in the church, the ceremony should be somewhat more elaborate than a home ceremony. If the marriage is to be solemnized in the pastor's study or in some other private room, the ceremony will be simple. Even in the simplest wedding, however, there should be at least two individuals present to serve as witnesses.

The pastor will be wise to encourage the use of the church as the ideal place for a wedding. This location tends to give a spiritual emphasis to the marriage relationship. Young people who give God His proper place at the outset of their lives together are less likely to make shipwreck of their marriage than those who do not recognize Him. The next most suitable place for a wedding is the home, with its hallowed associations and memories. But no matter where the wedding is, the pastor should seek to obviate the growing tendency today of making the marriage ceremony something to be hurried, thus minimizing its sacredness.

He ought also to lend his influence toward making the marriage service as impressive and beautiful as possible. Certainly the ceremony which joins two people together in a relationship which is a type of Christ and His Church is worthy of careful planning. When a congregation gathers to witness a wedding ceremony, they should witness a service in keeping with the high importance of the marriage union and worthy of the house of God. Included in the service should be suitable musical numbers, instrumental and vocal, the processional, the ceremony with its Scripture reading, prayers, and giving of vows, and the recessional. Since the bridal couple will have a lifetime to look back upon this happy occasion, let it be of such character as to provide a most satisfying reflection.

In the pastor's conference with the couple to be married, he will ascertain whether it is to be a single or a double-ring ceremony. He will ask what given names the contracting parties want to have used in the ceremony. He should also discuss with them the form of service to be used. Usually the pastor has a form which he likes best, but it can be changed somewhat to please the couple. Most wedding ceremonies have many things in common, but no two are exactly alike, and the pastor will not find it difficult to alter a form a little here and there in order to suit the whims of certain individuals.

Moreover, at this conference the pastor will want to learn the time of the rehearsal. There *must* be a rehearsal before any church or home wedding. Sometimes two rehearsals are needed. The rehearsal quite often is directed by the bride, who at such times asks someone else to take her place in practice for the ceremony. There will be times when the pastor will be expected to take this leadership. He should be sufficiently acquainted with the procedure to be able to do this without difficulty. If he is not, his wife can usually help him in the situation. In all the planning for a wedding the pastor should let the bride take the lead as far as possible. She, above all others, is the one to be satisfied. The groom usually is not too much concerned about the details.

Since officiating ministers usually give a wedding certificate in addition to the official one isssued by the county clerk, it is good for the pastor to find out what kind of certificate is desired. The later ones are usually booklets which contain more than just the copy of the certification of the marriage. But some couples still prefer that older type which is often more decorative and suited to framing. The writer once gave a marriage book containing the certificate to a girl from Virginia. Detecting disappointment, he discovered that she wanted a certficate which she could frame. Needless to say, he gave her what she wanted!

Seating at the Church Wedding

When the ceremony takes place in the church, the seating usually follows this arrangement: The front pews on the left, as one faces the pulpit, are reserved for the relatives of the bride and those on the right for the relatives of the groom. On some occasions there are reserved seats for invited guests who are seated on the right or left of the church behind the relatives, depending on whether they are friends of the bride or the groom. Then the rest of the available seats are for those who come in response to a general invitation, such as might be given in the church bulletin or from the pulpit.

The last person to be seated before the ceremony begins are the mother of the groom, who is escorted to her seat in the front of the church on the right, and the mother of the bride, who is escorted to her seat in the front on the left. The head usher cares for this. No person should be seated after the entrance of the mother of the bride. This plan of seating varies little from one locality to another.

The Wedding Procession

The seating of the bride's mother is the signal for the wedding march to begin. The "Lohengrin" march is most often used for the procession. In some places, as soon as the wedding march begins, the congregation arises and remains standing during the service; in other places, this is not done. It is best to conform to local customs in such matters. The ushers lead the march down the aisle, walking two by two or one by one about four paces apart. Next come the bridesmaids, singly or two by two, followed by the maid or matron of honor. The flower girl or girls, if there are such, come next. If there is a ring bearer, he may come after the flower girls. A distance of about six feet between each person in the procession should be observed.

Last, and most important of all, comes the bride, leaning on the right arm of her father, brother, or near male relative. Sometimes a page or pages assist in carrying the train of the bride.

Before the procession begins, the minister and the groom and the best man come from a side room. The beginning of the wedding march is the signal for them to come and take their stand in front of the pulpit, facing toward the procession. (In some localities, the ushers enter from the vestry door, following the best man, instead of preceding the bridesmaids in the wedding procession as described above.) Before the minister comes out, he should make sure he has in his possession the marriage license, for without it he has no legal right to perform the ceremony.

The arrangement at the front of the church depends upon the available space. But some such plan as follows is usually used: As the ushers approach the minister, they divide and take their positions half of them to the right and half to the left, leaving space for the bridesmaids, who also divide equally to the right and to the left and stand in front of the ushers. When the bride arrives at the front of the church, the groom, who has been standing by the minister, steps forward to meet the bride, who slips her left hand from the arm of her father and gives her right hand to the groom and together they take their stand immediately before the minister, and the wedding ceremony begins. It is the writer's opinion that it is far better for the minister to read the ceremony than to give it from memory, since this is no time to fumble. Embarrassing fumbling has resulted when ministers have tried to conduct the ceremony from memory. Let the minister read the service slowly and distinctly so that everyone present can easily hear.

The Wedding Ceremony

Any minister's handbook will contain sample forms of the ceremony. With these as a help, the minister should formulate one which will be his own. The ceremony should contain a brief address setting forth the origin, nature, and responsibility of the marriage relation. In connection with this address, preferably as its culmination, it will be well to read Ephesians 5:22-32, asking the couple if they are willing to accept this scriptural teaching on marriage.

Then usually there is the giving away of the bride in which the minister asks the question, "Who giveth this woman to be married to this man?" The response comes from the father of the bride or some near male relation in the words, "I do." Or the father says, "Her mother and I." The father then steps back and takes his place next to his wife at the end of the first pew on the left. In case the giver is someone other than the bride's father, he either takes a pew reserved for him or steps back to one side and remains standing during the rest of the ceremony.

The questions are then asked of the groom and the bride as to their willingness to take each other as wife and husband. All the forms are similar at this point. In the questions asked of the bride there is variance as to the usage of the word "obey." The writer uses it when he performs a ceremony, and he sees no reason why it should be objected to when the full significance of the Ephesian passage referred to is understood. The bride whose groom promises to love her as Christ loves the church should have no difficulty in promising to obey him in the Lord.

Next come the vows which the bride and groom say to each other. As these are spoken, the bride and groom should face each other, joining right hands. It is best for each member of the bridal pair to repeat the vows phrase by phrase after the minister. It is a great risk for nervous young people to plan to recite their vows from memory. The writer remembers instances of young people who insisted on doing this and who under the stress of the moment forgot their lines. When the couple insist on reciting the vows from memory, the minister had better be ready to fill in if their memory fails. It will save embarrassment for all concerned if the couple will let the minister read the vows phrase by phrase, with the bride and groom repeating them. First the groom repeats his vows, then the bride hers.

The ring ceremony follows. The minister asks the groom, "What token and pledge do you offer that you will faithfully perform these covenant vows?" The groom should then receive the ring from the best man and say, "This ring." The minister then says to the bride, "If you are willing to accept this token of the performance of these vows, allow it to be placed on the proper finger of the left hand." While holding the bride's hand, the groom should say after the minister, "With this ring I thee wed, and with all my worldly goods, and my heart's faithful affection, I thee endow, in the name of the Father, and of the Son, and of the Holy Spirit."

Then the minister should briefly explain the symbolism of the ring in words such as these: "As this ring of gold is circular in shape and has no beginning or ending, so it is a symbol of love that knows no bounds, and should be given and received as such. Let it continually remind you of that endless life which you have in Christ Jesus our Lord." (The last sentence should be omitted if the contracting parties are not Christian.)

Where there is a double-ring ceremony the procedure for the single-ring ceremony is repeated. The minister's remarks concerning the symbolism of the ring should be made at the conclusion of both placings.

The most solemn moment of the entire service comes with the pronouncement of the marriage union. The bride and groom should join right hands for this, and the minister should place his right hand on their joined hands, saying, "Forasmuch as John and Mary have consented together in holy wedlock and have witnessed the same before God and this company, and thereto have given and pledged their troth, each to the other and have declared the same by giving and receiving a ring and by joining hands, by my authority as a minister of the Lord Jesus Christ, I do now pronounce them husband and wife in the name of the Father, and of the Son, and of the Holy Spirit. Whom therefore God hath joined together, let not man put asunder."

Then follows the prayer and benediction. The bride and groom may or may not kneel for this part of the ceremony. If they are to kneel—and this seems to the author more impressive, preparations will need to be made for the kneeling, that is, a kneeling bench or white silk pillows will be placed for the purpose. The prayer should invoke God's richest blessing upon the union just solemnized. It should contain a request that God will help the newly married couple to be true to the vows which they have taken. It will also ask Him to guide them in the establishment of their new home. Then, too, it may well contain a petition that the Lord will help them to honor the Lord in every aspect of their lives together. Either before or after the prayer, while the couple is still kneeling, an appropriate hymn is commonly sung. "O Jesus I Have Promised" (making the "I" plural) is especially effective.

Upon completion of the prayer the bride and groom may embrace, if they wish to—they usually do! This is perfectly proper if done with dignity and in a manner befitting the House of God.

The newly married couple will now turn about, facing the audience, and the minister may say, "It is now my pleasure to present to this congregation Mr. and Mrs.————." If there is to be a general reception at the close, as there usually is, the minister may add, "They will be glad to greet their friends immediately," designating the place.

Then the organ begins playing. The bride takes her bouquet from the maid of honor, and the recessional begins. Usually Mendolssohn's "Wedding March" is used. The bride and groom lead the processional, walking at a brisk gait, the bride taking the right arm of the groom. Then follows the maid or matron of honor, and she is followed in turn by the bridesmaids and the ushers in the proper order. The best man may retire with the clergyman or, as is sometimes done, he walks out with the maid or matron of honor. Immediately upon the conclusion of the recessional, the ushers come forward to dismiss the congregation row by row.

When the wedding is in a home, at its conclusion the wedding party simply turns about and the couple receives the best wishes and congratulations of those who are present. Usually the family is first to do this, the intimate friends second, and the acquaintances last.

After the Ceremony

At the conclusion of the ceremony, the minister has several responsibilities. Three of these are of special importance.

1. He should give the bridal couple a signed certificate. He ought to attend to this as soon as possible following the ceremony. This is more important than is sometimes realized. This certificate is the only proof the couple has that they are married until the record is filed in the court house, which may involve several days. This, of course, has to do with the official certificate. The more elaborate and ornate form, provided by the minister in the form of a booklet or a certificate for framing, may be given at this time, or even before the ceremony.

2. He must send the designated certificate to the county clerk. The law specifies a time limit for this to be done. The minister had better attend to this immediately lest the matter be forgotten in the press of other duties and he become a breaker of the law. This form will be different in various states. In some states the document which the couple brings to the minister is in three parts, perforated at the proper places so that the parts can be readily separated. One part, authorizing the minister to perform the ceremony, is for him to keep for his file; the second is for the couple being married and is their official license; and the third is the portion to be filled in by the minister and returned to the county clerk for a permanent record. In other states there is no part to be retained by the minister. Some states require further information from the one performing the ceremony regarding the lives of those being married. A questionaire is provided when this information is required.

3. The minister should visit in the newly established home as soon as convenient following the wedding. By this contact he may help to tie the young people to the church. Very likely he can also help them in beginning their Christian lives together.

The matter of remuneration is something that should not be forgotten in connnection with the wedding. Fees for the organist, church caretaker, or for use of the church should be cared for by the family of the bride. It is the groom's responsibility to give a fee to the minister. This is usually handed to him in a white envelope by the best man. The minister should never make a charge for a wedding, although in some states the law stipulates a definite amount as due the one performing a marriage ceremony. It will be best for the minister always to leave this solely on the free-will basis. The writer was once asked to marry a couple on the "promise-to-pay" basis and he was paid! Let the minister receive gladly what is given to him, whether much or little, and use it for the glory of God, whether it be to buy his wife a new hat or purchase for himself some much needed books for his library.

A SUGGESTED ARRANGEMENT AT THE ALTAR

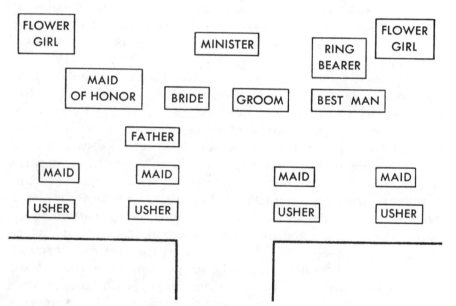

RECOMMENDED READING

BRAND, NORTON F. and INGRAM, VERNER M. *The Pastor's Legal Adviser.* New York and Nashville: Abingdon-Cokesbury Press, 1942.

CAPPER, W. MELVILLE and WILLIAMS, H. MORGAN. *Toward Christian Marriage.* Chicago: Inter-Varsity Press, 1958.

ERDMAN, CHARLES R. *The Work of the Pastor.* Philadelphia: Westminster Press, 1924. Pp. 109-112.

HEWITT, ARTHUR WENTWORTH. *Highland Shepherds.* New York: Harper and Brothers, 1939. "Rural Weddings," pp. 54-68.

LEACH, WILLIAM H. (ed.). *The Cokesbury Marriage Manual.* Rev. and enlarged edition. Nashville: Abingdon, 1959.

MAIER, WALTER A. *For Better Not For Worse.* St. Louis: Concordia Publishing House, 1939.

PIKE, JAMES A. *If You Marry Outside Your Faith.* New York: Harper and Brothers, 1954.

POST, EMILY. *Etiquette.* New York and London: Funk and Wagnalls Co., 1945. Chaps. 19-22.

RICE, JOHN R. *The Home—Courtship, Marriage, and Children.* Wheaton, Ill.: Sword of the Lord Publishers, 1945.

VANDERBILT, AMY. *New Complete Book of Etiquette.* New York: Doubleday and Company, Inc., 1963.

Chapter 15

THE FUNERAL

AT NO TIME is there a greater call for the pastor's sympathetic and spiritual service than in the hour of death. The pastor needs to pray for a special preparation of heart for this ministry. He may exert an influence for Christ and the church at such a time that will be of untold value. Or he may by neglect or carelesssness do irreparable injury to the cause he represents. The time of bereavement offers special pastoral opportunity. The pastor with a true shepherd heart will manifest it at this time.

His Immediate Ministry

When the pastor is notified of a death in his parish, what should be his response?

1. He should make a visit in the home of the deceased as soon as possible. This should not be delayed. The visit may be very brief, but it ought to be long enough to manifest his concern. The family should sense that the pastor really cares and is ready to be of any help he can give them.

2. The question of funeral arrangements need not be brought up at this early visit. The family may be in such a state of shock that they are not prepared to consider them. Often some members of the family are located in distant places and need to be contacted before such arrangements are made. However, there are occasions where the plans for the funeral have been settled long before death occurred. Death came as no surprise and the bereaved were prepared for it. In such cases the family may want to discuss the funeral at the pastor's first visit.

3. At this immediate visit the pastor should present some Christian truth, such as the sufficiency of God's grace, the comforting ministry of the Holy Spirit, the prospect of reunion with loved ones who are now present with the Lord, in cases where the departed one

162

was a Christian. Where the latter situation prevails, the pastor may stress the blessed truth that the loved one is "absent from the body, [but] . . . present with the Lord."

4. The minister should be prepared to deal with the various problem situations which he may meet, such as cases where the bereaved demonstrate a rebellious spirit, or cases where it is felt that the deceased one was not prepared to die. There are other situations where death has had a very solemnizing effect upon a careless family. This is likely to be the pastor's finest opportunity to point the loved ones to the way of living which will be according to godliness. The spiritual neglect of certain members of the deceased loved one may stand in bold relief at such a time, and they will listen to the counsel of the man of God. The pastor will need to depend wholly upon the leadership of the Holy Spirit at such times, and He will not fail to give the earnest pastor the right words to say and the proper manner to manifest.

5. When he comes to the home of death, as soon as possible after learning of the decease, the pastor should seek to be as helpful as possible. He may find himself in a situation where the bereaved ones are altogether at a loss to know what to do. It may be the first such experience in the family. In a case where the writer ministered, the elderly husband had just died, leaving his wife alone in the home. She was so bewildered that she did not even call the doctor to pronounce her husband dead, and she did not realize that she ought to get in touch with a mortician. Her pastor, whom she did have the presence of mind to call, aided her in these matters.

Then there may be a need to send telegrams to distant loved ones or to notify folks nearer at hand by telephone. The pastor will offer his services in every way possible and will be utterly sincere in his offer.

Preparations for the Funeral

The pastor will confer with the family about the funeral service at a later visit, if this was not cared for at the first visit, assuming, of course, that he has been asked to conduct the service. By this time the family will have had time to compose themselves and to consider together as a family group the details of the service.

As the pastor talks with the family about the last rites, he should learn their desires and seek to comply with them as far as possible.

Even little things mean much at such a time. Perhaps the deceased had requested to have a certain passage of Scripture read. Sometimes even a text is chosen to be used for the sermon. Often the family requests the hymns to be sung. Possibly the family desires someone besides the pastor to have part in the service. As far as possible, the pastor will seek to conform with all wishes of the family. Not often will any request be made which will be contrary to his convictions.

In the conference the pastor has with the family some of the things he will want to learn or get clearly in mind are:

1. Where is the funeral to be held? At the home, the church, or the funeral parlor?

2. What is the time of the service? Is there to be a brief service in the home prior to the service in the church? If so, what is the time for that?

3. Will the body lie in state at the church before the service begins? If so, how long?

4. Who is to assist the pastor and how? In order to avoid any possible embarrassment, the pastor should know if others are to have part in the service. Each participant should be notified of his part in plenty of time in advance of the time of the funeral. The writer, upon one unforgettable occasion, came to a funeral service and discovered that another minister, much older than he, expected to conduct the service. Unknown to the writer, this good man, a former pastor of the deceased, had been asked to come to the service and take part in it. He misunderstood the intent of the invitation and supposed that he was to have charge of the service. Fortunately, the difficulty was ironed out shortly before the service began, and it progressed smoothly, and those who attended the funeral were unaware of the difficulty. The writer, who was a very young pastor at the time, learned through this experience the importance of having everything carefully arranged ahead of time in order to avoid any possible embarrassment.

5. Is there to be an obituary? If so, who is to prepare it? Practice as to the use of an obituary varies in different communities. The author feels that there are distinct advantages to using an obituary in some cases. It provides for the setting forth of some of the details of the deceased's life which do not fit in well with the pastor's sermon. People are interested in these facts and a well-written account of the departed one's life will answer many questions in the minds of

people present in the service. The obituary is usually prepared by some relative or close friend who possesses the necessary facts. When this is the case, the pastor will want to make sure that he has an opportunity to read it through carefully before presenting it in the public service. He may need to correct some faulty grammar or make some other changes. In any case, he should familiarize himself with the obituary so that he can read it well. There are times when the family feels that no one among them is competent to write such an account, whereupon it will be the pastor's responsibility to do it, unless he can prevail upon his wife to write it! When the responsibility is the pastor's, he must make sure to get all the facts accurately.

Included in an obituary are such items as the full name of the deceased, the names of his father and mother, his birthplace and date of birth, his schooling, the facts about his marriage, the names of his children and possibly his grandchildren, the character of his work, his church relationship, and the time and place of his death. Quite often the deceased's favorite Scripture verse or chapter is mentioned and, sometimes, the first verse of his favorite hymn. A small bit of well-chosen poetry may also be used.

6. Who is to sing? And what hymn or hymns? The wrong music can spoil the service. Hymns lacking a definite Christian message, such as "Beautiful Isle of Somewhere," should not be used. Where wrong selections have been made, the pastor can usually tactfully suggest some other hymn which will fit in better with his sermon. He probably will not ever face such a ludicrous situation as one young pastor did in the mountains of Kentucky. Before a funeral service he asked a lady of the bereaved family if there was any hymn she especially wanted sung at the service. She thought a minute and then said she thought "Marching Through Georgia" was right pretty! Though this is an exaggerated case, yet it is surprising what little taste some folk demonstrate at times like this. The minister will seek to rectify wrong selections.

7. Is there to be a service at the home of the deceased before the service in the church? This implies that the main service is to be held at the church. A service in the home is the regular custom in some communities and is usually very brief, consisting of Scripture reading and prayer. In some instances, however, the simplicity and inclusiveness vary to quite an extent. The writer recalls one such service in rural Indiana in which practically the whole neighborhood

was present and in which three special numbers were sung, the Scripture was read with remarks by the officiating minister, and prayer was offered. Following this the funeral procession moved to a large church in town where the main service was held. Usually, however, the home service is more simple than this and is attended only by the immediate family and close friends.

8. Who are to act as pallbearers? Sometimes the pastor is asked to aid in procuring these. Usually they are individuals who have been rather closely associated with the deceased, such as members of his Sunday school class or neighbors.

The minister should know the answer to these and similiar questions before he leaves the conference with the bereaved family.

The Church Funeral

The details of the church funeral may vary considerably. Sometimes the casket is placed in the church for a period (perhaps an hour) prior to the service so that friends may come and pay their last respects to the deceased. In other cases, as previously indicated, before the service in the church, there is a short service in the home, in which case the casket remains there until this service is completed, at which time it is moved into the funeral car and transported to the church for the service there. As the body is removed from the home the minister or ministers accompany it to the funeral car, walking at the head of the casket. He (or they) stands with bared head until the casket is deposited within the funeral car. In times of inclement weather the minister need not remove his hat, but will put his hand to his hat in token of respect. He then will go to the car which is to convey him to the church.

Upon arrival at the church, the minister leads the processional into the church. The pallbearers and the casket come next. In some places the pallbearers will carry the casket. Some funeral directors use a modern conveyance to wheel the casket into the church and down the aisle, then the pallbearers precede the casket. The members of the deceased's family follow immediately after the casket. Then come the intimate friends.

While the procession is moving into the church, the organ or piano should be playing appropriate music to soften the effect and ease the tension. As soon as the procession appears at the door or entrance to the auditorium of the church, the congregation should rise to their feet as a mark of respect to the bereaved. Sometimes the funeral director will give the signal for the congregation to stand. At other times, without a signal those present rise to their feet in accordance with their usual practice. This is not always done; the writer considers it a good procedure because it is not only an expression of respect to the bereaved family but it also tends to break the tension of such an occasion.

As the procession moves into the church, the members of the family and intimate friends' sit in seats reserved for them on the right side of the church as they go in. The pallbearers sit in seats reserved for them on the left.

The minister (or ministers) takes his place behind the pulpit, and the service opens.

Upon occasions where the casket has been in the church for some time and there is no procession into the church, the pastor may either come with the family into the church and make his way to the pulpit, or he may come directly from his study to the rostrum at the proper time. There is no rule as to this.

The Order of Service

The service should be carefully planned to run smoothly and not take too much time. Preachers need to learn that the effectiveness of a service is not determined by its length. They should realize also that the bereaved ones very likely have been under a severe strain for quite a period of time. The preacher should not take advantage of this situation by prolonging the service. Some ministers have gone to the other extreme in this matter and have made the service too brief, sometimes elimating the sermon altogether. The writer believes this to be a mistake, for such an occasion offers a great opportunity to give forth Gospel truth to some who very seldom, if ever, darken the doors of the house of God. There is a happy medium between length and brevity which the wise minister will seek to observe.

Some such order in the service as the following may be used with variations to suit the particular occasion:

Scripture reading		Invocation
Hymn		Hymn
Obituary		Scripture reading
Prayer	or	Obituary
Sermon		Hymn
Hymn		Prayer
Prayer		Sermon

It is well to see that each participant in the service has a typewritten copy of the order of service so that there will be no confusion. In this way the service can go forward unannounced from part to part.

The Funeral Sermon

In a funeral service time should be allowed for a message from the minister. It is the tendency in some places to dispense with the funeral sermon and have only soft music, the reading of Scripture, a prayer and, possibly, a flowery obituary. In the mind of the author this brevity is unfortunate. At such a time people need to hear something from the man of God; some likely will never hear the Word of God preached if they do not hear it at such times.

In characterizing the funeral sermon, several things deserve to be noted:

1. Let it not be too long. In fifteen or twenty minutes, a well-prepared minister can say what needs to be said and leave a profounder impression than if he prolongs his preaching. Remember that at such a time the emotions of folk, especially the bereaved, are under great stress. The minister, if he wants to be kind and considerate, will not prolong the service unduly, though it ought to be long enough to leave with the people a message from God.

2. Let the message be thoroughly scriptural. This is no time to present the uncertainties of men. A "thus saith the Lord" is what folk need to hear. Good chapters from which to develop funeral messages are: Psalms 23, 46, 91, and 103 with their assuring note; John 11 and 14, with their stories of resurrection power and matchless comfort; I Corinthians 15, the classic chapter on the resurrection in its various aspects; II Corinthians 5:1-10 with its urgent argument to be ready to "appear before the judgment seat of Christ"; I Thessalonians 4:13-18 with its graphic description of what takes place in the experience of the believer when Christ comes for His saints; II Timothy 4:5-8 with its account of the Apostle Paul's readiness to depart this life; and Revelation 21 and 22 in which blessed truths concerning the "better country" are presented. There are many other precious passages to which the faithful minister will be directed by the Spirit of God as he performs his task in the hour of bereavement.

3. Surely it is appropriate at this time to emphasize the great Biblical truths concerning the future. Subjects dealing with Heaven,

judgment, the resurrection, the brevity of life as compared with eternity, rewards, the second coming of Christ, and others may be dwelt upon with profit. This is the time to relate all of man's doings upon earth with his responsibility to God and the future. The pastor's message ought to be something more than pretty poetry and vague suppositions. The certainty and authority of God's Word should characterize his message.

4. The funeral sermon should be directed to the living. The dead cannot hear. The time for preaching to them has passed, but the living present a special challenge to the minister to appeal to them at such a time concerning their relation to God. Occasions like this should be used to present a call to each individual to so number his days that he may apply his heart unto wisdom (Ps. 90:12). The minister's time should not be taken up with a long eulogy of the deceased. But where there has been a great transformation of the Gospel in the life of the departed, it is appropriate to call attention to that. The word "eulogy" is simply a compound of two Greek words meaning *good word*. Surely, it is proper to speak a good word about the deceased, especially if it can be turned to a practical application to the living who need to incorporate the same virtues in their lives. Such reference to the deceased will be greatly appreciated by the relatives and close friends. Some preachers, however, have been guilty of such extremism in a eulogy that members of the congregation have wondered if they really knew the deceased! Let the minister preach to the living. That is always proper, and it is sure to save him possible embarrassment.

5. Then the funeral message ought to have something in it to tell people how to be saved. As previously stated, there are usually some people at a funeral service who seldom attend a service in a church. Therefore, it is the minister's responsibility to point the way to Heaven. Let him be definite about it, setting forth the Lord Jesus Christ as the Way, the Truth and the Life.

6. The funeral message ought to be full of tenderness and sympathy. The pastor needs to remember how Jesus wept at the grave of Lazarus. A cold, professional demeanor at such a time only manifests the minister's failure to be like his Lord. By word and manner the minister will endeavor to express sympathetic concern for those who are passing through the experience of special sorrow.

The Closing Part of the Service

As soon as the service at the church is completed, the funeral director takes charge. He is responsible for the physical aspects of the service. In many instances he directs the casket to be removed to the rear of the church for the final viewing of the body. The minister should either accompany the casket to the rear of the church and stand by while the body is being reviewed, or he should wait until the family is ready to see the body for the last time and accompany them. It seems to the writer that the former is preferable. However, the minister should be willing to accomodate himself to the customs of the community where he serves.

The funeral director takes charge of the movement of the congregation to the casket, beginning with those sitting in the rear of the church and arranging for the bereaved family to be the last to see the body. In cases where the casket remains in the front of the church, those in the back come to the front first to view the body. There is less embarrassment for the family in this method. Pent-up emotions often become manifest at this time, and it is best not to have a congregation observing.

When all have viewed the body for the last time, the casket is closed, and the minister accompanies it to the funeral car and stands there with bared head until the casket is deposited in the car. He then, along with the family and all others, makes his way to the car assigned to him, and the procession to the cemetery soon follows. This procession is carefully arranged by the funeral director, who gives the necessary instructions.

The Home Funeral

When the funeral is held in the home of the deceased, much the same procedure is followed as in a church funeral. However, the service is somewhat simplified. Usually the minister will want to speak to the bereaved family before the service starts in words of comfort and assurance. He may want to have private prayer with them if they are in a room by themselves. Upon word from the funeral director, he should be ready to open the service and carry it through smoothly. He should stand where he can be heard most easily by all who are present. He may have to speak to people in several rooms. Some may be upstairs and in favorable weather others may be on the front porch.

After the service is completed and the funeral director has the casket in readiness, the minister will walk in front of the casket to the funeral car. As soon as all are in the assigned cars, the procession to the cemetery is ready to begin.

The Funeral Parlor Service

The practice of holding funeral services in specially prepared funeral parlors is becoming more prevalent. The reasons are obvious. A big burden is removed from the family of the bereaved when they are able to receive the condolences of friends at the funeral parlor instead of at home. The chapel is attractively and suitably arranged and appropriate musical instruments are provided for the service. The parlors are so built that the bereaved family has a place of privacy during the service and thus is relieved of the embarrassment of many eyes being focused upon them. Funeral chapels are also easy of ingress and egress and commodious enough to care for the average size funeral service.

In a service of this kind the family is taken to the parlor at the appointed time by the funeral director or one of his associates. The pastor comes to the parlor either with the family or alone. Usually upon arrival he is taken to a private room where he waits an indication from the funeral director that it is time to begin the service. Then the pastor takes his place at the lectern or at the head of the casket and proceeds with the service. After the concluding prayer, he nods to the mortician, who takes charge as at the church or home funeral. After the final viewing of the body, the procession soon moves toward the cemetery.

Graveside Service

Upon arrival at the cemetery, the pastor should go at once to the rear of the funeral car where he will await the removal of the casket, which he will precede to the grave. At most cemeteries he will be accompanied by the custodian of the cemetery so that he will arrive at the right position for his graveside ministry. Following the casket to the grave, of course, will be the relatives and friends of the deceased. They take their places about the grave in locations provided by the cemetery management.

The minister usually stands at the foot of the grave which looks toward the head of the casket. If it is arranged for him to stand at the head of the casket, he will, of course, comply. As soon as all of the relatives and friends are properly situated, he begins the commital service. Various commital forms are available. Every denominational handbook includes them, and good ideas can be gleaned from them. However, for Bible-believing ministers of the Gospel what can be better than to use selected passages from an open Bible? For example, the account of the raising of Lazarus in John's Gospel, chapter eleven, may be read with great comfort. Or portions of Revelation 21, which looks forward to Heaven, may be read with peculiar blessing at such a time. Or portions of the great resurrection chapter, First Corinthians 15, may be read with telling effect. Let the pastor prepare his own commital service, using those passages of Scripture which seem most appropriate to him.

Following the reading of the Scripture and the giving of the additional remarks he may feel led to present, he should close the graveside service with prayer and a fitting benediction, such as Hebrews 13:20-21 or Numbers 6:24-26. After this completion of the commital service, the pastor ought to have a brief word with the bereaved friends, assuring them of his continued interest and prayers. He should also promise to call upon them soon.

Quite often ministers are confronted with what to do with fraternal organizations which desire some part in the last rites. It may be that the deceased belonged to some such organization and the relatives request that the fraternity be used in some way. Whether the minister likes the idea or not, he had better conform to the wishes of the family. This is no time to discuss the lodge problem. However, he will do well to insist that the fraternity confine its participation to the committal service, with the minister concluding his ministry at the church, the home or the funeral parlor. Trying to mix the two services will not prove satisfactory either to the pastor or the fraternal order. Let the minister have full charge of the service in the church or wherever the service is held. Then the order should be given opportunity to have their part at the grave. If the order calls upon the minister for the concluding benediction, he should pronounce it.

After the Funeral

The days immediately following the funeral service are usually very lonely and trying for the bereaved. They are then faced with the stark reality of their loss. The familiar voice is no longer heard, and the vacant chair is a constant reminder that the loved one is gone, not to return. The calls of friends who flocked in at the time of death taper off. The adjustments that have to be made increase the bewilderment that comes at such a time. The minister should not forget the family in this hour. He should call soon after the funeral to bring encouragement and to offer any help he can in making the necessary adjustments.

As to the matter of remuneration for pastoral care extended in connection with the funeral service, ministers take different views as to what is proper. Some take the extreme view and never accept any gift at any time. Others take the opposite view and expect remuneration upon every such occasion. It seems to the writer that there is a better plan than either of these. Let the minister expect no remuneration in any case. Certainly this is one of the services to which his members are entitled free of all payment. However, if folk are able to give and insist upon giving something to their pastor who has served them faithfully in time of real need, they doubtless find pleasure in giving, and the gift should be received gratefully as a gift from the Lord and used accordingly. There will doubtless be some occasions when the pastor will want to return gifts which are presented to him.

When ministers serve people who are in no way connected with the church, it is no more than right for them to reimburse the minister for his time and effort. Equally good ministers differ in their convictions on these matters. It will be advisable for each minister to adopt a policy which to him seems best and then abide by it.

RECOMMENDED READING

BLACKWOOD, ANDREW W. *The Funeral*. Philadelphia: The Westminster Press, 1942.

CUYLER, THEODORE L. *How to Be a Pastor*. New York: The Baker and Taylor Co., 1890. Chap. 3.

ERDMAN, CHARLES R. *The Work of the Pastor*. Philadelphia: Westminster Press, 1924. Pp. 112-115.

HEWITT, ARTHUR WENTWORTH. *Highland Shepherds*. New York: Harper and Brothers, Publishers, 1939. Pp. 69-81.

HOPPIN, JAMES M. *Pastoral Theology*. New York and London: Funk and Wagnalls, 1901. Part IV, Sec. 21.

LEACH, WILLIAM H. (ed.). *The Improved Funeral Manual*. Grand Rapids: Baker Book House, 1956.

MURPHY, THOMAS. *Pastoral Theology*. Philadelphia: Presbyterian Board of Publication and Sabbath School Work, 1897.

RILEY, WILLIAM B. *Pastoral Problems*. New York: Fleming H. Revell Co., 1936. Chap. 8.

Chapter 16

AS A PUBLIC SERVANT

THE MINISTRY OF THE PASTOR has an outreach far beyond the confines of his own parish. He belongs to the public in a very literal sense. His first responsibility, of course, is to his own church. But by reason of his calling as a servant of the Lord whose concern is for a lost world, he is a public man and dare not restrict himself to a prescribed field. If he surrenders this idea of the farther outreach, he is apt to become a second-rate man.

The dignity and deference with which even the unchurched citizens of the community regard the minister cause them to turn to him for leadership in many facets of community life. He dare not hide his light under a bushel or restrict his witness to a select few. Our Lord's commission to His disciples was a worldwide commission. Paul exhorted his spiritual son Timothy that "supplications, prayers, intercessions, and giving of thanks, be made for all men" (I Tim. 2:1). When Christ was here upon earth, His compassion went out to the multitudes—and still does—and was not confined to favored groups. It is utterly inconsistent, in view of these facts, for the ministry of a pastor who has received "the ordination of the pierced hand" to be restricted to a local church membership.

Let the pastor therefore recognize that he should have a concern for the whole world which knows not God's grace. Let him also recognize that he has a particular responsibility to the local church of which he is the pastor and which in a definite way supports him materially and in spiritual ways. But between these two responsibilities there is his obligation to the community in which he resides. This constituency is much broader than the organization of the local church and presents various facets. The pastor with a vision should be available to the limit of his ability to minister to human need wherever he finds it in the community. The writer feels that it is a mistake for the pastor to project himself, by way of membership, into every organization in the community or to seek prominence in them. But he should be available to minister wherever he can in community interests, and it should be known that the pastor is behind every influence for good in the community. Let us consider, therefore, some of the areas where the pastor may be a public servant.

Consider, first, the area of the public schools. It has often been said that the three institutions indispensable to democracy are the home, the church, and the school. It should be evident then that the pastor should be interested in the schools of his community. He will make himself available to minister from time to time in their public assemblies. If he has children, he and his wife will be faithful in attendance at the local Parent-Teacher Association meetings. Doubtless there will be times when he will be asked to offer prayer at such meetings and invited to speak to the group on certain occasions in a vital though nonsectarian manner. Such contacts will often mean more than is realized at the moment for the cause of righteousness and the church.

In some communities the pastor will be invited to speak at the junior or senior high school assembly. This provides a great opportunity to bear a faithful witness for the Lord and holy living. He will likely make some friends among the young people in this way, perhaps resulting in lives dedicated to the Lord and His service. On certain occasions he may be asked to deliver the baccalaureate sermon at commencement time. He will, of course, thank God for such an opportunity and seek His guidance for the right message for the occasion. This is a time of reflection, when memory goes back over the years spent in bringing the graduating class to this event. How wonderful for the minister to challenge these young people to "remember Jesus Christ" as they go forth into life with all of its varied experiences!

Invitations will also come from time to time for the pastor to deliver commencement addresses in high schools and even in colleges. Upon such occasions, when education and preparation for life are emphasized, the minister has a fine opportunity to speak about the Word of God, without the knowledge of which no person can claim to be educated in the fullest sense. In all such addresses the wise preacher will stay away from sectarian issues. Failure at this point will likely do more harm than good and will limit his future ministry. The place for the sectarian emphasis is in the local church.

In short, the pastor should make it clear that he is the friend of the schools—their teachers, principals, boards of trustees, and, not least important, the children and young people for whom the schools exist. Where there are Christian day schools in the community, the pastor will be at liberty to exercise a larger ministry than in the public schools and will seek to make the most of his privilege.

A second area of influence in communities of average size can be found in service clubs. What should be the attitude of the pastor toward Rotary, Kiwanis, Optimist, Lions, and other service clubs? There is no doubt in the writer's mind that such clubs serve a worthwhile and constructive ministry in the community. He has enjoyed attending and speaking to some of their luncheon meetings. These clubs are engaged in philanthropic enterprises and are nowise in opposition to the church. They provide a wholesome fellowship for businessmen and leaders in the community. Many ministers feel that personal membership in a local club provides a good contact and affords a splendid oportunity to gain the confidence of men of stature to the end of reaching them for Christ and the church. Other ministers appear to hold a less favorable opinion of these clubs and refuse to have anything at all to do with them. The writer has chosen to assume an attitude different from either of these. He finds much that is good in all of these clubs as far as his knowledge goes. He is willing to attend their meetings upon invitation and is glad to speak when asked. He has done both and has been impressed with much that he witnessed on these occasions. He is willing to commend the clubs for all the humanitarian service they are rendering for the community.

However, he has felt it the part of wisdom not to join any one of the clubs. Very likely the pastor may have representatives of several of these service clubs in his church. For the pastor to join one club to the exclusion of others might make it less easy for him to commend the work of all the clubs without partiality. However, he finds no fault with the pastor who feels that his situation makes it practical for him to belong to one of them. But he does feel that the pastor needs to guard himself against being a "joiner" of too many organizations. They will likely occupy too much of the time which ought to be devoted to the definite work of the church.

A third area of influence to be considered is that of politics. What part should the pastor take in this aspect of human affairs? Two extreme positions may be taken in this matter: one is that the pastor should have nothing at all to do with politics; the other is that he should give all possible attention to it. We believe both attitudes are wrong. Politics is defined by the dictionary as "the science and art of government." Surely, the pastor will have some interest in the government of his land and will be vitally concerned about the kind of laws which are passed. Jesus commanded, "Render therefore unto Caesar the things which are Caesar's; and unto God the things that are God's" (Matt. 22:21). From this it is clear that there are obligations toward the government which we ought to faithfully discharge, even as there are obligations to God which we should meet. The pastor will seek to be a good patriot, will pray for the rulers of the land, and will exercise his voting franchise regularly. Whenever moral issues are involved in the voting privilege, he will not hesitate to take a firm stand for the right and let his constituency know the nature of his stand. In this sense the pastor will surely maintain an active interest in politics and will seek to cultivate a like interest in his church. He will often refer to such passages of Scripture as Romans 13:1-7 and others which plainly set forth what the Christian's attitude toward government should be.

On the other hand, the word "politics" has often had a bad connotation. Someone has observed, "If you do not know how to lie, cheat, and steal, turn your attention to politics and learn."[1] It is most often connected with certain parties which either control or seek to control the affairs of government.

Because of the possible effect on some of his members, the wise pastor will refrain from vociferous declarations as to his party affiliation. Neither should he tell his people for whom to vote. This the people themselves should decide. If a pastor is interested in a short pastorate, he can likely achieve his ambition by taking sides on a political issue!

As previously stated, if there are moral issues at stake, the pastor will courageously take his stand, but he will be careful to avoid talking about the political party involved or its candidates. It will be his duty to thunder against the evil involved. He will have plenty of Biblical background for such procedure. The Old Testament prophets denounced sin and injustice wherever they found it, whether

[1]Quoted by Eugene D. Dolloff in his *The Pastor's Public Relations* (Philadelphia: The Judson Press, 1959), p. 144.

in relation to peasant, prince, or nation. Though their denunciations went unheeded, they refused to be silenced. Our Lord did not hesitate to denounce sin in high places. Nor did His followers who became leaders in the New Testament period, hesitate to cry out against every form of public and private wickedness. Let the pastor deal in principles, not in party politics, as he speaks from the sacred desk.

In standing for righteousness in the community, the pastor will be aware of times when he will need to visit public officials or urge the circulation of a petition in protest of something the church deems wrong for the community. The writer recalls feeling led to visit the leading official of the Alcholic Beverage Control Board upon one occasion when he was pastor in Washington, D.C. Liquor interests threatened to establish a tavern across the street from his church and within a block of a public school. The church was given the privilege of circulating a petition against such an establishment, with a good result. In all such matters it should be clearly evident that the pastor and his church stand for righteousness and good government in the community.

A fourth area where the pastor may exercise an outside contact is in hospital chapel services, nursing homes, homes for the aged, detention homes, jails, and other places where human need is desperate. As a representative of the Lord Jesus Christ and one who is called to minister to human need, he cannot refuse such calls. He will count it a privilege to respond to such invitations, though sometimes he will find the ministry difficult. He will seek the definite guidance of the Lord as to what message he should bring in each case and what other ministry he may perform. He will surely want to emphasize the love and care of God for those to whom he ministers. Quite likely he will want to arrange to take others with him to sing or to engage in personal visitation, taking into consideration the particular situation.

In some instances the institution involved invites the minister to come for a service. In other instances, the invitation may come from the ministerial association of the community. In any case, the minister will manifest all possible deference to those in charge as he renders service. Where doctors or nurses are concerned, their wishes will be ascertained and followed as closely as possible. In a jail service, the attendants will conduct him to the place of the serv-

ice and will give him many necessary instructions. Such ministries
will demonstrate the willingness of the pastor to go anywhere to proclaim the Gospel.

A fifth area of contact for the pastor outside his church has to do
with the public press. In order that he may broaden his ministry,
the pastor should seek the best possible relationship with this instrument of communication. The local newspaper is one of the most
potent media for spreading news, including the good news of the
Gospel and the church. Therefore, the good pastor will seek the
most congenial relations possible with the editor of the local paper.
In coming to a new church, one of the first business contacts the
pastor should make is with the editor of the local newspaper. In all
probability, this contact will pay rich dividends in the months and
years ahead. If no consideration is given to the editor by the pastor,
the chances are that no special favors will be given to him or his
church in the way of publicity. If there is more than one paper in
the community he will play no favorites but will try to maintain
cordial relations with each.

In addition to contacting the editor, the pastor can profitably
make friends with as many of the reporters as possible. In return,
they will likely ask for articles relating to his church activities. The
pastor should manifest a willingness to talk with reporters at any
time about subjects for press release. He will likely observe better
reporting as a result of such consideration.

The pastor ought also to supply the press with items of interest
for publication. A few churches have laymen who are good at this
sort of thing and can act as press agents. But in the majority of cases
it will be the pastor who will have to add this to his already long
list of responsibilities. But, after all, who knows the items of interest better than the pastor himself? This means that the pastor should
be aware of what makes a good news item, and pay attention to the
style in which it is written and how to attract attention. If the area
of good press relations is neglected, the influence of a church's ministry will not be as large as it might be.

As opportunity is afforded, a sixth area of outside contact can
become very effective for the minister of the Gospel, namely, the
area of broadcasting by radio and television. These increasingly powerful instruments for the dissemination of knowledge and information are now being used in a limited way to send forth the Gospel

message, the radio far more than television. In this technical age the day may not be far away when many more opportunities than now will be available to the average church for both radio and television broadcasts. Let the pastor be ready. Dr. Eugene D. Dolloff, in his book, *The Pastor's Public Relations*, has a chapter on "Opportunities of Radio and Television," in which he offers the following specific suggestions regarding the religious broadcast: (1) make ample preparation, (2) time your message, (3) employ plenty of illustrations, (4) have one central idea and make it one which is germane to life, (5) avoid a theological discussion, (6) keep up the tempo, (7) speak to the individual, and (8) avoid dead spots. It is evident that if a minister is to be a good broadcaster he must learn to discipline himself in the matter of time and will need to carefully consider the content of every message. And such discipline and care should characterize his whole ministry.

A seventh and final area for consideration in this chapter is that of the pastor's relation to other churches and pastors in the community. It seems altogether consistent with the scriptural doctrine of the unity of the true Body of Christ that there ought to be a sincere fellowship between all churches which hold to the fundamentals of the Christian faith. Though churches will not agree on all minor matters, there is no need for compromise of convictions. But where there is adherence to the divine inspiration of the Scriptures, the deity of Christ, His substitutionary atonement and bodily resurrection, salvation by grace through faith, and related doctrines, churches of "like precious faith" ought to have a common interest in one another, pray for one another, and labor together in forwarding the cause of Christ in the community. Such churches as believe these things in common ought to be able to get together for a Thanksgiving Day service, an Easter sunrise service, a special prayer service, the enjoyment of an oratorio such as *"The Messiah"* or even join hands and hearts in a community evangelistic service.

The pastors of such churches ought to know one another and be able to have sweet fellowship together. A very practical question faces many ministers regarding membership in the local ministerial association. Should they belong to it or not? In some large communities where there are separate associations for the evangelicals and liberals, there is not much of a problem. But what about the ministerium in the smaller community where at least a few of the ministers are modernistic? Should a new evangelical pastor coming into such a community join or not join? As is usual in such matters, there are two extreme views. According to one viewpoint, he should not join if there is so much as one modernist affiliated with it. Representatives of the other extreme viewpoint would say that he should join with the association no matter how many liberals there are in it, feeling that there should surely be a voice for evangelicalism in the one ministerium.

Possibly a position somewhere in between these two extremes is preferable. If the new pastor finds that the ministerium of his community is mainly composed of fundamental men, though they may not see eye to eye with him on every matter of the faith, he may feel it the part of wisdom to join with men who hold the truth in giving forth a clarion sound for the Gospel and the Word of God in the community. He need not compromise his convictions in the least, and he may find that his cooperation will give him a voice in spiritual matters that otherwise he would not have. Members of the ministerium will usually get their turn to speak over the radio, participate in baccalaureate and commencement exercises, write special articles for the newspaper, preach upon such occasions as Thanksgiving and Easter sunrise services, and to perform other ministries that take them beyond the confines of their own churches. At such times they can make their influence felt for the truth of God.

On the other hand, the new minister may find the situation so dominated by those with the liberal viewpoint that he will feel it best not to affiliate with the group. In such a situation he will want to find fellowship with the few ministers of like mind with his and possibly at some future time participate in the formation of an evangelical ministerium in the community.

Finally, in connection with all his outside relations, the pastor will want to remember that his chief business is to "preach the Word" and to be a faithful overseer of the flock of God. Let him always give priorty to these responsibilities. Fidelity to his high calling in relation to his own flock will dictate to him how much time and effort he can justifiably give to community interests and projects.

RECOMMENDED READING

BLACKWOOD, ANDREW W. *Pastoral Leadership*. Nashville: Abingdon-Cokesbury Press, 1949. Pp. 122-147.

Colton, C. E. *The Minister's Mission.* Dallas: Story Book Press, 1951. Pp. 170-187.

Dolloff, Eugene Dinsmore. *The Pastor's Public Relations.* Philadelphia: Judson Press, 1959. Pp. 94-186.

Hoppin, J. M. *Pastoral Theology.* New York: Funk & Wagnalls Co., 1884. Pp. 194-224.

Leach, William H. *Handbook of Church Management.* Englewood Cliffs, N. J.: Prentice-Hall, 1958. Pp. 243-257.

Spann, J. Richard (ed.). *The Ministry.* Nashville: Abingdon-Cokesbury Press, 1949. Pp. 119-129.

Thiessen, John C. *Pastoring the Smaller Church.* Grand Rapids: Zondervan Publishing House, 1962. Pp. 56-90.

"Faithful is the saying, 'If any one is eager to have the oversight of a church, he desires a noble work.'" (I Timothy 3:1, Weymouth).

Part III

THE PASTOR IN HIS ADMINISTRATIVE RELATIONSHIPS

Chapter 17

LOOKING TOWARD THE PASTORAL RELATIONSHIP: LICENSURE

WHAT IS MEANT by the terms licensure, license, and licentiate in relation to the Christian ministry? According to their derivation, these words come from the Latin verb *licere,* meaning "to be permitted." Hence, one who has a license is one who has permission to do something which otherwise he cannot do. A licentiate is one who possesses such a license. In Europe a licentiate is a person who possesses an intermediate degree, between that of a bachelor and a doctor.

In the realm of the ministerial profession the practice of licensure may be observed. Ministerial licensure is a provision whereby men who are not yet properly prepared or qualified for ordination may receive official authorization by the church to act as pastors, supply pastors, or in other capacities where a recognized minister is needed. Licensure is an intermediate provision for men who have not yet attained to the full status of eldership in the church—for men who have not fully arrived either as to preparation or experience.

By this provision a man is given opportunity to prove himself (II Tim. 4:5) as to ability and character. If he proves worthy, if he succeeds in his status as a licentiate, he will in all probability be considered eligible for election to the eldership and subsequent ordination.

Through this means the church is able to comply in a very practical way with the New Testament admonition to "lay hands hastily on no man" (I Tim. 5:22 A.S.V.). There have been numerous instances where the church has acted too quickly in the matter of ordination, with the result that they have ordained men in their membership who no longer are performing the duties of an elder or who have brought reproach on the ministry. In some instances, men like this only serve as ordained men a few years and then spend the rest of their lives in some secular pursuit. Undue haste is responsible for this incongruous situation and is disobedience to the plain Word of God. The church ought to beware of such disobedience.

On the other hand, situations often arise in which some official authorization of a man who is serving the Lord and the church proves very helpful. For instance, there is a student in the seminary who has taken a student pastorate. He may not be sure what the future holds for him. He is not ready for ordination but has answered a call to be of service as a pastor while he is in school. Licensure during this period will likely give him more authority in the eyes of the church which he serves. It will give him more prestige in the community. Then there are some matters with a legal aspect, such as marriage ceremonies, for which some states require that a man at least be licensed if he is to have a part in performing them. In short, licensure is the answer to a very practical problem that confronts ministers who as yet are not ready for ordination. It gives them standing which otherwise they would not have.

Then, too, when a church or ministerial group licenses a man they are apt to pay more attention to him. He will be the object of their prayers and observation. He will be the subject of needed counsel. All this will be good for both the licentiate and the ones providing this status. It will very likely give the licentiate a greater desire to make good and faithfully discharge his solemn responsibilities.

Its Limitations

Licensure has its limitations, limitations which are most easily seen by comparing it with ordination. How does licensure differ from ordination? There are two outstanding differences. First, licensure is temporary, whereas ordination is permanent. It is the practice among many denominational groups to license for one year at a time. The license may be renewed if the situation seems to warrant it.

The wisdom in this provision is apparent. If after the expiration of one year or one term of licensure it is discovered that the licentiate does not possess ministerial qualifications or has proved to be inconsistent in his life or possibly has come to feel that the Lord has not called him to the ministry, all that needs to be done is to refrain from renewing the license. This saves the embarrassment involved in having to unfrock an ordained man who has proved unworthy. Or it saves the church from the incongruity of having a man in the church as a minister who no longer serves in that capacity. The provision thus has distinct advantages.

It seems wise that there should be a limit as to the number of times the license can be renewed. Surely, after a period of three or four years in the status of a licentiate a man should demonstrate whether or not he is fit material for full ordination. For a man never to seek ordination and year after year ask for licensure seems to discount the value of order which has been established in the church. A man ought to grow in the ministry so that he is able to leave the ranks of the immature and find his place among those who have met the qualifications for eldership as laid down clearly in the New Testament. Furthermore, when a man fails to attain unto ordination, he deprives himself of the added authority which the rite gives him. Thus after a few renewals of his licensure, the minister ought to be ready for ordination. The fact of the renewals would imply that he is heading in that direction, except in certain peculiar cases.

Second, licensure does not allow the licensed man to take part in the ordination of other men to the ministry. There is a principle here that operates in many other realms. For instance, it would seem incongruous for a person to welcome another person into the membership of a particular church if he himself is not a member of that church. Nor does it seem fitting that licensed men should have part in ordaining men to the ministry.

There are a few other minor differences, such as delegate distinctions which are made at denominational conferences, but the two differences discussed above are the main ones. These, however, are important, and it should be the aspiration of every licensed minister to reach the ordained status as soon as possible. This is a worthy ambition. In ordination resides the opportunity for a more fruitful ministry because the prerequisites for ordination include careful preparation and proven ability and consistency of life.

But while the licentiate awaits the time of his ordination he should be encouraged by the fact that his limited status puts no restrictions on his ministry in preaching and teaching the Word of God or on his pastoral privileges. He can perform these functions with utmost liberty. There have been many men who have glorified God with most fruitful ministries over many years without the benefit of ordination. Usually there have been peculiar circumstances which have been responsible for this. But the exceptional cases do not violate the orderly provision laid down in the New Testament whereby men ought first to be proven and then set apart unto the ministry through the "laying on of hands" and prayer.

Licensure Procedure

There are two ways by which licensure may be obtained. First, the local church of which the applicant is a member by vote of its membership may license its own men without consulting any outside body. This is also true of ordination and is congregational church government manifesting itself in extreme independence or isolation. The second method is much better, especially if the candidate expects a wider recognition and ministry than in his own local church. According to this method, the local church seeks the approval of the district examining board before licensing. Such a procedure will give stature to the candidate's license and will preserve the interdependent attitude that should prevail in true congregational church government. The latter does not advocate absolute independency of the local church. It seeks to foster the need for fellowship and cooperation among the churches which make up the particular group. Requiring men who are seeking licensure to appear before the more representative group for examination and approval will tend toward preserving this idea. In some denominations the approval of a presbytery, a synod, or a bishop is necessary for licensure; a local church cannot act on its own.

When a young man makes known his desire for licensure to his pastor or the moderator of the church, his request should then be brought before the entire congregation in a regular or special business session for consideration. This is an important matter and should not be taken lightly by the church. A man should not be approved for licensure just because he has an attractive personality, because he is a good speaker, or because he has demonstrated a good degree of dedication. The matter should go deeper than this. Licensure is a definite step toward ordination. The church should therefore exercise utmost care to see that the candidate realizes the seriousness of the ministry and the responsibilities which are involved.

Hence, it seems wise for the congregation to vote that the applicant be subjected to an examination by a designated group within the church, which group should spend sufficient time with him to ascertain his true status. This examining group may be the official board of the church or a group especially appointed for this purpose. The pastor, of course, should be a member of the examining body. At the same time the church votes to commit the applicant to a particular group for examination, it may also vote that in case he successfully passes his examination he be approved and recommended to the district examining board for its approval. In the same meeting the church may vote to license him to the ministry provided he successfully passes the examination by the more representative body. The church may choose to wait until the district examining board has sent in its report before taking final action. Either method may be followed with the same result.

Because of the involvements of licensure, more care should be exercised in examining the applicant than is sometimes given. It is a serious mistake to take the attitude that since this is only licensure and only a temporary or preliminary step, it is not very important. Some seem to think that ordination is the act of real importance and that not much concern need be given to licensure. Such a superficial attitude may result in serious consequences. It may cause embarrassing situations to arise in the future. It may become apparent that the man who has been licensed does not have ministerial qualifications at all, and many will wonder why any group would license such a man. Carefulness in examination of the candidate will often help to obviate such a situation. Then if real care is exercised in examination, the applicant will be made to understand the seriousness of his position and will be influenced to pursue his preparation with more diligence. Some men have decided, after examination for licensure, that they did not wish to go on in the ministry. Before this they had not realized the serious responsibilities connected with this calling, and in the examination they became convinced that they were not qualified to shoulder such responsibilities. The ministry is no place for men who have little conviction and who are lacking in moral and spiritual courage. If a man is of this kind, it will be well for him and the church to know about it before he is licensed and possibly makes shipwreck of his ministry. A thorough examination is a good way to find out the situation.

Usually ministerial associations provide questionnaires which may be used in guiding candidate examinations. Any member of the examining group should be granted the privilege of asking other questions if the need arises.

Questions usually asked upon such occasions include queries about the applicant's call to the ministry, his Christian experience, his doctrinal beliefs, his ethical standards, his devotional life, his experience in Christian work, and his education. After a man has been asked questions of this character and has given his answers, the examining committee will in all probability have a pretty good idea as to the potentialities of the man before them. They will be able to make an intelligent recommendation to the church and to the district examining board.

Having successfully passed the examining group of the local church the candidate should then appear before the district or regional examining board for further examination. This group will have the benefit of the careful work which the local examining committee has done to aid them. The questioning in this second examination will probably be much like that in the first examination. But as the candidate appears before the district board, he will have a more representative hearing, and if he passes this examination he will have standing in a much wider area. The candidate who manifests a rebellious spirit in connection with any of the examination proceedings will not likely commend himself favorably to his examiners and may do himself great injury. He should gracefully recognize that they are the appointed representatives of the church to perform a helpful ministry in his behalf, and he should readily accept their counsel and recommendations.

Upon completion of the two examinations just described, the candidate is ready to be licensed. As previously indicated, some churches wait for a statement from the district examiners before they vote to grant licensure to the applicant. In others, the whole process of examination and licensure is cared for in one meeting on the local level. The approved man should receive a certificate of license to the ministry from his local church with the collaborating approval of the district examining board. It will read somewhat as follows: "This certifies that———————has been licensed for a period of one year from the date indicated on this certificate to perform the duties incident to the ministry, subject to the limitations delegated to ministers alone and according to the laws of the state in which the licentiate serves." It should be properly signed by both the moderator of the local church and the moderator of the district. Every licentiate as well as every ordained man ought to be provided with an appropriate certificate. There is no service held for the licentiate such as in the case of the man receiving ordination. The licentiate immediately enters upon his duties as an officially recognized minister of the church.

Recommended Reading

Books and articles are not often written upon the subject of this chapter. One who wishes to enter more deeply into this study should consult the various denominational and ministerial handbooks and discuss with denominational leaders the practice that prevails in the different groups.

Chapter 18

LOOKING TOWARD THE PASTORAL RELATIONSHIP: ORDINATION

By ORDINATION is meant the public setting apart of a man to the ministry or the solemn induction by the church into the pastoral office of one who is regularly called and chosen by the church to be its pastor. Usually the one to be ordained has had a definite call to a church as pastor or is under appointment to a mission field. The two Scripture passages which are the most definite in speaking of the setting apart of God's servants to the function of the office of elder[1] are Acts 14:23 and Titus 1:5.

The ceremony envisioned here is not to be confused with the heavenly ordination without which no man can serve the Lord. To be called of the Lord ·precedes the ceremony of ordination, which imparts no mystical power and is valueless apart from "the benediction of the pierced hand." The church cannot make a true minister of the Gospel. Only Christ can do this. Nevertheless, the importance of the rite should be obvious to all since it is apostolical. It is clearly set forth in the New Testament and is symbolic of the communication of the Holy Spirit, who qualifies the servant of God for a particular ministry.

Doubtless the ceremony can be overemphasized and given a significance never intended for it in the Scriptures. For instance, it is recorded that at the monastery of Etchmadzin in Armenia the mummy hand of St. Gregory the Illuminator is kept, which is used to this day in the consecration of every patriarch, who, being touched by it, receives grace direct from the founder of the Armenian church. This concept injects too much of the human into the ceremony and makes it mystical. But to go to the other extreme and neglect it al-

---

[1]Many denominational groups consider the pastor and the elder to be identical. Many who do not and who elect a board of elders consider the pastor to be both a ruling and teaching elder in the congregation. Thus, Scripture passages relating to elders pertain to pastors as well.

together does violence to good order in the church and tends to lessen the dignity, efficiency and permanency of the ministry. Ordination is not a matter of necessity. A man can be a good preacher without it. But it is a matter of expediency.

Prior to the time when a prospect for ordination applies for the ceremony in his behalf, some things should have been carefully considered and cared for. With variations due to differences in detail and practice among different groups, there are eight points of great importance—in fact, they are imperative—which should be considered before a man is ready to call for the service of ordination.

Preliminary Considerations

1. It is presumed that the candidate shall have considered well the *qualifications* of an elder. These are set forth distinctly in the Scriptures, particularly in I Timothy 3:1-7 and Titus 1:5-9. These passages set forth the type of man he should be in life, faith, temperament, disposition, reputation, judgment, family relations, ability, and experience. Not only should the candidate have studied these qualifications carefully but the church also should consider them well lest they lay hands on a man hastily (I Tim. 5:22). No novice is to be chosen by a church for this high and holy office (I Tim. 3:6). This means that those who are elected to this office should have shown themselves by life and experience to be men after God's own heart.

2. It is presumed that the candidate has acquainted himself with the *responsibilities* of the office. There are at least five main functions connected with the office of an elder: (1) *pastoral,* namely, to shepherd the church, feeding and caring for its members (Acts 20:28; I Peter 5:2 in Greek); (2) *administrative,* namely, the elder is to rule in the church, not as a dictator, but by precept and example (I Tim. 5:17; I Peter 5:2-3); (3) *educational,* namely, to teach the church (I Tim. 3:2; 5:17, A.S.V.); (4) *officiative,* namely, to preside and lead in the worship and activities of the church (James 5:14); and (5) *representative,* namely, to represent the church when need arises, as Paul did in Acts 20:17 where he dealt with the church through its elders. Unless a man has carefully weighed these responsibilities and found a willingness in his heart to undertake them with God's help, he should not apply for the service of ordination.

3. It is presumed that the candidate has felt a definite *call* to the eldership. Having felt God's call to this important office, a man may

properly seek the office (I Tim. 3:1). At other times the church may be used to stir up in the mind of a worthy man the desire for such a call (Acts 14:23, A.S.V.).

4. It is also presumed that the candidate shall have given himself to careful, practical *preparation* for the office. We have already noticed that the elder is not to be a "novice" (I Tim. 3:6) or to be impressed into service with undue haste (I Tim. 5:22). Titus 1:9 shows that he should be able to hold forth "the faithful word as he has been taught, that he may be able by sound doctrine both to exhort and to convince the gainsayers." This means preparation. It is considered by many thoughtful Christian leaders that a thorough Christian education in college and seminary is a good test of a man's sincerity of purpose. This seems especially true in these days of a rising standard of education even among the laymen of the church. The minister of the Gospel should not be behind them in his fitness, since he is to be engaged in the greatest business in the world. Furthermore, it is felt that a candidate's election and ordination should be delayed until such time as he has proved himself in this manner or by some definite Christian work (I Tim. 3:10). Candidates for the ministry will do well to reflect on the fact that Moses spent the first eighty years of his life in preparation, the last forty in service. Our Lord spent the first thirty years of His life in getting ready for the last three. The Apostle Paul retired to the desert of Arabia when called of God to preach the Gospel, thus preparing himself for the arduous years ahead. Others of the apostles had already become successful in various professions before being called of the Lord, and yet they had to spend three years under His personal instruction before taking up their future ministry.

Therefore, it does not seem too much to expect of young men who aspire to eldership in the church that they lay at the feet of Christ a period of educational preparation at least equal to that which other young men are willing to undertake for worldly professions.

5. It is presumed that the candidate has been carefully examined by his local church through its board or a special committee and that a written record of this action has been kept. Various denominational groups conduct this matter differently, but those operating under a congregational polity find that having the initial action toward elec-

tion to the eldership begin with the congregation tends to preserve the congregational idea.

6. It is to be presumed that the candidate, after having been approved by the local examining body, shall have been recommended by vote of his local church to a district or regional ministerial examining board for examination. This provision gives the candidate, if finally approved, the privilege of exercising his eldership rights beyond the precincts of his own church.

7. It is presumed that the candidate shall have successfully passed through the district examining board and, furthermore, that this board or council has sent a written report of the result of its findings to the local church.

8. Finally, it is presumed that the candidate has been elected to the office of elder by ballot vote by the church of which he is a member. This church will then proceed to recommend his ordination.

As previously indicated, procedure varies somewhat according to different denominational groups. For instance, some Baptist groups spend the major part of a day in bringing to culmination the ordination procedure. On this day the examining council examines the candidate. He is then subjected to a rather lengthy period of open questioning. If the examination proves satisfactory, he is ordained on the evening of the same day with an appropriate service. Among Presbyterians a committee of presbytery commonly examines the candidates and makes its report to presbytery, which then examines the candidate, decides whether or not to ordain him, and makes arrangements for his ordination. Bible churches and community churches have no district or regional group to consult; therefore they themselves arrange for all questioning of candidates for the ministry and their ordination. Commonly, however, such churches call in ministers of neighboring churches to assist them.

The Ordination Service

In planning for the public service, the details as to time, place, and participants will be worked out by the church in which the service is to be held, usually the candidate's home church, and the candidate, or by a denominational group, such as a committee of presbytery, in conference with the candidate. It is especially appropriate that such a service take place in the church with which the candidate's spiritual experience has been most closely connected. This very likely will be the church of which he was a member at the time of his call to the ministry. Such a choice is an appreciative recognition of this church's ministry in the life of the candidate. The service will also act as a fine object lesson on dedication to those who through the years have been closely associated with him. However, such an arrangement is not always possible or advisable. Sometimes it may be best to hold the service in the church to which the candidate has lately been called as pastor. It may be that he already has been serving this church for some time as pastor without formal ordination.

The service should usually be in charge of elders who are outside the local church. This tends to establish the candidate as an elder in all the churches rather than in the local church only. This is suggested by Paul to Timothy in the words: "Neglect not the gift that is in thee, which was given thee by prophecy, with the laying on of the hands of the presbytery" (I Tim. 4:14).

Liberty is allowed in the form of the service, since no definite form is set forth in the New Testament. This is especially true in churches which operate by congregational government. As long as the two essential elements of the imposition of hands and prayer are observed (Acts 6:6; 13:3; I Tim. 5:22), considerable latitude is allowed for the rest of the service. A suggested order of service follows.

1. *A devotional exercise.* This may consist of a regular church service at which one of the officiating elders may preach a pertinent sermon. All of the elders having part in such a solemn service should be carefully chosen. They should be men of proven ability, reputation, and experience. And in particular the one chosen to deliver the ordination sermon should be someone held in high esteem by the church, one who for a number of years has been a credit to the ministry. He may well be a former teacher or pastor of the candidate or someone else who has greatly influenced his life.

In some instances the ordination ceremony may be conducted with no sermon. Such services are sometimes held at denominational conferences where there are many sermons and addresses delivered throughout the conference and it does not seem necessary to have a special sermon for the ordination service. But in this event the service can well be opened with song and prayer.

2. *The authorization.* This is in the form of a definite statement read to the assembled congregation, setting forth the right of the candidate to receive "the laying on of hands." This is often a two-

fold statement consisting of a properly signed document from the candidate's home church indicating that he has been regularly elected to the eldership and a similar statement from the district examining board signifying its approval of him after careful examination. Such statements tend to assure the witnessing congregation that the candidate has passed through the proper channels and is entitled to the public recognition which he is about to receive. These statements may be read by the secretaries of the church and the district examining board, or they may be read by the one in charge of the ordination service.

3. *The Scripture reading.* With the candidate standing directly in front of the officiating elders, one of these elders should read the scriptural qualifications for the eldership as found in I Timothy 3:1-7, Titus 1:5-9, and II Timothy 4:1-8. Such passages take on special meaning at a time like this. Though they have been read many times before, yet upon this occasion they deserve to be heard again by the candidate and by the congregation. Both are apt to realize in a new way the solemn responsibilities that devolve upon the ministry by this reading.

4. *The questions and vows.* While the candidate is still standing before the elders, one of the latter asks the questions which the candidate should be ready to answer without hesitation. By this time he has considered fully all the responsibilities and privileges of the Christian ministry. These questions should relate to faith in the Scriptures, one's calling to the ministry, consistency of life, the responsibilities of the ministry, the devotional life, and the minister's homelife. Any good ministerial handbook will contain a suggested list of pertinent questions which may be used or modified. Upon such a solemn occasion it seems best to read the questions rather than to trust the memory. Much time and thought has been put into the questions as they appear in the handbooks, and it is doubtful if the officiating minister will be able to improve their wording upon the occasion of a particular service. However, the minister will do well to be so familiar with the content of the questions that he can look frequently into the eyes of the candidate as he asks the questions. This can be a very effective and moving part of the service. As the candidate answers in the affirmative the solemn questions which are asked of him, life commitment takes on a new meaning. It is especially good for young people to witness such a commitment. Doubt-

less there will be some young people in the assembly who ought to give themselves in like manner for preparation for the Lord's service.

5. *The imposition of hands and prayer.* These two things go together and are the two most essential parts of the service. A study of the Scriptures shows that the laying on of hands in both the Old and New Testaments was a symbolic action of deep significance. It carried the ideas of identification, transference, devotion to God, setting apart to a particular service, and the infilling of the Holy Spirit. See such passages as Leviticus 3:2, 8, 13; 4:4, 29; 16:21; Numbers 8:12; Mark 5:23; 16:18; Acts 8:17, 19; 13:2-3; 19:6. It is not to be supposed that there is any mystical power in the laying on of the hands. This act is symbolic of the setting apart by God of a man to His particular service and of God's enablement for that service, indicating that the prepared and qualified man is now to take his place among those who have been previously called into the ministry. Without that divine ordination which takes place when God calls a man into His service, human ordination will mean nothing.

As the laying on of hands takes place, the candidate kneels. Each officiating elder lays his right hand upon his head. That is, the first elder places his hand directly upon the head of the candidate, the next places his hand upon the hand of the first elder and so on, with all taking part. This should be done, of course, without undue pressure being exerted.

One or two of the designated elders then offers the ordination prayer. If two are to offer prayer, it will be well for them to have an understanding as to what phases of the ministry each will consider in his prayer so as to avoid needless duplication and yet give full consideration in the prayers to his ministry. In most instances one prayer is deemed sufficient. The content of the ordination prayer should be in complete harmony with the occasion. It should seek God's power for the fulfillment of the vows which have been taken. It should petition God for a faithful discharge of the stewardship which has been committed to the candidate including, of course, a faithful preaching of the Word of God. Then there should be a plea for a consistent walk on the part of the new pastor as he moves in and out among his people and for a homelife which will be a worthy example in the community. It will be well also to pray for a happy relationship between pastor and congregation, since the two must work together if much is to be accomplished. The prayer may well be concluded with a petition for the infilling of the Holy Spirit for the performance of the work of God by the new minister.

6. *The charge.* With the candidate standing, one of the elders should then take the candidate by the right hand and deliver the carefully worded charge to him. This is a very solemn moment and should leave a lasting impression on both the candidate and the congregation. The charge should be given clearly and with deep feeling. For the best effect the charge should be memorized so that the officiating elder can look directly into the eyes of the newly ordained man. Before the charge is delivered, all ordained ministers should be invited to stand. This tends to add impressiveness to the ceremony and dignity as well. The ministers should remain standing until the benediction has been pronounced.

Most ministerial handbooks contain a suggested form for the charge. The one with which the writer is familiar is as follows:

> My dear Brother ————, take thou authority in the church of God to perform the duties and offices of the elder; to preach and teach the Word of God; to be instant in season and out of season; to reprove, rebuke, exhort, with all longsuffering and doctrine; to administer the holy sacraments and ordinances of the church; to guard carefully the souls for whom Christ died; to make full proof of thy ministry; in the Name of the Father, and of the Son, and of the Holy Spirit. And when the Chief Shepherd shall appear, ye shall receive a crown of glory that fadeth not away.[2]

7. *The welcome.* Immediately following the charge the newly ordained man is usually welcomed to his position in the ministry by one of the officiating elders. The others join with a welcoming handshake.

8. *The benediction.* This is ordinarily pronounced by the new minister and thus becomes his first act of service following his ordination. The benediction is often preceded by a suitable hymn of consecration. The benediction concludes the service but usually there is a time of congratulation following the service. Many in the congregation at that time offer their best wishes for a blessed ministry.

[2]*The Brethren Minister's Handbook* (Winona Lake, Ind.: Brethren Missionary Herald Co., 1945), p. 22.

RECOMMENDED READING

EDWARDS, D. MIALL. "Ordain, Ordination," *The International Standard Bible Encyclopaedia*, IV, 2199 f. Chicago: Howard-Severance Co., 1915.

ERDMAN, CHARLES R. *The Work of the Pastor*. Philadelphia: The Westminister Press, 1924. P. 13 ff.

Handbooks, Ministerial. (Consult denominational ministerial handbooks for suggestive forms.)

HOPPIN, JAMES M. *Pastoral Theology*. New York and London: Funk and Wagnalls Co., 1909. Pp. 101-110.

McCLINTOCK, JOHN and STRONG, JAMES. "Ordination," *Cyclopaedia of Biblical Theological, and Ecclesiastical Literature*, VII, 411-420. New York: Harper and Brothers, Publishers, 1882.

ORR, JAMES. "Hands, Imposition," *The International Standard Bible Encyclopaedia*, II, 1335. Chicago: Howard-Severance Co., 1915.

PATTISON, T. HARWOOD. *For the Work of the Ministry*. Philadelphia: American Baptist Publication Society, 1907. Chap. 4.

Chapter 19

ESTABLISHING AN ADMINISTRATIVE RELATIONSHIP: CANDIDATING

THERE COME TIMES in the lives of all ministers when they are invited to preach as candidates for a pastoral relationship. This ministry need not be an experience filled with fear and apprehension. Nor should candidating be looked upon as undignified or humiliating. In it the minister should seek the guidance of the Holy Spirit that he may conduct himself in the proper manner and that he may have discernment as to what the will of the Lord is.

The Nature of Candidating

Candidating is the getting together of a prepared and available minister with a church which is in need of a pastor. Often the candidate is just out of seminary. He is unknown and inexperienced but is desirous of beginning a definite ministry in the pastorate. He may not have been ordained yet, but usually he is at least licensed by his denominational group to preach. In other cases, the candidate may have been in the pastorate for some years but has severed his pastoral relationship with the previous congregation for one reason or another and would like to enter another pastorate. He may not be very well known in the vicinity of an available church and so an acquaintanceship needs to be formed. Candidating may well provide this.

As to the church involved, its previous pastor may have resigned or died, or for some reason he may not have been reappointed. The church now needs another pastor. There are men available, but the church knows little or nothing about them. Its official board or pulpit supply committee may be authorized to contact one of the available men to come to the church to preach, looking forward to a possible pastoral relationship. Thus in one way or another a prospective pastor and a church without a pastor get together for mutual acquaintance.

The church should follow the policy of hearing and considering only one candidate at a time. Candidating should not be made a competitive matter. Either a call should be extended to the candidate who has been heard or his name should be dropped from consideration. In the event of the latter another candidate may then be heard.

Candidating is also a means whereby the will of God may be determined with respect to the exact place where the available minister should serve. On the other hand when a candidate is heard the church has an opportunity to make an intelligent decision about calling the candidate. The experience may prove to be very beneficial both to the minister and to the congregation, offering opportunity for mutual acquaintance. In what better way may a minister find out whether a certain place is suitable for his type of ministry or affords sufficient challenge? Then, too, how may a congregation better be enabled to learn whether a certain man is the right one for its pulpit? Surely a congregation has a right to know about the man who is to be their pastor! It has a right to know about his beliefs, his background, his family, his policies, his zeal, and so on. Some churches would have saved themselves a lot of difficulty and heartbreak if they had taken a little more time to consider the man whom they called to be their pastor. Some men just do not fit into certain situations, whereas they may do well in others. For instance, some men do not fit well into a rural church, but on the other hand, they will do well in a city church. Again, some men do not fit well into a new, home-mission church but will succeed in an old, established church. Since men are different and congregations are different, good judgment is needed in getting the right man in the right church. Through the experience of candidating, both the minister and the church can learn of these things and thus each will be better able to make a proper decision.

Moreover, candidating is an evidence of humility and a willingness on the part of the candidate to be led by the Spirit of God. The man who refuses to candidate sets himself up higher than he ought. Some men appear to think that candidating is beneath them. They take the attitude that their training and calling as a minister ought to be sufficient. Thus they frown upon putting themselves on trial, as they say, in the experience of candidating. Admittedly the position of the candidate is both difficult and delicate, but it may well demonstrate the minister's courage and adaptability as well as his humility. And through the experience the will of God has often been made clear. The latter is true both for the minister and the congregation. Often the congregation becomes enthusiastic in favor of calling the candidate after they have heard him. In other instances, it becomes clearly evident that the candidate is not God's man for the particular place.

The Conduct of the Candidate

First, he should act as an ambassador of Christ going forth to bring God's message to the people. In this respect he should be no different than at any other time he preaches. As he seeks to be God's ambassador at this rather critical time, he should, of course, endeavor to do his best. Again, this will be no different from the other times he preaches, for is there ever a time when the man of God is justified in doing less than his best? If he has quite an assortment of sermons, it may not be wise to preach the most brilliant ones in the collection lest later he might not be able to maintain that high standard as a steady production. Perhaps the advice of an old Methodist preacher is in order. He said, "When you go to a new place, never preach the best sermon you have the first time you are there. If you do, the people's expectations will be raised so high that you may never be able to satisfy them again. Don't preach your worst sermon either. Just give them a middling good stiff sermon, and you have got room after that to go in either direction."[1] Let the candidate "preach the Word" faithfully as a good Gospel ambassador should always do, and he will have nothing to fear.

He should be natural. He should not be guilty of putting on airs or acting like some other preacher. He should refrain from being a mere performer. Let him act the part of a "man of God," which he is called to be. Though the candidate be a very young man, his conduct should be of such character that no man will have reason to despise his youth (I Tim. 4:12). In short, the candidate should be his best self when it comes to preaching his trial sermon or sermons as the case may be. In the experience he will seek to keep his nerves under control, even though they may be playing tricks with him on the inside!

Let him enter wholeheartedly into the service as a worshiper. He should take a sincere part in the singing of God's praise, the reading

[1] Nolan B. Harmon, Jr., *Ministerial Ethics and Etiquette* (New York and Nashville: Abingdon-Cokesbury Press, 1928), p. 124.

of the Scriptures, the ministry of prayer, and every other part of the service insofar as it is possible for him to do so. The preacher needs to worship as well as the congregation, and they are quick to notice the preacher's sincerity or lack of it which he demonstrates as he conducts the worship service. A minister deprives himself of a great blessing if he fails at this point, and he will lessen his influence as the director of the service. Let the candidate remember this when he becomes the regular pastor.

The candidate should manifest an interest in every phase of the church work. An ideal pastoral relationship concerns itself with all departments of the church and all phases of the ministry to the congregation. The candidate therefore will not show himself overly interested in the young people to the exclusion of the older folk. He will not talk so much about the importance of a radio ministry that the members will wonder if he will have any time for parish visitation. He will seek to present himself as a well-balanced minister. An impartial interest in all phases of the church's activity is the ideal, for he is called to be an overseer of the whole flock of God in a given pastorate.

The candidate may well ask the church if there is some pastoral service which he may render while he is with them. It may be that the church has been without a pastor for some weeks or months. Perhaps a pastoral visit on some very sick member may be needed. Someone with a great burden would appreciate a word of counsel. An offer to be of help would likely be much appreciated and would indicate that he has a pastor's heart. The candidate should be happy to be of service in this way. If such opportunity is afforded, it will help to acquaint him with the congregation. Furthermore, it may be just the thing that will make clear to the congregation that this is the man they are looking for.

He should be friendly to everybody but be careful lest he show special interest in particular groups or individuals. In almost every church there are certain individuals or groups who like to curry the favor of the minister and bend him to their will. Certain organizations sometimes feel they are entitled to special favors from him. The candidate should be aware of this tendency and guard himself against being influenced by it. While at the church he will do well to inquire about every phase of the church's work and to show proper interest in all that is being done without displaying favoritism.

The candidate should leave to the church the matter of taking the first steps to a pastoral relationship. Let him not be overanxious. Such an attitude is likely to work against him. If the church is desirous of talking to him about a possible pastoral relationship, he should be glad for the opportunity and answer their questions to the best of his ability. This conference may be through a committee, the official board, or even the entire church in small congregations. He should express himself with respect to his convictions but should refrain from undue dogmatism. He should refrain from giving the impression that he knows all the answers, especially if he is a very young man. He will demonstrate his assurance that the Word of God is able to meet the entire need of the church, and express his determination to preach that Word without compromise. If he finds himself in a church where there has been trouble and division, he will guard against depreciating the previous pastor and the work he has done. He should remember that usually, no matter how miserably the previous pastor may have failed, he will have some friends who will continue to think highly of him. There is no use incurring their disfavor at the beginning. The candidate probably will know little of the actual facts in the case; therefore he should refrain from snap judgments. Let him take the forward look and plan for the future should he become pastor of the church.

Finally, he should leave the whole matter of the call to the Lord. If the candidate has from the beginning committed the experience of candidating to the Lord, he should be willing to let Him work out the consummation of the matter. If the church extends him a call, he should thank the Lord for this indication that his ministry has been appreciated. And then shortly he should either accept or reject the call. He should not keep the church waiting a long time for an answer. In most cases the candidate will accept the call, especially if it is unanimous or practically so. There may be situations regarding the church which will indicate to him that this is not the field which will best suit his capabilities or training. In such cases, he will courteously refuse the call, expressing the desire that the congregation will be able in the near future to secure the right man as their pastor. In case the candidate is not called, he should remember that this does not mean that he is a failure in the ministry. A man may not be suited for one place but may succeed gloriously in another. There are many such cases on record.

Installation of the Accepted Candidate

After a candidate has accepted a call extended to him and a date
is determined when the pastoral relationship will begin, the matter of
his installation into the pastorate should be arranged.

The difference between installation and ordination is that the
latter admits one to a permanent office while the former establishes a
relation to a particular church. The first occurs as many times as a
man has pastorates, the latter occurs but once. Installation to a pastoral relation may occur before a minister is ordained. The writer
knows of a very successful pastor who has had two thriving pastorates
and has never been ordained. He is only licensed. Installation has to
do with the new pastor's commencement of activity in the church to
which he has been called.

Installation is a mutual pledge between the pastor and the people
of the congregation. The pastor agrees to serve the church faithfully,
and the church promises to support the new pastor in every possible
way in harmony with the will of God. Installation serves to exalt
the importance of the pastoral relationship and at the same time
presses home the responsibility which the membership has for success
in this relationship. It is also a splendid and dignified way of introducing the new pastor to the community. The church misses a
good opportunity of advertising its ministry if it fails to conduct an
installation service.

The arrangement for this service is cared for differently in different
churches. In some denominations the presbytery or district ministerium or some such group has charge of the arrangements. In others,
such as independent churches or most Baptist churches, the local
church arranges for the service. In such cases the new pastor should
be consulted as to his desire concerning the time of the service and
participants in it. Usually it is wise to invite ministers outside the
local church to have part in such a service. This gives the installation
a wider recognition. Community representatives may also be invited
to be present and have part, even though it may be but to bring a
personal greeting. In order that these outside representatives may
attend, it will probably be wise to schedule the service at some time
which will not conflict with the regular public worship services. A
Sunday afternoon or some week night may be used.

An installation service should follow somewhat the following order, with a prominent minister in charge. The latter responsibility may be cared for by the moderator of the district where the church is located or by a minister who is a special friend of the pastor.

1. Devotional exercises, including a pertinent sermon.
2. Questions to the incoming pastor by the presiding officer or some other chosen minister.
3. Questions to the members of the congregation by the same minister or some other as best suits those planning the service.
4. The prayer of installation.
5. The charge to the pastor.
6. The charge to the congregation.
7. The benediction by the new pastor.
8. Personal greetings and congratulations.

A service of this kind can be made very impressive, and it tends to get the new pastoral relationship off to a good start.

In bringing this consideration to a close, it may be well to ask the question, How long should a pastorate be extended? Equally good men differ widely on this question. Normally a pastorate should not be severed under four or five years. A pastor can scarcely learn his field and do a constructive work in less time than that. Some churches benefit by a change after this length of time. This depends largely upon the man. Some men are constitutionally fitted to go on indefinitely with a consistently rich ministry. Others are not. Happy is the situation where the pastor can build solidly from the beginning of his pastorate and continue for a long period of time in a constructive ministry. Changing of pastorates involves loss of time and knowledge of the field. The writer is convinced that the long pastorate is the ideal.

However, there are circumstances which make it advisable for a man to change pastorates after a number of years. He should have a call to leave a church the same as he had to come. The pastor should not let a disturbance or trifling circumstance be an excuse for him to pull up stakes. The Lord is not fickle. He does not usually call a man to a field and then quickly tell him to leave. Neither should the pastor always be on the lookout for greener pastures. Dr. M. G. Kyle used to tell the young men who sat in his classes at Xenia Theological Seminary to avoid pastoral flirtation. He told them that they ought to go to a field with a determination to give their best without thinking about some other field. He further emphasized that it takes time to do a constructive work in a given field and this ought to be the goal of every pastor.

RECOMMENDED READING

Not many texts have been written exclusively devoted to the matters dealt with in this chapter. Short treatments may be found in such works on the ministry of the pastor as T. Harwood Pattison's *For The Work of the Ministry* and *The Work of the Pastor* by Charles R. Erdman. Ministerial handbooks which are published by various denominational groups often present a suggested program for an installation service.

Chapter 20

THE PASTOR AND THE ORGANIZATIONS OF HIS CHURCH

A GOOD MINISTER must be a good administrator in the church. The administrative responsibility is one of five main functions belonging to the eldership. These five functions are (1) the pastoral—he is to shepherd the flock of God, feeding and caring for its members (Acts 20:28; I Pet. 5:2); (2) the educational—he is to teach the church (I Tim. 3:2; 5:17); (3) the officiative—he is to lead in the worship and activities of the church (James 5:14); (4) the representative—he may be called upon to represent the church at certain times (Acts 20:17); and (5) the administrative—he is expected to rule in the church, not as a dictator but rather by precept and example (I Tim. 5:7; I Pet. 5:2-3).

This latter function is the subject of this chapter. The importance of it is suggested by the word itself, for it carries in its bosom the word "minister." And to minister is a vital part of the work of Christ's undershepherds, even as it was of the Chief Shepherd (Matt. 20: 27-28). While the word "minister" includes more than is suggested by the term administration as used here, yet the latter is included.

The work of administration has to do with the general oversight of the various departments of the church. No matter how good the church organization may be, it will not continue to run smoothly and efficiently without some attention and oversight. Since this principle is true in almost every realm outside the church, it should cause no surprise to discover that it is true within the church. The pastor is the main one to provide oversight in the church. The Apostle Peter in his First Epistle exhorted elders, "Tend the flock of God which is among you, exercising the oversight, not of constraint, but willingly, according to the will of God" (5:2, A.S.V.).

Such oversight on the pastor's part will require time and effort and much prayer. It will demand that he be closely associated with the leaders of his church to counsel with them and to learn what they are thinking. Furthermore, it will mean that the pastor will constantly be the directing head of all phases of his church. But he will seek to occupy this position in such a way as to foster good feeling and to forward the progress of the church. Let us consider the pastor's relation to some of the organizations of his church and see what are the responsibilities that he needs to discharge.

The Pastor and the Official Board

The Official Board is that group of individuals elected by the church to care for certain matters of business which it does not seem wise for the congregation as a whole to care for. It commonly acts for the church between business meetings. This group is known by different names in different churches, but for our purpose we will adhere to the designation as indicated. Its responsibilities vary somewhat in different congregations, but in the main the functions are similar.

Since church government varies so widely between denominations and independent churches, it is difficult to make generalizations in this chapter to cover even a large plurality of religious groups. In Baptist churches generally the official board is the board of deacons. Trustees take care of the temporal affairs of the church. Local Presbyterian churches are governed by a session, which consists of a board of elders. In addition there is a board of trustees and a board of deacons; the latter may or may not act as ushers for the church services.

In a Methodist church the governing body is called the Official Board and consists of trustees (who care for temporal affairs) and stewards (who care for spiritual affairs). There are no deacons. Ushers are not elected; nor do they constitute a special board. In the new Lutheran Church in America,[1] which came into being in January, 1963, the local congregation is supervised by a Church Council, members of which are called deacons. The deacons also assume the responsibilities of trustees. The Church Council arranges for the appointment of ushers. Among the Grace Brethren, of which the

[1]Consists of the old United Lutheran Church, Suomi Synod, American Evangelical Lutheran Church, and the Augustana Lutheran Church.

writer is a member, the Official Board is composed of the pastor, moderator, vice moderator, the Sunday school superintendent, and chairmen of various boards and committees and presidents of some of the church organizations, as spelled out by the church constitution. Whatever the name of the official board, the pastor has some responsibilities in regard to it.

The pastor should see that the membership of the Official Board is clearly defined. The church constitution usually makes it clear just who is supposed to sit on the Board. However, some churches do not have a constitution. Until one is adopted, the pastor should have a definite understanding with his membership as to who are members of this Board.

The pastor should see that the Board is properly organized. There should be at least a chairman and a secretary. In some churches the moderator and secretary of the church automatically become the same officers of the Official Board. Whatever the situation may be, the pastor should see that these officers are functioning and that the proper committees of the board are appointed.

The pastor should also see that the Board holds meetings when they are needed. Some churches have stated times for these meetings. Others have meetings only when they seem necessary. At the present writing, church boards customarily meet once a month, with the exception of the summer months.

The pastor should see that the Board performs its various duties. He must be acquainted with the constitution of the church so that he knows what duties are outlined therein, and he should check to see that the Board fulfills these. Some of the duties usually handled by the Official Board include advising the pastor in time of need, acting for the church in business matters between congregational meetings, preparing recommendations to present to the church for consideration, and caring for cases of discipline. In some cases this board acts as the nominating committee of the church. In many churches, it is the Board's responsibility to recommend a pastor to the congregation when the need arises. In some instances, its responsibility also includes approving of committee nominations, particularly in cases where it is the prerogative of the moderator to select them. Increasingly the Official Board is assigned the duty of setting up the committees for the entire church organization.

When the pastor has a recommendation to present to the church, it usually will be well for him, first, to bring it before the Official Board for consideration. The content of the recommendation will likely carry more weight if the congregation knows that this body of individuals has considered the matter and is favorable to it. Then, too, it is a mark of deference to the Board which the pastor can well afford to show.

The pastor should exercise all possible care to recognize all the ideas expressed by the members of the Board. This is a wise procedure, especially if the pastor is chairman of the Board. He will gain in the long run if he takes time to listen to all the ideas the members wish to present. If some of these ideas seem shortsighted or impractical, the Board as a whole is likely to rectify the matter and thus the pastor is in the clear. There is likely to be unfavorable reaction if it becomes known that the pastor is accustomed to silencing free expression.

The pastor should pray for grace to keep him from becoming involved in arguments with his Board. There will be times when he will need to wait for the fulfillment of his desires in some matters of policy. But better to wait than to create friction or a divisive spirit on his Board. Often when it is evident that the Board is not unanimous in some matter, it will be far better to hold the issue in abeyance until it can be more fully considered and prayed over. The pastor does not always have to get his own way!

The Pastor and the Deacon Board

The deacons and the deaconesses of the pastor's church should be his very best helpers. They ought to be Spirit-filled men and women. In the New Testament they are shown to be God's servants in the fullest sense of this designation. The pastor cannot make them to be all that has been suggested, but he does have some oversight of their labors in the church. Concerning these the writer wishes to make the following remarks:

1. The pastor needs to make sure that the Board of Deacons is properly organized. There should be a chairman of the Board as a whole, and often a chairman of the deaconesses, for this latter group commonly has duties that belong to it alone. A leader for this group will be helpful. Experience teaches that groups without a head usually do not function properly.

2. It is also the responsibility of the pastor to outline the duties of the deacons. These officials should not have to wait to be told what they are supposed to do. In order to set forth the work of the diaconate more efficiently, it will be well for the pastor to read some material regarding the subject of the diaconate, such as *The Deacon at Work* by Frederick A. Agar, or the chapter in Eugene Dolloff's *The Efficient Church Officer,* entitled "The Work of the Diaconate." Sometimes the church constitution or denominational handbook spells out the duties of this board.

As to these responsibilities, some things are very clear, both negatively and positively. First, it is evident from the study of Acts 6:1-7 and I Timothy 3:8-13 that the office of deacon is not simply a position of honor. Neither is it limited to service at the time of Communion or baptism. The root meaning of the word "deacon" suggests the more positive aspects of the office. The word carries within it the definite idea of service or ministry. The passages cited above suggest any service in the church that might aid in a fuller preaching of the Gospel by those especially designated for that purpose. The "serving of tables" in the Acts passage would suggest the more temporal or physical aspects of the work of the church. However, we must not carry this idea too far so as to prohibit deacons from ministering the Word of God. At least two of the men mentioned in the first group of deacons were outstanding exponents of Scripture, namely, Philip and Stephen. Stephen has left us the longest sermon recorded in the New Testament.

Then the instruction in the First Timothy passage that deacons are to "hold the mystery of the faith in a pure conscience" (v. 9) and to possess "great boldness in the faith" (v. 13) would suggest more than a ministry in temporalities. It should be a deeply spiritual ministry but include matters of a physical nature which are absolutely necessary for the welfare of the church.

Usually included among the duties of the diaconate are such matters as service at times of baptism and Communion, visiting the sick, caring for the poor, instructing new converts, teaching the Word to various groups, and many other types of service that will help the pastor. Theirs ought to be a busy ministry. A. T. Robertson suggests that the word deacon comes from two Greek words *dia* and *konis,* meaning 'through' or 'by' and 'dust,' carrying with them the thought that deacons are to be so busy that they stir up a dust because of their activity!

3. The pastor should also see that new deacons or deaconesses are publicly dedicated to the service of the church. In connection with the setting apart of the first deacons in Acts 6, there was the laying on of hands by the apostles, doubtless a symbol of the impartation of the gifts and graces needed for their office. It was also in the nature of a prayer to God for divine blessing for the discharge of the included responsibilities. A similar service may be conducted at a Sunday worship service or at a midweek prayer service. Or a special service may be arranged at another time. The time is not the important thing, but the pastor should make sure that the matter is not overlooked.

The Pastor and the Board of Trustees

It has seemed wise in many churches of today to have a group of men in the church whose sole responsibility is to care for the property of the church. In New Testament times, when there were no church buildings, the office of trustee was not needed. But today, with increased numbers of buldings, the trustees of a church have a great deal of responsibility, and the pastor's oversight should include them in the following ways:

1. The pastor should see that they are properly elected. The church constitution usually provides that they shall be elected one or two or three each year, for a two- or three-year term, so that continuity will be maintained on the Board. The size of this group is usually determined by the size of the church and should be stated in the constitution. From three to six members is probably the average size of this Board.

2. Then, too, the pastor will want to make sure that the trustees are properly organized with at least a chairman and a secretary. The chairman is responsible to take the lead in calling needed meetings, and the secretary is expected to take any minutes that should be preserved and be prepared to present any recommendations that should be considered by the Official Board of the church.

3. Most important of all, the pastor should see that the trustees discharge their duties. He may find it necessary to outline carefully their duties at the beginning of each term of office so that the new members will know just what their responsibilities are. These duties

include an overall care of the physical property of the church. Happy is the situation if the pastor can get his trustees to realize that their responsibility is a sacred trust. Since they have the care of the Lord's property, they are the Lord's custodians.

More specifically, this care includes repairing of any property damage, such as broken windows or a stalled furnace. The trustees should be persuaded to make periodic inspections of the church property to see what needs to be done to keep it in the best possible shape. They then should fulfill the need or take steps to meet the need if church action is necessary. Most churches allow their trustees to proceed with necessary repairs without special action. If an unusual amount of money is needed, special church action usually is necessary.

Their duties also include the insuring of church property and the employment of a sexton, purchase of fuel, and the like. The trustees may well be the ones to initiate recommendations as to improvements to the church, presenting such recommendations to the church for their final action. It may be better still to present them first to the Official Board and then to the church. In some states there must be an annual filing of the names of the trustees at the county court house.

In all of these matters, the pastor will exercise a watchful oversight, not attempting to do the things that the trustees are delegated to do, but making sure that none of their duties are overlooked.

The Pastor and the Ushers

Dolloff says that "the ushers, as a group, act as host for the congregation."[2] He goes on to show that when this is properly understood the importance of their position will be more fully appreciated. Happy is the church which has a group of dedicated, loyal ushers. They are the ones who in a definite way represent the church to the folk who attend its services. Often the first impression visitors get of a church is through the usher who greets them at the door. In a real sense he is a salesman for the church. The pastor will be wise to do all that he can to encourage their work and to help them make it more efficient.

The pastor should see that there is the proper number of ushers. What this number is, of course, depends largely upon the size of the church. He should make sure that there is a head usher. He may

[2]Eugene Dinsmore Dolloff, *The Efficient Church Officer* (New York: Fleming H. Revell Co., 1949), p. 20.

well be elected by the church. This gives dignity and importance to the position. It makes him responsible not only to the pastor but to the church as a whole. In larger churches there should be at least one assistant head usher. Following the choice of a head usher, the necessary number of helpers should be appointed, preferably by the Official Board, and after consultation with the head usher.

The pastor should know the qualifications of good ushers so that he can advise wisely with respect to their choice and appointment. Desirable traits are dependability, punctuality, good memory, neat appearance, cooperation and, most of all, a love for the Lord.

The pastor should outline the duties of the ushers so that they will have a full comprehension of their task. These duties include meeting and welcoming strangers, assisting in the seating of the congregation, receiving offerings, ventilating properly, aiding the sick or quieting disturbances, and distributing the church bulletin. In short, the ushers should do everything possible to make the service reverent and worshipful. The pastor will do well to encourage his ushers to read a good manual on the art of church ushering, such as Sylvester's *Church Ushers' Manual.*

The pastor can well afford from time to time to encourage his congregation to cooperate with the ushers. Some folk are very thoughtless in their treatment of these hosts of the congregation and greatly embarrass them at times. Sooner or later every usher will have the experience of leading the way down the aisle of the church to show folk available seats, only to discover after arriving at the selected place that they have chosen to go another direction! The usher will, of course, overlook the incident, but the pastor can help in educating his people as to the proper consideration of ushers so that such incidents will be kept to a minimum.

Some pastors have found it worthwhile to have a social gathering for the ushers and their wives occasionally. Such an event may serve to impress upon this group its importance and to tie them to the pastor in a more intimate way, resulting in a more effective service. Extra attention shown in such ways often does much to bring about an increased sense of loyalty and a desire to reciprocate.

The Pastor and the Committees

Much of the work in a normal church is delegated to committees. Some of these committees may be standing committees provided by the constitution. Others may be special committees created by the church to care for some special project. In either case, the pastor has some responsibility in the way of oversight.

The pastor should see that the committees are properly constituted. As previously stated, the standing committees are usually set forth in the church constitution. Often these are appointed by the Official Board, sometimes by the pastor himself with the approval of the Board. A few committees, such as the nominating committee, may be elected by the church itself. Churches differ as to their procedure at this point. Common committees in churches are the music, the missionary, the publication, the finance, the auditing and the educational committees.[3] In addition to these there may be any number of special committees to care for special projects, such as a building committee, which may be elected or appointed depending upon the wishes of the congregation. The pastor, irrespective of how these committees may be created, needs to make sure that they are all properly appointed.

He should also make sure that the committees are properly organized. At the beginning of the church year it may be his duty to ask all the committees to meet and organize. He may want to designate the first named individual in each case to act as chairman to get the several committees organized. If someone other than the pastor takes all this responsibility, well and good. But the pastor should make sure that it is done. A committee with no chairman is about as good as no committee.

Furthermore, the pastor should see that the duties of the different committees are made clear to them. A midweek prayer service may well be devoted to presenting the committees and their work to the church, and then having special prayer for them in the pursuance of

[3]Increasingly churches are adopting a plan for the educational work of the church similar to that of the United Presbyterian Church in the United States of America. That denomination has devised a plan to unify the total educational work of the local church which involves the establishment of a Christian Education Council under the general leadership of the Christian education director. Members of the council include members of the Official Board (the session), representatives of the Sunday school (generally the superintendent), the youth work, the music program, the women's work, the scouting program (if there is one), and the like. Generally the representatives of the various areas of Christian education are themselves chairmen of subcommittees, i.e., the representative of the youth work is chairman of the youth committee.

The pastor is an exofficio member of the Christian Education Council. As such, he can influence its decisions, although he does not have voting power. He can also give directions to the council through the members of the Official Board serving on it, one of whom is probably chairman of the council.

their duties. Subsequent to this, there may be times when the pastor will need to urge his committees to a more diligent attention to the work which has been committed to them. He should not undertake to do the work of the committees but should make sure that they do it.

If the pastor can get all of the committees in the normal church to working properly, he will have a splendid group in whom leadership, effectiveness, and interest will be developed. Dwight L. Moody had a good idea in mind when he said, "It is better to put ten men to work than do the work of ten men." In some churches it seems that the pastor has to do everything. He cannot even call on anyone to lead in prayer. Somewhere along the line leadership has not been developed.

Finally, at this point, the pastor should seek always to keep spiritual objectives before his committees. Let him encourage them to open their meetings with prayer so that the spiritual welfare of the church will be ever kept in view. Incidentally, as an aid to this end, the pastor should be considered as a member ex officio of all committees in his church.

The Pastor and the Church Choir

Since the pastor is the overseer of the entire church, it is clear that he should have oversight of the ministry of music in his church. A factor so important to the success of the church's program warrants his careful supervision. Since the music program to a large extent centers in the choir, the writer is limiting his discusson to that group with its contributing personnel.

The pastor's ministry in this phase of the church's work can help to overcome the common reputation of choirs throughout the years, namely, that they are the war department of the church! The pastor's supervision may well include the following:

1. Let him meet with the music committee from time to time as it deals with matters concerning the choir. By such action he may ward off difficulties that might otherwise arise. In such contact he can impress the committee with the importance of the choir's ministry and encourage it to expend every effort to make this ministry as effective as possible.

2. Moreover, the pastor should insist that all the members of his choir be Christians. Those who lead in the singing of God's

praises should be those who love the Lord. The pastor may find a situation in his church which does not measure up to this ideal. It will take time and wisdom and tact to rectify such a situation, but it must be corrected if God's service of praise is to be what it ought to be.

3. The pastor should also insist that the choir loyally support the services of the church in which they participate. It is demoralizing to any church service to have choir members leave the church after they have finished their singing. This is sometimes witnessed when the choir is permitted to leave the platform so that it may be in front of the preacher while he preaches. Some choir members have been known to leave the church by a side door; they don't stay to hear the sermon! Better have no choir at all than one which does not support the worship services.

4. The pastor can help to correct such an unfortunate situation by impressing the choir with the importance of their task. Their service, like that of the pastor, can be a ministry of evangelism and spiritual nurture. Their ministry may reach certain individuals who would not be reached by the ministry from the pulpit. If somehow the pastor can get his choir to realize this, he will have achieved much toward making it an effective spiritual instrument.

5. Then, too, the pastor should foster all possible cooperation between himself and the choir leader in the selection of hymns and special music from Sunday to Sunday. If this is to be accomplished, the choir leader will need to be informed of the pastor's sermon subjects. This needs to be done early enough in the week so that the director can make his plans accordingly. The music is much more effective if it fits in with the thought of the message.

6. Finally, but not least important, the pastor ought to pray with his choir before it enters the sanctuary for the service. This will tend to make the choir realize the significance of its service. This ministry is so important that it ought to be rendered in the atmosphere of prayer.

The Pastor and Church Business Meetings

The pastor needs to be a good administrator when it comes to the business meetings of his church. Business meetings are sometimes difficult, but they afford an opportunity to the pastor to manifest the graces of the Spirit in this phase of his work. In some churches the pastor is not the moderator of the church business meetings. Some pastors prefer not to be. But whether or not he is the moderator, he has the responsibility of oversight in these meetings. In this brief discussion the writer supposes that the pastor is the moderator. Even though he is not, still many of the following principles should prevail:

1. He should see that the meetings are properly announced. Although the times for these meetings are clearly stated in the church constitution and bylaws, many never read this document, and many who do easily forget. Therefore, the pastor, from the pulpit and in the church bulletin, should urge his members to attend these meetings. Especially in a church with congregational rule, it is desirable for as large a representation as possible of the members to discharge the business of the church. This tends to make the church as a whole feel its part in the work of the church and helps to keep down friction.

2. He should also see that these meetings are well planned. He should make sure that the financial and other reports are ready. He should see that the Official Board has had its preparatory meeting well ahead of the congregational meeting. The business meeting will run more smoothly if the Board gives careful consideration to matters which need to come before the church and makes suitable recommendations. If there are any special committeees with work entrusted to their care, the pastor should check to see that they are ready with their reports. It is always disconcerting in a business meeting to have no reports from those who have responsibility to report. This dampens the spirit of the meeting and hinders the progress of the church.

3. The pastor should make sure that each business session is opened with a devotional period. This period should not be long, but the business meeting should be bathed in the atmosphere of the Word and of prayer.

4. Furthermore, the pastor should do what he can to see that the scriptural injunction that all things be done "decently and in order" (I Cor. 14:40) is carried out. To this end the observance of some such order in the progress of the business session as follows is suggested:

(1) After the opening devotions, it should be ascertained if a quorum is present.

(2) The moderator should call for the reading of the minutes of the last meeting (and any special meetings) and have them approved.

(3) He should next call for the reports of the financial officers, the heads of the various organizations, and the committees. If there is a pastor's report to be given, it also should be submitted at this time. These reports provide a cross section of the work of the church and in no case should they be considered unimportant. These reports should be acted upon by the meeting.

(4) Unfinished business should then be considered. This is usually noted from the reading of the minutes.

(5) Then comes the call for the presentation of new business. In this category come recommendations from the Official Board, from other organizations of the church, or even from individuals. It is usually best for new business to come through the Official Board, which group has had time prior to the meeting to consider carefully the matters to be presented. But in congregationally governed churches this is not absolutely necessary. Any member has the right to present matters for consideration.

(6) Finally comes the adjournment, followed by a closing prayer seeking God's blessing upon the actions which have been taken in the meeting.

In the conduct of business meetings, it will be well for the moderator to have at least an elementary knowledge of parliamentary law. And surely he should have a complete acquaintance with the content of the church constitution and bylaws.

Moreover, in this phase of his pastoral oversight, as well as in all others, the pastor should demonstrate the grace of self-control. A pastor who loses his temper and is inconsiderate of those who may disagree with him loses irreparably in the esteem of his people and in future influence. Maybe at this point a lesson can be learned from Martin Luther, who at the Leipzig debate always maintained his composure and good nature, although at times he used bitter words. He held a bunch of flowers in his hand, and when the discussion became heated he looked at it and smelled it.

Recommended Reading

Agar, Frederick. *The Deacon at Work*. Philadelphia: The Judson Press, 1923.

Benson, Clarence H. *The Church at Work*. Chicago: Bible Institute Colportage Association, 1929.

——. *Techniques of a Working Church*. Chicago: Moody Press, 1946.

BLACKWOOD, ANDREW W. *Pastoral Leadership*. New York and Nashville: Abingdon-Cokesbury Press, 1949.

CASHMAN, ROBERT. *The Business Administration of a Church*. New York: Harper and Brothers, Publishers, 1937.

DOLLOFF, EUGENE D. *The Efficient Church Officer*. New York: Fleming H. Revell Co., 1949.

ELFORD, HOMER J. *A Guide to Church Ushering*. Nashville: Abingdon Press, 1961.

ERDMAN, CHARLES R. *The Work of the Pastor*. Philadelphia: Westminster Press, 1924.

GARRETT, WILLIS O. *Church Usher's Manual*. New York: Fleming H. Revell Co., 1924.

LANG, PAUL H. *Church Ushering*. St. Louis, Mo.: Concordia Publishing Co., 1957.

LEACH, WILLIAM H. *Church Administration*. New York: George H. Doran Co., 1926.

McAFEE, CLELAND B. *The Ruling Elder*. Philadelphia: Presbyterian Board of Christian Education, 1931.

RILEY, W. B. *Pastoral Problems*. New York: Fleming H. Revell Co., 1936. Chaps. 8, 14-16.

ROBERT, HENRY M. *Robert's Rules of Order*. Chicago: Scott, Foresman and Co., 1915.

SYLVESTER, B. F. *Church Usher's Manual*. Cincinnati, Ohio: Standard Publishing Co., n.d.

Chapter 21

THE PASTOR AND THE FINANCIAL
PROBLEM IN THE CHURCH

EVERY CHURCH has a financial problem with which to deal. In some churches the problem is more difficult than in others. But whether difficult or not, it must receive careful attention. The Bible, in both the Old and New Testaments, has much to say about money and the support of God's work. The writer is convinced that there are principles laid down in the Scriptures regarding the support of God's work which ought to be followed. When they are followed, the maintenance of God's work becomes a joy, not an oppressive burden.

In Exodus 35 and 36 we have a striking example of how the work of the Lord should be supported. It is the account of securing materials for the building of the tabernacle in the wilderness. This sacred structure was to be built with materials to be provided by the people themselves. In other words, it was to be erected as a result of an offering presented unto the Lord. Moses made it clear that the method to be used in obtaining the offering was from the Lord.

Six things about this offering deserve to be carefully studied. First, it was an offering from the Lord's people (35:5). They were not to appeal to any people outside their own borders. Moses said, "Take ye from among you an offering unto the LORD." There is a principle here to the effect that God expects His people to support His work, a principle operative in both Testaments and in the church of today. Second, it was to be a voluntary offering. Whoever was of a "willing" heart was to give for this purpose (35:5). Again and again this idea is presented in chapter 35. It makes one think of the statement in II Corinthians to the effect that "God loveth a cheerful [hilarious] giver" (9:7). Third, it was an offering according to ability (35:5ff.). Not all the people brought the same offering. A careful reading of the account makes it clear that they brought as they were able, some more, some less. This same principle is enunciated in the New Testament where believers are instructed to give as God has prospered them (I Cor. 16:2). Fourth, it was to be an offering prompted by zeal for God's service (e.g. 35:21, 26). The expression, "whose heart stirred him up," indicates that God wanted His people to be enthusiastic about His work and thus to give gladly. Fifth, it was to be an offering *unto the Lord.* Ten times in Exodus 35 reference is made to "an offering unto the Lord." In short, their giving was to be an act of worship. Sixth, it was an offering sufficient to meet every need (36:5-7). So fully did the people respond to the need that finally they had to be restrained from bringing further gifts for the project—surely a unique situation in God's service!

If such a plan were followed in the program of the church today, the financial problem would for the most part be solved. There would be sufficient funds to care for every need, and much of the stress and strain which so often attend the raising of money for church support would be banished.

Twelve Foundation Stones

There are twelve basic rules or regulations to be observed in caring for the finances of the church. If followed, these rules would greatly ease the financial burden so many churches have. Moreover, there would be a great deal more joy in the support of God's work. Let us call these rules the foundation stones of church finance. We will analyze them briefly.

1. Pastors ought to preach and teach the Biblical method of supporting God's work. This rule has broad implications, some of which will be treated in later considerations, but it is placed first because of its importance. Every pastor owes it to his ministry and to his church to include the money aspect of the Christian's responsibility in his preaching and teaching. To fail at this point is to be guilty of a serious neglect in one's ministry.

No pastor should apologize for speaking about finances from the pulpit. The Bible has much to say about money in both testaments. Our Lord devoted a third of all His parables to dealing with the matter of possessions. A sixth of all the verses in the Gospels have to do with this subject. With the Bible as his authority and the Lord Jesus Christ as his example in such matters, the pastor should not hesitate to tell his people God's plan of financing His work here on earth.

It is clear from the Scriptures that God's plan of financing His work is not through taxation, assessments, pew rents, sales, socials, bazaars, or whatnot. Dr. W. B. Riley has said, "Such sales effect an anti-Christian influence; they dry up the fountains of benevolence, and they leave the church of God on a financial basis little better than that of the beggar."[1] The whole tenor of the Scriptures is against the commercialization of the House of God.

The methods just referred to doubtless have their place in the raising of funds for worldly institutions and projects, but for the cause of God there is a better way. His work is to be supported by the freewill offerings of the people of God.

The Apostle Paul devotes two whole chapters, II Corinthians 8 and 9, to the grace of giving. The climax of his appeal in this section is exemplified in the person of the Lord Jesus Christ, who gave His best for man's redemption. In the spirit of His giving and with a grateful heart for God's "unspeakable gift," Christians ought to give as God has blessed them for the support of His work.

Let the pastor therefore be faithful in setting forth the grace of giving, the Biblical method of supporting heaven's work on earth. This is the only method that is worthy of His name. The pastor should be careful, however, not to be talking about finances constantly.

2. Let him stress the importance of regular offerings to the Lord's work. The Apostle enforces this idea by his statement, "Upon the first day of the week let every one of you lay by him in store, as God has prospered him, that there be no gatherings when I come" (I Cor. 16:2). Paul instructed the Corinthians that they ought to give regular, weekly attention to this matter of the Lord's offering. He knew that if this were done he would not be embarrassed by having to make a special appeal for funds when he came.

There is a principle here that ought to be emphasized in our day. The first day of the week is a good time to put the Lord first. It is the time when God's people should go to His house, seek to be in the attitude of worship, and bring with them an offering unto the Lord. Expenses in the Lord's work come by the week, and income should be by the week, too.

[1]W. B. Riley, *Pastoral Problems* (New York: Fleming H. Revell Co., 1936), p. 152.

As an aid to such regular giving the pastor will do the church a service by encouraging the use of the envelope system, according to which packets of envelopes are provided to each individual or family of the church (and to others if desired). There is a dated envelope for each Sunday of the year, a weekly reminder of the Christian's responsibility to support the Lord's work. These envelopes should provide opportunity for the donors to indicate to what purpose they wish their offerings to go, whether to current expenses, missions, Christian education, or whatever it might be. From time to time the pastor will need to urge his members to use the envelopes, showing the advantages of using them. Not only are they an aid to systematic, regular giving as the Lord has instructed but they also make it easier to report to the federal government at income tax time what has been given to the church. Such a method will appeal to good businessmen. And, after all, the cause of Christ is the biggest and most important business in the world.

3. The pastor should insist that the church adopt a budget for each church year. A budget is deemed necessary in government, in the program of education, in all sorts of business enterprises, in social clubs, and other organizations. Should the church be less careful than the institutions of the world?

There are at least five outstanding advantages of having a budget: (1) it provides a goal for the church to reach, (2) it encourages systematic, weekly giving by the people in order to meet the demands of the budget, (3) it will help to eliminate the bizarre methods often used to raise funds for the church, (4) it helps the church systematically to plan its program for the coming year, and (5) it helps to secure a balanced church program so that every legitimate item is cared for.

The budget should be carefully prepared by the finance committee, the official board, or other appropriate group, and presented to the congregation at its annual business meeting for its consideration and approval. In this way the people who give have a voice as to how the money will be used. This will create a greater interest in the financial aspects of the church's work with the result that the people will be more likely to give liberally for its support.

The adoption of a budget enables the pastor to know what the average weekly income of the church should be. He can thus appeal to his congregation publicly and through the church bulletin to meet the amount of the budget. If there is a slipping below the average needed, he can appeal to his members for greater liberality. If they are meeting the average or going beyond it, he can commend them and look forward to a larger ministry in giving.

The budget should include all the normal running expenses of the church, such as the pastor's salary, office expense, church maintenance, telephone, repairs, music ministry, and the like. Some churches prefer to leave certain offerings, like those for missions, on a purely freewill basis, not putting them in the budget but setting a goal to be reached, if possible.

The preparation of a budget is doing the thing suggested in the Scriptures, which speak of counting the cost before undertaking work that needs to be done (Luke 14:28ff.). The idea therefore is scripturally sound and should have the encouragement of pastoral leadership.

4. The pastor should cultivate the cooperation of all the members of the congregation in the financial support of the church. Paul's admonition to the Corinthian church was, "Let everyone of you lay by him in store, as God hath prospered him" (I Cor. 16:2). If every member shares the burden of supporting the work of the church, no one will need to be overburdened, and much more can be done in the way of outreach.

This every-member support includes, of course, all of the resident members. It also includes the nonresident members. As long as individuals wish to be identified with a certain congregation, they have responsibility in supporting its projects. It includes members who may be away from the church temporarily on vacations or for other reasons. It includes the young as well as the old. As soon as children are old enough to assume membership in the church, they should be taught the ministry of giving. Their offering may be in pennies instead of dollars, but children and young people as well as adults should support the church. Many churches provide special packets of envelopes for the children in which they take peculiar delight. Insofar as possible, let every one in the church have part in the privilege and joy of giving.

5. Let the pastor stress giving as an act of worship. Giving is so set forth in the Scriptures. We have previously noticed the part that worship had in the offerings which were brought for the building of the tabernacle. The sacred record tells us that when the wise men

came to Jesus after His birth, in connection with their worship of Him "they presented unto him gifts; gold, frankincense, and myrrh" (Matt. 2:11).

Giving is lifted out of the realm of the commonplace when it is viewed as an act of worship. This concept sanctifies and dignifies it. The taking of the offering on Sunday morning is just as much a part of the total worship experience as the singing, the praying, or the preaching. Happy the pastor who can get his people to understand this! Since this is so, he should never feel as though he should apologize for taking an offering.

6. The pastor can help the ministry of giving in his church by providing literature on the subject of giving for his people to read. One successful pastor made available to his members, especially the new ones, an attractive pamphlet entitled, "Our Plan of Church Life," in which was included the Biblical plan of church finance. This is a good way to keep such matters before the congregation. The pastor can write material himself, or he can obtain tracts and pamphlets on the subject of giving from various sources, such as church publishing houses or agencies that specialize in the production of tracts. Periodically a page in the weekly church bulletin may be devoted to the presentation of such material.

7. The pastor will ease the financial problem in his church by urging his people to make tithing the basis of their giving. The system of tithing is a Biblical system found in both the Old and New Testaments. It antedates the Law, which sets aside the objection that tithing is a legal system. Abraham paid tithes in his day (Gen. 14:20). So did Jacob (Gen. 28:22). We read of tithes after the Law was instituted (e.g. Mal. 3:10) and in New Testament times. That the Lord Jesus Christ approved of tithing is indicated in Luke 11:42, where we read that He reprimanded the Pharisees for some of their failures but approved of their tithing.

Tithing should be only a basis for giving in the Christian dispensation, not the ultimate. It is inconceivable that Christians should give less than believers gave in other dispensations. A Christian should not allow himself to go below the minimum standard of the tithe. Some Christians who have no standard but give spasmodically according to the situation in which they find themselves or the appeal of the moment probably would be surprised if they knew exactly what proportion of their income they actually give in a year. Maybe they would discover themselves to be like the good sister who said, "Oh, I give more than a tenth. I give a twentieth!"

Multitudes of Christians have derived great blessing from tithing. And where tithing is the rule in church, there you will find the financial problem at a minimum. Folk ought to have some standard by which to gauge their giving. What better one can be found than that set forth in the Scriptures?

8. The pastor should teach his church to pay its bills as it goes. A church will quickly lose its testimony in the community if it gets the reputation of being careless in meeting its financial obligations. It is too bad that churches in many places have the reputation of being poor risks. It has been said that the two things that have caused the downfall of more ministers than any other things are debts and women. There have been too many cases where churches have followed the example of some preachers in money matters.

The pastor therefore will urge his financial officers to care for church bills promptly. Such promptitude will make it much easier for the church to fulfill its spiritual responsibility in the community.

9. The pastor should do all that he can to keep his church from going into excessive indebtedness. A reasonable debt may be a good thing for a church. It may act like a project, keeping the membership busy in order to discharge its responsibility. In certain parts of Africa the natives, in crossing swift streams often carry a heavy burden upon their heads in order to keep from being washed downstream. A moderate indebtedness on many occasions will enable a church to grow, whereas if it had to wait until it had sufficient cash in the bank to complete a project, valuable time would be lost and the outreach of the church curtailed.

The scriptural injunction of Romans 13:8, "Owe no man anything, but to love one another," is no argument against having debts. The context shows this. It recognizes that we all have "dues" and we ought to pay them. But when all of these obligations have been paid, the debt of love always remains with us. Moreover, a better translation of the verse would be "Do not continue to owe any man anything." In other words, there is no sin in owing money as long as it is repaid according to the terms of contract, charge account, or mortgage.

Excessive indebtedness can discourage a congregation. When the debt is so large that the church can scarcely do more than meet the interest, the spirit of the members is likely to be broken, and they will be hindered in reaching people outside the church. Sometimes churches in the flush of enthusiasm are tempted to go beyond their ability to pay. If the temptation is yielded to, the church will likely find that it has a white elephant on its hand. The pastor will be wise to advise moderation in these matters, even if it means that the church must meet in partially completed quarters for a time. Many churches have done the latter and have found that the incompleted structure acted as an incentive to work toward a finished building. And during this period of waiting they were saved a crushing burden of indebtedness.

10. The pastor should do all within his power to encourage a wise selection of persons to serve as financial officers in the church. It is vitally important that the financial secretary, the treasurer, the members of the finance and auditing committees, and board of trustees be persons of competence and undoubted dedication to the service of the Lord.

The financial secretary has to do with the intake of funds. He keeps records of the different funds to which money is given and of the giving of individuals. If individuals give through the envelope system, a good financial secretary can tell what each member has given in the course of the year and for what purposes. He also writes warrants for expenditures.

The treasurer has mainly to do with the outgo of funds. He writes the checks and, of course, keeps a record of the money that the financial secretary turns over to him, and of all expenditures. These two officers act as a check upon each other. It can readily be seen that they occupy very responsible positions and therefore should have some ability in handling money and keeping books and be individuals of undoubted integrity. These two men and possibly one or two others will very likely form the finance committee whose responsibility it is to keep the church informed as to its financial status and to make recommendations having to do with financial matters in the congregation.

In order that the financial officers may be protected and that everyone will have complete confidence in the financial structure of the church, the pastor should insist that the books be regularly audited. The writer recently heard of an inmate of a state's prison who declared that he learned to steal when he was treasurer of a Sunday school where his accounts were not audited, and he carried the practice into the bank where he was apprehended. This is a sober reminder of the importance of extreme care in money matters in the church!

11. Let the pastor be faithful in insisting that the financial officers be absolutely honest in the matter of handling designated funds. Designated money must not be used for other purposes than those for which it was given. It is not right, for instance, to take money designated for missions and use it to repair the roof of the church! Such a procedure is dishonest, and once it becomes known that money given may possibly not be used as designated, gifts may be withheld or directed elsewhere. Only by the consent of the donors can changes from the designated use honestly be made.

12. Last, and of great importance, let the pastor make sure that he sets a good example before his flock in the matter of giving. If the pastor is not a generous giver himself, he had better not preach giving to others. If he is not a tither, he had better not urge others to tithe. Some pastors have presented a weak argument to the effect that they have given their whole lives to the church and thus are exempt from giving of their income the way their members ought to give. Since pastors usually receive a salary as do others, by their giving they ought to be good examples to their members. A stream will rise no higher than its source, and it is not likely that the membership of a church will excel in the ministry of giving if the pastor is not exemplary in it.

In concluding this consideration, let us note the testimony which the Apostle Paul has left concerning the Macedonian believers. Of them he said, "And this they did, not as we hoped, but first gave their own selves to the Lord" (II Cor. 8:5). Every pastor should realize that such devotion means more than all rules and regulations. When people are truly dedicated to the Lord, their financial support of the church follows naturally.

Recommended Reading

Agar, Frederick A. *Church Profit Making*. New York: Fleming H. Revell Co., 1929.

Barndollar, W. W. "The Scriptural Tithe." Unpublished thesis submitted for the degree of Doctor of Theology at Grace Theological Seminary, Winona Lake, Ind., 1959.

BENSON, CLARENCE H. *Techniques of a Working Church.* Chicago: Moody Press, 1946.

DOLLOFF, EUGENE D. *The Efficient Church Officer.* New York: Fleming H. Revell Co., 1949.

ELLIS, H. W. *Christian Stewardship and Church Finance.* Grand Rapids: Zondervan Publishing House, 1953.

KING, JULIUS (compiled and annotated by). *Successful Fund Raising Sermons.* New York: Funk & Wagnalls Co., 1953.

LANSDELL, HENRY. *The Tithe in Scripture.* Grand Rapids: Baker Book House, 1963.

LEACH, WILLIAM H. *Handbook of Church Management.* Englewood Cliffs, N. J.: Prentice-Hall, Inc., 1958.

McGARRAH, ALFRED F. *Modern Church Finance.* New York: Fleming H. Revell Co., 1916.

RILEY, WILLIAM B. *Pastoral Problems.* New York: Fleming H. Revell Co., 1936.

Chapter 22

THE PASTOR AND THE
SUNDAY SCHOOL

THE IMPORTANCE OF SUNDAY SCHOOL scarcely needs to be argued. It is the church studying the Bible. It is the church reaching out for new recruits. It is the church dealing constructively with each age of life in ways suitable to the respective ages. It is a glorious part of the church, its most fertile field of evangelism.

The pastor has a vital responsibility in relation to the Sunday school just the same as to every other part of the church.[1] Henry Clay Trumbull, a great Sunday school enthusiast of a past generation, expressed this relationship in a way unexcelled since his time: "The Sunday School" in the pastor's church is his Sunday-school in the same sense that the pulpit of his church is his pulpit. This being so, it follows that if the pastor is what he ought to be, or what he needs to be, in knowledge, in ability, in spirit and in purpose, his school will be what it ought to be in plan, in scope, in organization, and in

[1]The discussion of this chapter applies primarily to the smaller church, in which the pastor serves as his own director of Christian education. When a church has a professional director of Christian education, the situation is quite different. Then, the person hired to administer the educational work of the church will have general supervision of the Sunday school superintendent, and the pastor, director of Christian education, and Sunday school superintendent should meet together for frequent conferences concerning the work of the Sunday school.

The fact that another paid worker of the staff now has primary responsibility for the educational work of the church should not mean that the pastor is removed from responsibility for the success or problems of the church school. He should be available for conferences with members of the staff, should be actively involved in the training of the staff, should be concerned with the curriculum used, and should be familiar with the actual workings of the Sunday school. The latter may be achieved partly by occasional visits to various departments of the school.

Of course the Sunday school is only one aspect of the total educational work of the church. Youth groups, the women's work, adult week-day Bible classes, and the like, also come under the general supervision of the director of Christian education. This whole program is now increasingly being implemented through a Christian education council, which provides the kind of oversight for the educational work of the church that the official board does for the church's total organization. For a fuller discussion of the subject see the chapter on the organizations of the church.

methods of work. It will be this before he is through with it even if it is not all this when he takes hold of it." [2]

Dr. E. Y. Mullins, former president of the Southern Baptist Theological Seminary, in a published creed on the importance of the Sunday school, stated the matter in this forceful manner: "The chief teacher of the teachers and trainer of the trainers of the Sunday-school is the pastor." [3]

The writer's purpose in this chapter is to discuss some of the relationships in which the pastor should exercise oversight in the Sunday school.

The Pastor and the Sunday School Superintendent

The logical place to begin is with the relation of the pastor to the Sunday school superintendent. Marion C. Lawrance, one of the great Sunday school workers of the past and a superintendent himself for forty years, said on this point, "I cannot emphasize too strongly the proper relation that should exist between the pastor and superintendent. No two men in any church can accomplish so much if they will pull together, nor can any two men in a church mess things up worse when they get their horns locked. It has been my great joy to have had the very closest fellowship with my pastors." [4] Happy is the pastor who has a superintendent with whom he can congenially work, and happy the superintendent who has a pastor with whom he can work. The situation works both ways.

The pastor needs a Sunday school vision. Unless he envisions the Sunday school as a tremendous arm of the church for the purposes of evangelism, instruction in the Word of God, and training for leadership, he is not likely to be of much help to the school. It is a tragedy to see a pastor who chooses to have little or nothing to do with the Sunday school of his church. The result will inevitably be disastrous to the school and to the church as a whole. Statistics again and again have proved that a large proportion of those who eventually come into the membership of the church come through the Sunday school. Therefore, the pastor who neglects this phase of his responsibility will hinder the growth of his church.

---

[2] Quoted by Marion Lawrance in *My Message to Sunday School Workers* (New York: George H. Doran Company, 1924), p. 219 f.
[3] *Ibid.*, p. 219.
[4] *Ibid.*, p. 223.

It is equally true that the Sunday school superintendent needs to have a church vision. Unless he realizes that his Sunday school is not an organization by itself but an arm of the church, he will not perform a constructive ministry. Too many Sunday schools have developed into organizations almost separate from the church with no vital connection between the two. Such a situation may easily develop unless the superintendent has a clear vision of the whole work of the church. His business is to lead the membership of the school into a vital relation with the church. Pastor and superintendent working together, seeing eye to eye, on these matters, can bring about this happy relationship.

These two should counsel together about their respective problems. If there are wrongs to be righted in the school, let the pastor and the superintendent discuss them privately before airing them publicly. It is amazing what satisfying results can be accomplished in this way. One pastor known to the writer met with his superintendent regularly for an hour every Saturday morning to counsel with him about the work of the Sunday school and to pray over the problems and the work of the school. Such a practice builds confidence and results in constructive growth.

In his continued contacts with the superintendent, the pastor should ever keep before the superintendent the importance of his task. Next to the pastor (and the director of Christian education, if there is one) there is no one in the church who ordinarily exerts more influence than does the Sunday school superintendent. The pastor will bend every possible effort to make this influence a positive factor in the building of the church.

To this end he will encourage the superintendent to read helpful literature which will set forth the duties and responsibilities of a good superintendent. Every denominational Sunday school board has a supply of such material, and there are several interdenominational agencies which can supplement denominational literature. Then, too, the pastor ought to encourage his superintendent to attend Sunday school conferences and rallies where ideas and inspiration are likely to increase the latter's perspective. The superintendent has a big job, and in order to do it efficiently, he will need all the encouragement his pastor can give him.

The Pastor and the Teachers

Of similar importance is the pastor's relation to the teachers of his Sunday school. It is well-nigh unthinkable to suppose that the pastor of a church will have no interest in those who teach the Word of God in his church. Yet too often this relationship has been neglected.

He should have a voice in the choice of those who teach in the Sunday school. This may be cared for in different ways. Sometimes a committee composed of such individuals as the Sunday school superintendent, the Sunday school secretary, and the pastor approve all teacher selections. The different departments, of course, have the privilege of recommending prospective teachers. In other places, the Sunday school superintendent and the pastor care for this matter. In still other places the Bible school or educational committee, elected by the church with the pastor as an ex-officio member, cares for this approval. Though the method of selection may vary, the pastor should always have a part in it, else how can he fulfill his responsibility of being an overseer of all phases of the church's work?

In some places the choosing of teachers, especially in the older classes, is left entirely up to the classes concerned. This is a mistake and may easily cause the selection of a teacher to develop into a popularity contest. In one such case a pastor was greatly disturbed to learn that one of the classes in his Sunday school had chosen a popular high school teacher who was a Christian Scientist! We conclude at this point by saying that the pastor has a right to some part in the choosing of the teachers of his Sunday school.

He should also have a part in their training. Every pastor should see to it that there are training classes in his school. Only in this way can he develop an efficient corps of teachers. Many of his teachers will have had no opportunity to attend Bible institutes, colleges, or seminaries. Some of them probably will not have taken Bible courses anywhere. It will be the pastor's responsibility, working together with the superintendent and other officers of the school, to make training available in his own church.

No institution can truly be called a school without real teachers, and real teachers are impossible without teacher training. An increasing amount of material is available these days for courses in teacher training. The pastor and his associates will do well to consult some authorities on this matter before introducing a curriculum. For instance, Clarence H. Benson in his *The Sunday School in Action* has an excellent chapter entitled, "Teacher Training," in which the author outlines the possibilities in this field. The pastor will likely discover that some of his most fruitful work will be this ministry of training the teaching force in his Sunday school.

The pastor has responsibility to exercise oversight of the curriculum taught in the school. He will be fighting a losing battle if he preaches one type of message from the pulpit, only to discover that the material his teachers are teaching is at variance with that message. Benson, in the work cited, has an excellent chapter on the curriculum in the Sunday school which surveys the possibilities in this realm. It is the pastor's duty to insist that the proper Bible-centered, Christ-exalting materials are studied in his school.

The pastor should also appear before his teachers and officers from time to time to emphasize the importance of their task. If there is a Sunday school cabinet or council, he should speak to that group occasionally to inspire them with greater zeal for their work. In these appearances he ought to hold before them the high and holy purposes that every Sunday school should have of reaching people for God and in directing them along paths of Christlike living.

Furthermore, he will do well to impress upon them the importance of cooperating with all the efforts of the church as far as possible, including attendance at all the worship services on the Lord's Day and at the midweek prayer service. The example they set in these matters will largely determine how their pupils will respond. Many a pastor's heart has well-nigh broken as he has seen a large proportion of the Sunday school leave for home immediately following the Sunday school hour. Too often this exodus includes many of the teachers and officers of the school. This situation should be changed. Let the pastor talk frankly about such matters to his Sunday school cabinet.

The pastor should also embrace opportunities to talk privately to his teachers about their work. Let him ask them how they are getting along in their teaching. Are there some individuals in their groups who are about ready to make a confession? Are there any problem cases that need some pastoral counsel? This sort of attention will tend to keep the teachers diligent, and they will be encouraged by knowing that the pastor is interested. As he talks to them he may well impress them with the bigness of their task, which will pay rich rewards.

The Pastor and the Sunday School Cabinet

The importance of the Sunday school in the total program of the church requires regular meetings of officers and teachers to carry on the work. Sometimes these meetings are called the Sunday School Cabinet, sometimes the Sunday School Council, and at other times the teachers and officers meeting of the Sunday school. The name is not of major importance, but the work to be accomplished is. The pastor of the church should see that the organization does its work.

If there is no such organization in his Sunday school, he ought to see that one is organized. It takes planning to operate a successful Sunday school. Problems must be faced and solved. These and other responsibilities belong to the council. For the organization of such a council, valuable help can be obtained from Benson's aforementioned book (chapter 15) or from James DeForest Murch's book *Christian Education and the Local Church* (chapter 23). The pastor may ask his superintendent to read chapters like these to acquaint him with the purpose and work of such an organization. In connection with its organization and beginnings, the pastor will need to oversee its work so that it gets off to a good start and accomplishes its intended purpose.

The pastor should let the officers of the Sunday school run the council. He should not take over the leadership, but should be ready at all times to offer suggestions when the need arises. He should not be dictatorial but helpful in every possible way. The superintendent usually should be the chairman of the council meetings.

The pastor should be prepared to address the council when called upon. At such times he may discuss the relation that ought to exist between the Sunday school and the church. He can then use his influence toward keeping the school closely associated with the total church program. He can discuss some of the problems that face the school from time to time. The quarterly and annual reports may reveal weaknesses that the pastor can profitably discuss at such a time, offering suggestions as to improvement.

The pastor may also lend his influence toward the creation of some standards for the workers in the Sunday school to follow. It will be best, however, if he only advises in this matter and leaves it to the council to create its own set of standards. Those involved will be more likely to abide by standards which they themselves adopt than standards imposed upon them.

Let the pastor encourage an annual public installation service for teachers and officers of the school. Such a service may be a part of a regular Sunday morning worship service or of an opening exercise in the Sunday school. The former is preferred because it tends to tie the Sunday school and the church more closely together and does not interfere with the regular program of the Sunday school. With different departments meeting separately it disrupts the opening exercises of these departments to have an installation service in the opening part of the Sunday school hour.

The pastor should be asked to conduct this service. He will set before the teachers and officers their definite responsibility, ask their cooperation in discharging it, and have a prayer of dedication as they stand in front of the congregation. The congregation should also be charged with its responsibility of supporting the Sunday school staff by prayer and cooperation in every possible way. No matter how efficient the teachers and officers are, they cannot do an effective job without the support of the church constituency.

The Pastor and the Organization

The pastor, as the leading administrator of the church, has responsibility with respect to the organization of his Sunday school. Not only should he use his influence to see that the school itself is as adequately organized as possible but he should also see to it that there is a vital connection between the Sunday school and the church. Too often this relationship is overlooked. In overseeing the organizational aspect of the school, he should give attention to the following four things:

1. He should urge the election of the main officers of the school by the church, not by the school itself. There is sound reasoning behind this. The Sunday school is a vital part of the church. It is the church studying the Bible. This being so, the church ought to elect its officers. This method will tend to unite the church and the Sunday school. It will obviate the election of officers who are not vitally interested in the total program of the church. Popularity has too often been the basis of the election of certain officers. Sometimes Sunday school officers are totally deficient in church loyalty.

Election of officers by the church will head off difficulties of this sort. One of the points in the attainment of the Standard of Excellence in Southern Baptist Sunday schools is the selection of officers and teachers by the church with the further stipulation that regular reports of the Sunday school shall be made to the church. This provision makes the Sunday school a vital part of the church organization, and this is as it should be.

2. The pastor should see that the Sunday school is departmentalized in the best possible manner according to the conditions that exist in his church. His school will necessarily have to progress in this regard according to its facilities. The pastor will ever keep before himself and his school the goal of procuring the facilities for a fully departmentalized school. He will realize, as all public schools realize, that different age groups must be dealt with according to their several capacities.

A fully departmentalized school will be divided as follows:

    (1) Cradle roll, birth to one year
    (2) Nursery, two and three years
    (3) Beginners (preschool), four and five years
    (4) Primary, six, seven and eight years
    (5) Junior, nine, ten and eleven years
    (6) Junior High (Intermediate), twelve, thirteen and fourteen years
    (7) Senior, fifteen, sixteen and seventeen years
    (8) Young People, eighteen to twenty-four years
    (9) Adults, twenty-five years and up
   (10) Extension (Home), for shut-ins and shut outs.[5]

3. In order to keep the unity of the school and to acquaint the church membership with what is going on in the Sunday school, the pastor will do well to encourage the occasional meeting together of all departments of the school. This should not be done too often lest it disrupt the departmental work. On such days as Rally Day, Decision Day, or Children's Day this sort of thing may be done with great interest and profit.

4. Then, too, he should oversee what is being taught in the several departments of the school. As has been previously intimated, he will insist that what is taught in every department will be thoroughly in

[5]Clarence H. Benson, *The Sunday School in Action* (rev. ed.; Chicago: Moody Press, 1941), p. 54.

accord with the beliefs of his church. He will frown upon certain teachers going off on tangents and introducing irrelevant material. If one teacher is allowed to do this sort of thing, others will likely want to follow suit, and before long the result will be confusion in the teaching ministry of the Sunday school.

The Pastor and the Sunday School Secretary

The pastor should realize the importance of dependable records of the work of the school and will exert his influence in every way possible to see that the school has a capable secretary. A good Sunday school secretary is often an unsung hero, but this officer can perform an invaluable service and will surely be appreciated by the pastor and the officers of the school.

Careful weekly, monthly, quarterly and annual reports show the progress of the school. A study and comparison of these reports with previous reports will make it possible to determine whether or not the school is growing. Weaknesses and successes can be observed. These should be carefully considered by the Sunday school council when it meets, and efforts made to strengthen the weak places in the program. Perhaps the reports will show that the percentage of the active enrollment in weekly attendance is very low, or that few visitors attend the school, or that there has been no appreciable gain in attendance over the previous quarter or year, or—even worse— a loss. These and other facts revealed by the secretary's reports will make clear what needs to be done to improve the work of the school.

In these and other ways a good Sunday school secretary is of inestimable value to any school, and the pastor will encourage proficiency in the secretary's work. In larger schools there doubtless will be several secretaries—one for each department, with one person acting as the general secretary to gather into one report all the departmental reports.

An annual Sunday school secretary's report, based upon weekly, monthly, and quarterly reports for the year should include:

> total attendance for the year
> average attendance per Sunday
> total visitors present for the year
> average number of visitors a Sunday
> total active enrollment at the end of the year (all departments)
> average number of active pupils present per Sunday

average number of active pupils absent per Sunday
total attendance of inactive pupils during the year
percentage of teachers present per Sunday
percentage of attendance of officers per Sunday
total offerings (all departments) for the year
average offerings per Sunday
number of confessions of faith from the school
number of baptisms from the school
number of accessions to the church from the school

The secretary should also be able to give a comparative report from the previous year or years so that the school and the church may know whether there is an encouraging growth.

The Pastor and the Equipment

No longer is it accepted that most any kind of equipment will do for the Sunday school. Churches are coming to see that the best possible equipment is none too good to get across the greatest message in the world.

The pastor should encourage the procuring of whatever materials are necessary for a more efficient teaching of the Word of God and a more reverent spirit in God's house. He will study the equipment needs of his Sunday school, talk with his Sunday school superintendent about the matter, and then do all within his power to get his church to supply the need.

He will study the needs of the several departments. Do they need movable chairs, tables, cabinets, chalkboards, flannel boards, pianos, songbooks, mottoes, maps, pictures, charts, or coat racks? If so, he will set in motion the means to secure them.

He will visit the various classrooms and see what is needed to make the rooms more attractive and the work of the teacher more effective. Is it rugs for the floor, pictures for the walls, chalkboards for purposes of illustration and outlining, or maps to aid in teaching the lesson? It is amazing what some teachers have done without in times past! Many of these have succeeded in a measure at least in spite of inadequate equipment and facilities. But the pastor's job is to aid teachers in getting a better job done and his vision is often what is needed to point out a real need.

In case the pastor is called upon to have part in the erection of a new church building or a Sunday school annex, he should consider very carefully the needs of a growing school. He will do well to consult plans which have been suggested by Sunday school experts like Clarence Benson, DeForest Murch, and P. E. Burroughs before he consents to any plan. Furthermore, it will be helpful for him, together with the Sunday school superintendent and other leaders of the church and school, to visit other churches with up-to-date Sunday school facilities in order to get good ideas. It is better to take plenty of time to consider this matter thoroughly than to spend years regretting a hasty construction of an inadequate plant.

The Pastor and the Sessions of the School

The pastor, of course, will have a definite interest in the Sunday sessions of the Sunday school. This interest should manifest itself in various ways.

1. He should attend its sessions. Because of his responsibilities in connection with the worship service which usually follows, he may feel it wise not to remain throughout the entire period. Moreover, he may not feel it best always to attend the same department in a larger school. The pastor's attendance at sessions of the school will tend to emphasize the importance of the school.

2. He may or may not teach in the Sunday school. Opinion and pastors differ on this point. Some maintain that the pastor should teach because of his training, his example, the opportunity it affords of contacting people with the Word of God, and because of the more vital connection it gives him with the school.

Some equally good pastors maintain that the pastor should not teach and give as reasons that he should conserve his strength for the pulpit, that it is difficult for a person to concentrate his mind on two different lines of thought in such a short space of time, that it ties the pastor to one particular group too much, whereas he should be free to serve the entire school and to inspect its work. Furthermore, some seem fearful that if folk hear the pastor teach in the Sunday school they will not be disposed to hear him again in the preaching service.

Probably the ideal is for the pastor not to have the added responsibility of teaching in the Sunday school. But the writer has found that very often the ideal is not realized!

3. The pastor should make it a point from time to time to stress the importance of the Sunday school from the pulpit. He should

urge support from everyone, not just the children and the young people. Some continue to have the idea that Sunday school is only for the children. The pastor can do much toward dissipating this false notion. He can suggest that when any of his hearers have come to the place where they know all about the Bible, then they might have some justification for not coming to Sunday school! Until then they need it.

4. He should encourage decision days in the Sunday school from time to time. This can be done in connection with the Easter season, at Christmas time, or at the time of a revival meeting. Since the Sunday school is a most fertile field of evangelism, there ought to be definite times when the net is cast for an ingathering. Often the pastor himself should be the one to cast the net.

5. The pastor can well afford to have a "Sunday School Night" once a year in his church program. Let him ask the superintendent to be in charge upon such an occasion. Have a roll call of the classes. Let the special music and other special features come from the Sunday school. The climax of such an occasion should be the message from the pastor. Such occasions not only stress the importance of the Sunday school but they also bring to the church service some who do not ordinarily attend, providing a definite opportunity for evangelism.

6. Above all, the pastor should leave no doubt in the minds of any that he is a friend and promoter of the Sunday school. The pastor's enthusiasm for this phase of his work is bound to be contagious. His enthusiasm will spread to others, and a good school will be developed.

The Pastor and Sunday School Problems

Problems of one kind and another will arise in the work of the Sunday school, as well as in any other organization of any importance. The larger the school and the faster it grows, the more problems there are likely to be. Whatever the problems, the pastor ought to manifest an interest in their solution. Some of the more prevalent problems are as follows:

1. The problem of the summer slump. This problem tends to be more acute in city churches where large numbers of people get several weeks of vacation. They are likely to take this vacation in the

summertime, which is the season of the year most suited to a time in the mountains or by the seashore.

It will do little good to frown upon the idea of vacations. The members of the church and Sunday school are entitled to a vacation the same as the preacher is. It will be far better for the pastor to work together with the Sunday school superintendent and his staff to arrange as attractive a summer program as possible. They should avoid giving the impression that the Sunday school is practically folding up for two or three months and should work against the idea that a slump is inevitable and nothing can be done about it. A pessimistic attitude invites a slump.

An attractive program in the summertime will tend to draw visitors who will help to compensate for the regular members who are away. Some city Sunday schools have more visitors in the summertime than at any other time of the year. More and more schools are encouraging their pupils to attend Sunday school when they are on vacation by promising that they will be given credit in their own school if when they return they present a signed card from the school they attended. If all Sunday schools would do this, the problem of the summer slump would be largely alleviated.

Many Sunday schools have faced the problem frankly and have so solved it that the summertime has proved to be one of the most interesting and profitable seasons of the year.

2. The problem of ineffective teachers. This is a problem that cannot be solved quickly. But it can be solved by persistent attention. As previously suggested, the pastor should encourage the Sunday school superintendent to institute a long-range teacher training program. In accordance with this plan, a cycle of courses is offered for the benefit of those who would teach. If this plan is carefully pursued, the standard of teaching will rise little by little. To meet the immediate situation, the pastor may find it wise to suggest a weekly instruction period when the lesson for the following Sunday is taught by a competent person, quite likely the pastor. Where it is evident that some teachers are having a particular difficulty, the pastor may feel led to have some private interviews with such teachers to help them in their lesson preparation and in methods of presenting the lesson.

In some such ways, accompanied by prayer and patience, this problem of inefficient teachers can be solved to a marked degree.

3. The problem of the Sunday school "exodus." In reference to this difficulty, W. Curry Mavis has said: "George Truett once said that the saddest parade in all the world is the parade of Sunday school children that marches from the church to their homes just as the church service is beginning. This parade that leaves the church each Sunday at 11:00 A.M. symbolizes the church's failure to take seriously its mission of soul-winning and Christian nurture." [6] While this disturbs many a pastor, often nothing is done about it. Perhaps the following suggestions will help to solve the problem:

(1) Lay the matter clearly before the Sunday School council. Let the pastor tell the officers and teachers how much he is counting upon them to help in building up the worship service, how important is their example in this matter, and what is the place of the worship service in the whole plan and program of the church. God has ordained that through preaching men shall be saved.

(2) Employ the merged service idea, according to which there is really only one service with two parts, the Sunday school merging into the church service without an intermission between the two. The intermission is a definite invitation for folk to go home. In the merged service there is no singing of such a song as "Sunday school is over and we are going home"! The merged service has its problems, but they can be and have been worked out.

(3) Make use of the six-point system or a similar system, one point of which is church attendance. The awards offered in connection with such a plan often appeal to children to such an extent that they will remain for the church service in order to qualify.

(4) Let the pastor plan his sermons so that they will not be too long and so that they will be simple enough to appeal even to the children. Overlong sermons can discourage some from attending the Sunday morning service. The pastor should discipline himself to close the service on time.

(5) Some pastors and churches have instituted the unified service as a solution to the problem of the "exodus." According to this plan, the worship service comes first, and its opening exercise serves as the opening exercise for both the church and the Sunday school. By this plan many churches have found that attendance at both services increased perceptibly, particularly the church service. There

[6]W. Curry Mavis, *Advancing the Smaller Local Church* (Winona Lake, Ind.: Light and Life Press, 1957), p. 165.

are advantages and disadvantages to the unified service. These should be carefully weighed and a plan adopted that will best meet the need of the particular church.

4. The problem of the Sunday school census. The taking of a religious census of the community is a vital part of the plan suggested by Louis Entzminger in his book, *The Sunday School Transformed,* for increasing Sunday school attendance and reaching the unsaved.[7] According to this author the greatest need of the average Sunday school today, from the standpoint of outreach, is to take a census of the locality, find the prospects, then grade them and adequately organize for the purpose of reaching them. Such a plan makes good sense, and it has succeeded when put in operation. The pastor should work together with his Sunday school on a census, suggesting the best time for it in view of previous censuses that may have been taken and advising as to the content of the census card that will be used. In Entzminger's book, a good sample of such cards is included on page 27.

5. There is also the question of the proper time for the actual study of the lesson. In some schools many extraneous things have been allowed to encroach upon the time needed for a good presentation of the lesson. This is a mistake, and the pastor ought to use his influence toward preserving at least thirty minutes for the teaching of the lesson each Sunday. He should speak to his superintendent and to the council about this, impressing upon them that the most important part of the Sunday school session is the teaching of the Word of God. Let him show them that they ought to guard against opening exercises that are too long and against many features that tend to shorten the study period.

6. The problem of dropouts. This is a most serious problem and fraught with tragic implications. According to the 1962 nationwide survey of the *Youth and Research Commissions* of the National Sunday School Association, 80.7 percent of evangelical churches report dropouts for one reason or another. This same report showed that 17 percent of the young people who attend evangelical churches decide not to go back. This is one of every six. Nor are dropouts confined to young people. They appear in every age group in lesser proportions.

[7]Louis Entzminger, *The Sunday School Transformed* (Philadelphia: The Sunday School Times Co., 1925), chap. 3.

If it is important to reach people for the Sunday school and the church, it is just as important to hold them. How may this be done in the Sunday school?

(1) There needs to be a program that is attractive and well organized. Young people find their public schools in most instances well ordered and with qualified teachers. They are likely to be repelled by a situation in the Sunday school where there is lack of organization and a staff of incompetent teachers.

(2) There needs to be contact with the pupils other than a few minutes on Sunday morning when the lesson is taught. This may take the form of social activities, athletic events, Bible clubs, personal visitation in the homes, and so on.

(3) The pastor, along with the Sunday school superintendent, should urge his young people to have part in the Hi-C Club meetings in the local high school if there are such. If there are none, he should urge his own young people to take the initiative in organizing such a club. He may also urge them to participate in the area Youth for Christ program.

(4) The pastor should urge his young people to attend the youth rallies which are held regularly under the direction of some denominational groups. He himself should maintain an active interest in these rallies, lending his influence to keep them the spiritual force they ought to be.

(5) The pastor will do well to give special attention to the camp program of his district and urge as many of his young people as possible to attend. This program ought to be stressed weeks in advance of the actual camps. Great things are being done for young people of different age groups in these camps. Quiz programs have become especially popular in recent years, and they have a great ministry in acquainting young people with the Word of God.

(6) Most churches nowadays conduct vacation Bible schools in the summertime. Here is an opportunity to keep many of the young people together for a small part of the summer for good instruction and Christian associations. Some of the older young people can be used as helpers in this program.

In these and other ways the wide-awake Sunday school and church can do much to alleviate the dropout problem. Our main concern in this treatment has been related to teen-agers and older young people among whom the largest proportion of the dropouts occur.

However, attention should be given to those of all ages who absent themselves from the Sunday school. They should be contacted immediately when a lack of interest is noticed in order to deal with any difficulty that may be present. A proper contact will save many from the tragic ranks of permanent dropouts.

Because of the magnitude of the task of the Sunday school, and because of its great potential, the pastor will want to do all within his power to foster its success.

RECOMMENDED READING

BARNETTE, J. N. *The Place of the Sunday School in Evangelism*. Nashville: Sunday School Board of the Southern Baptist Convention, 1949.

BENSON, CLARENCE H. *The Sunday School in Action*. Rev. ed., Chicago: Moody Press, 1941.

———. *The Christian Teacher*. Chicago: Moody Press, 1950.

———. *History of Christian Education*. Chicago: Moody Press, 1943.

DOBBINS, G. S. *Building a Better Sunday School*. Nashville: Convention Press, 1957.

———. *The Church at Worship*. Nashville: Broadman Press, 1962.

———. *How to Teach Young People and Adults in the Sunday School*. Nashville: Baptist Sunday School Board, 1930.

———. *Winning the Children*. Nashville: Broadman Press, 1953.

EAVEY, C. B. *Principles of Teaching for Christian Teachers*. Grand Rapids: Zondervan Publishing House, 1940.

EDGE, FINDLEY BARTOW. *Teaching for Results*. Nashville: Broadman Press, 1956.

ENTZMINGER, LOUIS. *The Sunday School Transformed*. Philadelphia: The Sunday Times Co., 1925.

LAWRANCE, MARION. *My Message to Sunday School Workers*. New York: George H. Doran Co., 1924.

LEBAR, LOIS E. *Children in the Bible School*. Westwood, N. J.: Fleming H. Revell Co., 1952.

MASON, HAROLD C. *Abiding Values in Christian Education*. Westwood, N. J.: Fleming H. Revell Co., 1953.

MURCH, JAMES DEFOREST. *Christian Education and the Local Church*. Cincinnati, O.: Standard Publishing Co., 1943.

———. *Teach or Perish!* Grand Rapids: William B. Eerdmans Publishing Co., 1961.

PERSON, PETER P. *The Minister in Christian Education*. Grand Rapids: Baker Book House, 1960.

SCHMAUK, THEODORE E. *How to Teach in Sunday School.* Philadelphia: The United Lutheran Publishing House, 1920.

SHERRILL, LEWIS J. *The Rise of Christian Education.* New York: Macmillan Co., 1944.

TRUMBULL, H. CLAY. *Teaching and Teachers.* Philadelphia: John D. Wattles, Publisher, 1887.

Chapter 23

THE PASTOR AND THE SEVENTY GROUP

AN IMPORTANT PART of the pastor's work is to develop the members of his church into soul-winners. It is apparent that in the early church each member conceived it as his responsibility to witness for Christ. In those days this business was not left entirely to the ministers of the church but was a united effort in which everyone had a part. Numerous illustrations of this are to be found in the New Testament story. In the Book of Acts, chapter 8, we read that when persecution broke out in Jerusalem the church was scattered abroad throughout the region of Judea and Samaria, except the apostles, and those who were scattered abroad went everywhere preaching the Word (Acts 8:4). From this it is plain that not all preaching in the first century was done by those commonly called preachers.

Writing to the church in Thessalonica, the Apostle Paul commends them for their faithful witnessing, saying, "For from you sounded out the word of the Lord not only in Macedonia and Achaia, but also in every place your faith to God-ward is spread abroad; so that we need not to speak anything" (I Thess. 1:8). A truly remarkable statement! In it he asserts that laymen of the Thessalonian church had done such a complete job of witnessing in the stated territory that it was not necessary for him and his associates to do anything along this line.

The example of the early church clearly refutes the idea held by many that giving out the Gospel is only for preachers, not laymen. Some have been so bold as to say, "Let the preacher do it, that's what he is getting paid for." All too soon the church ceased following the early example, with sad results. Today in many so-called evangelical churches very little definite soul-winning work is being done by the membership.

253

If the pastor is to get his members active in this sort of thing, he must not only set a good example before them by doing this work himself but he must also train them and send them forth.

Many pastors have found the "Seventy Group" idea a workable plan. It is based upon the method used by the Lord as set forth in Luke 10:1-12. According to this method, He sent forth seventy disciples in pairs to minister in His name. In order to carry on this sort of work in the local church, it is not necessary, of course, to have seventy workers. The pastor will get as many as he can, train them, and send them forth two by two. If the pastor can stir up enthusiasm in a sizable portion of his membership for this kind of work and keep them at it, there will be a continuous harvest of souls all through the year. Soul-winning will not be limited to special efforts of evangelism.

Preparation Before Organizing a Seventy Group

Assuming that there is no such organization at work in his church and the pastor desires to create one, he should do some preparatory work before he undertakes an organization. Otherwise he is likely to be disappointed by lack of cooperation. The pastor will be wise to take plenty of time in breaking the ground so that when he seeks to form a Seventy Group he will have at least a measure of cooperation. A few of the things he may do in preparation are:

1. Preach on the privilege, responsibilities, and joys of personal evangelism. In many churches this phase of Christian service has been sorely neglected. Let the Word of God speak to the hearts of the people. Unless it does, there will not be much point in going further in this matter. The membership needs to realize that God expects those who have named His name to bear witness to His saving grace. Because witnessing for Christ may be a new thing to many of his people, the pastor will need to approach the subject carefully seeking the definite guidance of the Holy Spirit. He will find numerous passages of Scripture from which to preach. In the introduction to this chapter two fine texts were cited, namely, Acts 8:4 and I Thess. 1:8. Others include Acts 1:8; Matt. 28:19-20; John 1:42; Rom. 1:14-16; Luke 5:4; Matt. 9:36; Mark 2:1-12; Ps. 126:6; Ps. 142:4.

2. Counsel with some of the most spiritual of the church leaders on the matter. It will make the task much easier and give much more promise of success if the pastor can gain the cooperation of a few

of his most spiritual and able members from the very beginning. This nucleus may well include the Sunday school superintendent, an elder, the chairman of the deacon board, the teacher of an adult Bible class, or any other members in the congregation who have spiritual vision.

3. Then if the pastor can persuade some of his leaders to read a book like *Every-Member Evangelism* by Conant it will likely fire them with enthusiasm for this type of effort. It will show them what can be done when folk who love the Lord become definitely interested in the winning of others to the Saviour.

Organization of a Seventy Group

After the groundwork has been carefully done and the pastor feels that the time has arrived to organize a Seventy Group, he should arrange for a meeting. If some of those with whom he has talked about such a group offer the suggestion that a meeting be called, such interest shows half the battle is won.

1. For the initial meeting the pastor had better get the promise of a number of his most dependable workers to be present. Otherwise, he may be disappointed by a small attendance. Folk have a tendency to shy away from this sort of work. Later others should be asked to join the group. But at the beginning you want to be sure to have the right sort of workers. Some pastors have found it wise to extend the invitation at the outset to all who will volunteer for this sort of work.

2. As the group gathers for its first meeting, the pastor will want to lay before them his plan, namely, systematic personal work carried on month by month or week by week, with the group divided into parties of two each with a record to be kept of each case visited.

3. It will be very important to bathe this effort at its very beginning with much prayer. At this first meeting it will be well to have a season of prayer, everyone present taking part if possible, seeking the Lord's direction in the organization and the carrying out of this enterprise. This will be hard work. Satan will fight it from the beginning, seeking to discourage the Lord's servants as they attempt to snatch various individuals from his realm. Therefore reliance upon God in prayer is of tremendous importance.

4. At this organizational meeting the group should settle upon a regular time of meeting, whether monthly, bimonthly, or weekly. It probably will be wise at first to meet monthly. As the work grows

and the efforts become more definite, it may be well to meet oftener than once a month. But individuals are very busy, and it will be better to meet less often and maintain interest and cooperation than to try to meet too often and find lagging interest.

5. Officers should also be chosen at this first meeting. The organization should be kept very simple, but there should be at least a chairman and a secretary. It may be wise for the pastor to act as chairman, at least at the beginning. However, if there is someone else in the group who is capable of the responsibility, it will be well to choose him as the chairman, leaving the pastor free for other things. The secretary should keep minutes of the meetings and do such other work as usually belongs to this officer.

6. In connection with the organization of the Seventy Group, it may be expedient to arrange for a simple course in the elements of personal evangelism. Some willing workers have never had any training in this field. In a few short lessons the pastor can outline the basic principles. In subsequent lessons he can deal with some of the problems often met with in this type of work, such as how to deal with the cults. There is an abundance of sources from which to choose material in preparing lessons in personal evangelism. Works by R. A. Torrey, William Evans, and Eugene Harrison are excellent examples of such material.

The Monthly Meeting of the Seventy

Let us now see what takes place in connection with a regular monthly meeting of the Seventy Group.

1. First, the pastor, or whoever is chairman of the group, must prepare the prospect list so that assignments for calls can readily be made. The list may be gathered from numerous sources, such as the Sunday school secretary, the visitors' book, the young people's organizations, the pastor's calling, observation of those who have been attending some of the services of the church who have spiritual need, and a canvass of the community. Some cities make available to churches lists of persons newly arrived in the community; sometimes these are identified by denominational preference. As the work of the group proceeds, they will gather prospects from their calling which they will want to add to the list.

This list will include the unsaved, those who have drifted away from the Lord, sick folk, newcomers to the community, and others who are in need of a spiritual ministry. Not all the calls will be upon the unsaved. It is as important to conserve the present membership of the church as to add to it.

2. The time and place of these meetings will vary. When a decision has been made as to the most convenient time, the members of the group should be urged to set aside this time for the important responsibility of visitation. In most cases it will probably seem advisable to hold the meetings in the church. In some churches which have operated this sort of work successfully, the group gathers at the supper hour in the church, eats a simple meal, attends to its business, including the visitation assignments, and then spends the rest of the evening in calling. This plan has the advantage of combining the business of the group and calling in one evening. It also provides the fellowship of a meal together, although the latter should not assume major importance.

In many places, however, the supper idea is not followed. The group meets later in the evening of the date decided upon, the business is attended to, and the calls are made at times most suitable to the members of the group between the meeting times.

3. The group meeting should open with prayer, followed by the reading of the minutes of the last meeting. The group should be divided into teams of two. Care should be exercised in this division so that suitable persons are paired together. It is best to pair an experienced worker with one who is less experienced. It is never wise to appoint two timid souls to a team. Because of possible crticism, a man and a woman, except a husband and wife, should not be appointed as a team. Usually it will be best to arrange teams of two men, two women, or a man and his wife. If folk who are congenial are put together, the work will be more pleasant and more effective.

Not only does going out two by two have scriptural support but it also makes good sense. Two individuals on the same mission tend to add to the impression that is made upon those contacted. And then, what one member of the team may not be able to produce in the way of effective testimony, the other may. One member encourages the other. There is abundant reason, therefore, to follow the example of the Lord, who sent forth His disciples "two by two" to minister in His name.

4. Reports of previous efforts may well be made in these Group meetings. These reports will encourage the group, and if there are

disheartening circumstances, some counsel can be given by the pastor or leader of the group. Doubtless the reports given will provide definite matters for prayer. The leader should guard against permitting the meeting to resolve itself into a gossip session. Discussion of the problems should be wholly for the purpose of helpfulness and should be kept within the group.

5. A very important part of the regular meeting is the making of assignments for the visits to be made between then and the next meeting. In this connection, it will be well to ask members of the group for names of those they would like to have visited. Their calling since the last meeting may have brought to their attention some good prospects. Some reassignments will probably need to be made at this time. One team may not have been able to fulfill the desired end in a particular case. Another team may be able to complete what the first team began.

The chairman of the group should make these assignments on the special assignment cards. On one side of the card there should be a place for the date, the name and the address of the prospect, and the indication of the reason for the person being on the prospect list. On the other side there should be room for team reports after calls are made. The form of the assignment card is shown below. These

ASSIGNMENT CARD

Date. . . . .

Name . . . .

Address . . . .

REASONS FOR BEING ON PROSPECT LIST

. . . . Comes to Sunday School   . . . . Member Elsewhere

. . . . Children Come to S.S.   . . . . Other Members of Family in

. . . . Comes to Church   Our Church

. . . . Baby on Cradle Roll   . . . . Attends Youth Groups

. . . . Preference for our Church   . . . . Came to Summer Bible School

. . . . Other Reasons . . . .

. . . .

(over)

cards are very important, and when the work has been completed in any given case, they should be filed for future reference. It is always a cause for rejoicing when it is possible to write upon the report card the words, "Mission accomplished!"

In giving out assignments, it should be noted that these are of different kinds. There are many different reasons why folk may be on the prospect list. The assignment card will provide some information along this line which will help in making contacts easier. For instance, if it is known that the individual to be called upon has children in your Sunday school, the callers have a ready point of contact. Or if it is known that certain parents have a baby on the cradle roll of your Sunday school, access to these parents becomes comparatively easy.

How many assignments should be given to a team at one time? If too many are given, the task will appear burdensome, and if too few are given, the efforts may appear inconsequential. We suggest that not more than six prospects and not less than three be assigned. The teams should be urged to make their calls as soon as possible.

Date............................   Date............................   Date............................

Team........   Report............   Team........   Report............   Team........   Report............

Reverse Side

Some calls will need to be repeated because individuals will not be at home at the time of the first visit.

6. At the conclusion of the Group meeting, there should be a season of prayer for God's blessing upon the visits about to be made. The group should be made to feel that this is truly God's business and God's blessing can be claimed for it.

Advantages of Seventy Group Work

This work has many advantages. Some of them have already been suggested; others are self-evident. In summary fashion seven of these advantages are listed, with very little comment.

1. It stimulates soul-winning work among the people and helps them to do that which they know they ought to do. Nowhere in the New Testament are unbelievers commanded to go to church, but all Christians are commanded to take the Gospel to the unconverted. Seventy Group work gives guidance in accomplishing this obligation. Dwight L. Moody had the proper conception when he said, "I would rather put ten men to work than to do the work of ten men." This is the New Testament ideal.

2. It acquaints the congregation with the needs of the field. Apart from this sort of work, there is no adequate realization of the number of unsaved and unchurched people in the community. Acquainted with these needs, the people will be more apt to enlarge the evangelistic outreach of the church.

3. It opens up new homes for the church. Contacts by the personal workers are bound to result in reaching some homes where there is great spiritual need.

4. It gets new children for the Sunday school. Often parents who are not willing to come to church or Sunday school themselves are delighted to have their children in Sunday school. They don't want them to "grow up as heathen." Eventually through the interest of the children parents often become interested and find their way to the house of God and accept the Saviour.

5. It gets new babies for the cradle roll. The cradle roll department of the Sunday school affords real opportunity to get new members for the school and eventually to win parents to the Lord. Every Sunday school should seek to develop this department. Many parents in the community are glad to have their infants on the cradle roll of the nearby church, even though they themselves never darken the

doors of the church. They appreciate the visits of the superintendent, the attractive certificate that is given, and the fact that something is being done for the welfare of their child. Soon these little ones will begin attending the Sunday school. Then, as was formerly stated, these children may lead their parents to the church and hence to the Lord.

6. It supplements the work of the pastor. It will not substitute for the calling the pastor should do but will add to it. One pastor said that he would rather have his Seventy Group than an assistant pastor if he had to make choice between the two. Preachers are *expected* to call, but visitation by laymen in the interest of the church is bound to impress those who are visited in an attractive way.

7. Finally, it brings in people for the pastor to preach to. If nothing more was accomplished by the Seventy Group than inviting people to the house of God, it would be well worthwhile, for it is under the sound of the Gospel that people are saved. Almost without exception a calling church will be a well attended church.

For these and other good reasons the work of the Seventy Group or of some similar group is of great value and merits the pastor's careful attention. It will keep the church from becoming self-centered and make it a church with open arms of welcome for all.

Instructions for the Group

As in all other phases of the church's work, the pastor should exercise careful oversight of this visitation program. He should do this even though he may not be the chairman of the group. The following things will merit his attention:

1. The pastor will need to emphasize again and again that the main business of personal workers is to witness for Christ, not to get folk to "join the church" or to "go forward" in the public service. While these matters are important, it is of primary importance that folk get into a right relationship with Christ. Then these other decisions will usually follow without much urging.

2. He will also need to show his workers how to meet the various difficulties they are bound to face in the work of personal evangelism. There is the self-righteous man who feels no need of a Saviour. There is the man who has tried before and failed. There is the one who thinks he has committed the unpardonable sin. Then there are those who have been tainted by one or another of the religious cults or

isms of the day. The pastor should be able to counsel with those who have faced problem cases such as these. In order to meet many of the most common difficulties, the pastor may feel it wise to conduct a series of studies in personal work at some convenient time in the church's program.

3. He will doubtless need to encourage his workers from time to time. Satan will exert every possible effort to thwart this kind of work. Personal workers are sometimes rebuffed in their work. Sometimes they receive cool treatment. Sometimes they experience lack of results. These and other circumstances often cause discouragement. When this is the case, the pastor will want to urge the workers to be faithful, leaving the results to the Lord. He will show them that though the task is difficult, it is glorious. Compared to this work that Christians are especially commissioned to do, other things are of minor importance in the work of the church.

4. From time to time it will be well for the pastor to relate some of his experiences in personal work and to point out some of the most effective passages of Scripture to use in personal work. Let the pastor make sure that he leads the way in this work. He should be an "ensample to the flock" (I Pet. 5:3) in this phase of Christian service as well as in many others.

In conclusion, it should be remarked that there are other methods of carrying on a program of personal evangelism in the church. The Seventy Group method has been outlined because of the experience the writer had with it in his own church in Washington, D.C. The pastor should survey the various methods available and then choose the one which he thinks will work most sucesssfully in his field.

RECOMMENDED READING

BRYAN, DAWSON C. *A Workable Plan of Evangelism.* New York: Abingdon-Cokesbury Press, 1945.

CONANT, J. E. *Every-Member Evangelism.* Philadelphia: Sunday School Times Co., 1926.

EVANS, WILLIAM. *Personal Soul-Winning.* Chicago: Moody Press, 1910.

GREENE, WILLA. *Visitation Evangelism.* Chicago: Moody Press, 1955.

HARRISON, EUGENE MYERS and WILSON, WALTER L. *How to Win Souls.* Wheaton, Ill.: Van Kampen Press, 1952.

LEAVELL, ROLAND B. *Evangelism, Christ's Imperative Commission*. Nashville: Broadman Press, 1951. Chapter 11.

LOVETT, C. S. and EDWARDS, GENE. *Census Manual for Operation Manhunt*. Baldwin Park, Calif.: Christian Supply, 1961.

MACAULEY, JOSEPH C. and BELTON, ROBERT H. *Personal Evangelism*. Chicago: Moody Press, 1956.

MAVIS, W. CURRY. *Advancing the Smaller Local Church*. Winona Lake, Ind.: Light and Life Press, 1957. Chap. 14.

SANDERS, J. OSWALD. *The Divine Art of Soul-Winning*. Glasgow: Pickering and Inglis, n.d.

SWEAZEY, GEORGE E. *Effective Evangelism*. New York: Harper and Brothers, 1953.

TORREY, R. A. *Personal Work*. New York: Fleming H. Revell Co., 1901.

WHITESELL, FARIS D. *Great Personal Workers*. Chicago: Moody Press, 1956.

DEAN, HORACE. *Visitation Evangelism Seminar*. Chicago: Moody Press, 1962.

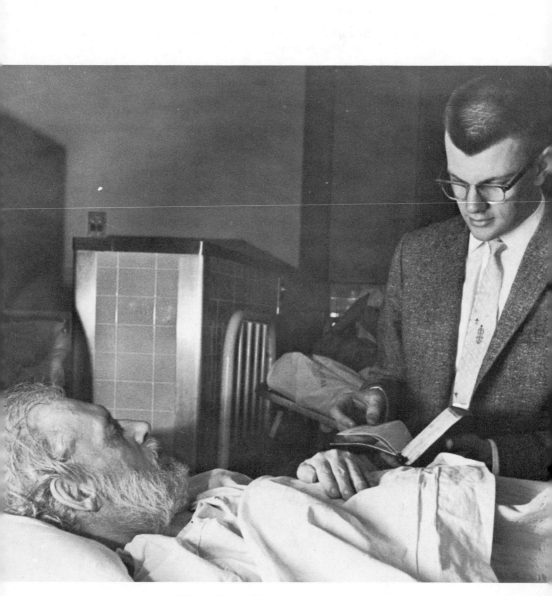

"I was sick and ye visited me" (Matthew 25:36).

Part IV

THE PASTOR AND HIS VISITATION AND COUNSELING OPPORTUNITIES

Chapter 24

PASTORAL VISITATION

IT IS SAID OF EZEKIEL, the prophet who ministered to his people in captivity in Babylon, that he "sat where they sat, and remained there astonished among them seven days" (Ezek. 3:15). The pastor who would minister effectively to the needs of his community will profit immeasurably by spending time in the homes of both his parishioners and the unchurched. There he can see how the people live, what are their problems, their sins, their temptations, and their general surroundings. In this sort of ministry the pastor, like the prophet of old, will often be astonished at what he sees. He will then be better able to adapt his pulpit ministry to the needs of his hearers.

In Jeremiah 23:1-2 a woe is pronounced against the shepherds of Israel because among other things they had not visited the flock of God. The reference here, no doubt, is to the rulers of Israel who had remained so aloof from the people that they did not know their real problems and burdens. Hence they could not be the kind of rulers they ought to have been. There is a principle here that applies to the ministers of the Gospel as well. It is possible for a pastor to live so far removed from his people that he does not know their real needs at all. Usually the arrows such ministers use in their preaching shoot wide of the mark, and the vital results of their ministry are few.

In Matthew 25:36 the Lord promises a special blessing upon certain ones because they had *visited* Him in His need. Likewise judgment is pronounced upon others because they had failed to *visit* Him in sickness and imprisonment. While there is a dispensational reference in this passage, the idea of visitation for purposes of comfort and ministry seems to be clearly set forth here and elsewhere in the Word of God.

The writer makes bold to assert that pastoral visitation is a vital part of the minister's work. Some pastors discount its value, probably largely because such work is distasteful to them. Some phases of modern life often make it very difficult. Some calls if made at all must be made at night or at other times when it is usually not considered the ideal time for calling. To reach some it seems necessary to see them at their place of business. There are other hindrances; nevertheless pastoral calling offers tremendous opportunities for effective ministry in many ways.

In this matter we have the example of the early apostles, who "daily in the temple, and in every house, . . . ceased not to teach and preach Jesus Christ" (Acts 5:42). So busy a man as the Apostle Paul found time for this type of work. In speaking to the Ephesian elders about his ministry in the vicinity of Ephesus, he said, "I kept back nothing that was profitable unto you, but have showed you, and have taught you publicly, and *from house to house*" (Acts 20:20).

Let us consider, first, some of the purposes of pastoral visitation. Why is it eminently worthwhile? What may be accomplished in this ministry?

Each visit should be made with a purpose in mind, not simply in order that the pastor may have a good record to report to his church at its periodic business meetings. The minister needs to be on guard against merely perfunctory calling. Before each visit is made he will do well to ask himself some such question as this, What do I want to accomplish in this visit? If there is no aim, there probably will be no hitting of the mark. It is sometimes true that the Lord will add to or subtract from the purpose or purposes the minister has in mind when he goes to a certain place. God may speak definitely to the minister after he arrives in the home through the situation he finds existing. Well and good, he will surely follow the Lord's leading. But the minister still needs to go with a purpose in his calling and with a willingness to be used beyond the purpose he has in mind if the Lord so leads. There are at least nine reasons for making pastoral calls:

1. To comfort and encourage the sick. It is a heartless shepherd indeed who has no concern for the sick sheep of his flock. More is said in another chapter on the pastor's ministry to the sick of his congregation. Suffice it to say here that no minister can afford to neglect the sick of his congregation. If he does, he will lose the respect of his church and the community in which he serves.

2. To seek out absentees. The pastor's concern over the failure of

some to put in an appearance at the regular services of the church should be evidenced by a visit to the home. The reason may be illness, opposition in the family, discouragement because of the loss of employment, the appeal of some cult which is making inroads in the community, or any one of a number of other reasons. The pastor, by a visit in the home, can often help to resolve the difficulty of whatever sort, and the absentee will soon be back again in the services of the church.

3. To welcome new members. The pastor is provided with a great opportunity to minister in spiritual things when folk are received into the membership of the church. He should get into such homes as soon as possible to welcome them, to instruct them as to their privileges, duties, and responsibilities in the church, and generally to help them get a good start in their church relationship. Neglect at this point may easily cause discouragement and subsequent loss of members to the church.

4. To contact prospects. The minister should be constantly visiting in the interests of evangelism. He should not expect his members to be faithful in this sort of work if he does not lead the way. The faithful pastor will discover that a large percentage of those who come to Christ in his church will come because he or someone else has dealt with them personally. Where personal contacts are not made, there is usually a dearth of confessions of faith. It takes the personal touch to win individuals to the Lord. The New Testament bears this out. Pastoral calling opens up magnificent opportunities of witnessing to the saving Gospel of Christ.

5. To bring cheer to the aged and those who are unable to come to the house of God. There are some in every parish who never can attend the services of the church. This may be because of advanced age, physical condition, working conditions, distance, or a number of other reasons. Should such as these be deprived altogether of pastoral care and the ministries of the church? The man of God will answer "no" to such a question and will endeavor to contact such as these as often as possible.

6. To learn the home conditions of the members of his church. Some attitudes which are manifested in the church cannot be understood unless the home conditions are known. For instance, a pastor may wonder why a certain young person who has been faithful in attendance in Sunday school and other services of the church and

has made a profession of faith at some time does not submit to baptism and enter into the membership of the church. A visit in the home may reveal violent opposition on the part of one or both of the parents to such an affiliation. By his visit the pastor may be able to effect a change of attitude upon the part of the parents. If not, he will at least gain a sympathetic understanding of the young person's problem and will wait and pray for the time when the situation will be different. When the pastor knows how his people live, he will be much better able to point his sermons to meet their needs.

7. To encourage the family altar. A particular visit of the pastor may be in a home where prayer and the reading of the Word of God is a regular thing. The family altar is already established. It will be his privilege in this situation to commend his members for their faithfulness in this matter and to encourage them never to let the pressure of outside interests crowd out family devotions.

Visiting another home, the pastor may find a family where there has been carelessness in this regard. Or it may be that the idea of the family altar is a new thing. As he encourages the members in the home to grow in the Christian life, he can properly instruct them as to the importance of giving attention each day as a family unit to the Word of God and to prayer. He can suggest a plan of Bible reading and prayer. There will be times in the pastor's calling when the whole family will be together. As he closes his call with the reading of a brief portion of God's Word and prayer, he may suggest that it would be a helpful thing if each day at a suitable time the family engage in a similar period of devotions. Thus a family altar will be established.

8. To stimulate church attendance. Dr. W. B. Riley has said with respect to the pastor's calling, "His house-going will produce church-goers." Common civility will lead those called upon to return the visit. Thus in time they may be led to spiritual conviction, and some will find Christ as Saviour through attendance at the house of God. Other things being equal, the church of the calling pastor will have a larger attendance than that of the non-calling pastor. In concluding a call it is good to say, "Good-bye, and God bless you. I'll be looking for you in church next Sunday." Such an expression will bear fruit.

9. To represent Christ and the church. The pastoral call should be distinct from other calls. The pastor should never forget that he

is an ambassador for Christ. After he leaves the home, those visited should feel that a man of God has been present.

Pastoral Calling Characterized

Let us now consider the nature of pastoral calling. How may it be characterized? It is hard to lay down hard and fast rules in this matter, since the needs of people vary so widely. But God will guide the pastor as to what to do in each case if he is willing to be led by the Spirit of God. And there are several general principles to keep in mind.

1. The pastor should seek to fulfill the purpose of each call. What this purpose is should be determined before the call is made. Unless he is definitely guided by the Spirit to depart from this purpose, he should pursue it. Also, as he goes, he should be prepared by prayer and a heart full of pertinent Scripture to use in fulfilling the purpose of the call.

2. The call need not be long, but it should be long enough to fulfill the purpose at hand. In the city an average call should be fifteen or twenty minutes in length. In the country they are usually a bit longer. The value of a call is not dependent upon its length but upon the minister's manner and ministry while there.

3. The conversation in the call should be directed along spiritual lines. There is a place in the pastoral call, of course, for everyday pleasantries. The minister will take an interest in the things about the home, the health of the members of the family, the work they are doing, the schooling of the children, and the recent happenings connected with the household. He should have an intense interest in people. But he should be quick to take advantage of opportunities to turn the conversation to spiritual advantage. He should determine to discourage all gossip in the visit. When he notices a tendency to gossip, it is a good thing if he has an important sick call to make! Talk much about the goodness of God and the privilege of serving Him.

4. Interest should be shown in the personal problems of every member of the family. No one should be overlooked. A son or daughter may be away at college. Perhaps a son is in the armed service of his country. The father may be unsaved. Someone in the home may have a health problem. The minister will seek to make each problem his own and show best how to face these problems. When

the call is completed, these problems should be remembered before the throne of grace in prayer.

5. Usually each call should conclude with the reading of a short portion of Scripture and the offering of prayer. This is a wonderful opportunity to direct the attention of the members of the household to the things of God and to pray God's blessing upon it. These moments may be the means of drawing some who have been indifferent or careless closer to the Lord.

6. A record should be kept of all the calls the pastor makes. This record should include the date of the call and any special items of interest in connection with the call that might be of help for future contacts. It will be well for the pastor to provide himself with a pocket-size notebook in which to list his calls and the pertinent information regarding them. Such a record will be valuable, and with it he can check on the progress of his calling. What families have been missed? How long has it been since he has been in this home or that? What response did he receive from his last visit? Such questions can be readily answered from the little notebook, if the pastor faithfully makes notations in it. Then, too, when it comes time for the quarterly report for the church business meeting, the minister can quickly present the desired information on this phase of his work if he keeps such a record. While an effective notebook record of pastoral calls is a must for a pastor, he should keep in his office a more detailed card file on his visitation program.

7. If folk are absent when a call is made, the pastor should leave his calling card. Every minister should have suitable calling cards with his name, his address, his telephone number, and the name and location of his church. A short verse of Scripture may be used at the top or bottom of the card, but one side of the card should be left blank so that the pastor can write a personal note to people who are not home when he calls. Often the card will do the work of an actual visit, such as prompting absentees to come to church again. It is not uncommon for a pastor to shake hands at the close of a Sunday service with a parishioner whom he has not seen for some time and be greeted with the words, "I received your card last week and was sorry I wasn't home, but here I am!"

8. An occasional letter should be written by the pastor to those upon whom he cannot call. By reason of distance or other circumstances, there are always some in every congregation who cannot be

reached by the pastor in his pastoral calling. A letter to such as these often is deeply appreciated and will accomplish much in the way of keeping such folk in contact with the church and the things for which it stands. Dr. George Truett, the great pastor of the First Baptist Church of Dallas, Texas, counselled pastors to write several letters every day of a pastoral character in which a spiritual message is included. Stewart Harral in his book *Successful Letters for Churches* has reflected this idea in many of his splendid pages. The pastor can well afford to develop the art of personal letter-writing. It will pay off in rich dividends for the glory of God.

In the ministry of calling the pastor should seek to shed abroad the radiance of Christ. Once, after Dr. Thomas Chalmers had called upon a woman, she said to her neighbor, "Our pastor called today and the day seems brighter since then."

Methods of Pastoral Visitation

Most pastors are agreed that visitation is a good thing, even that it is absolutely essential for a successful ministry. But a very practical question begs for an answer: How should it be done? What is the best plan to be employed? Dr. W. G. T. Shedd has said, "The clergyman should be *systematic* in pastoral visiting, regularly performing a certain amount of this labor every week."[1]

It is difficult to lay down rules as to how this work should be done, what system should be used. Successful pastors do not agree as to method. But each pastor ought to have some plan for the doing of this work, or in all probability he will not get it done.

Some ministers like the *seasonal* method. According to this plan an intensive effort is made to visit the entire membership of the congregation in the fall of the year. Thus they concentrate their efforts along this line into a few weeks, depending upon the size of the church. They feel that this gives impetus to their work after the vacation season. Some of these pastors repeat this plan in the spring if their congregations are not too large. Those who use this plan arrange their schedule so that other things are put aside and every possible hour is spent in visitation.

After this concentrated effort is completed, only new contact calls, sick calls, and emergency calls are made during the rest of the year.

[1]William G. T. Shedd, *Homiletics and Pastoral Theology* (New York: Charles Scribner's Sons, 1895), p. 391.

Some pastors operate this plan very successfully. The plan does have some apparent advantages. However, some pastors feel that this method leaves too many weeks of the year without the continuous contact with the congregation that is desirable.

Then there is the *weekly goal* plan by which the pastor aims to make a definite number of calls a week. One teacher of pastoral theology has said that the pastor should aim at no less than twenty-five calls. Some of our home mission boards demand some such plan as this, for they realize that there will be no growth unless folk in the community are definitely contacted. To reach his goal the pastor must arrange his program so that a sufficient number of afternoons and evenings are set aside for visitation.

Many pastors like the *time-budgeted plan*. This plan calls for certain periods of the week, usually afternoons, to be set aside for pastoral calling. There is much to be said in favor of this plan. The minister who has been in his study all morning needs a change in type of work. Calling will provide this change. Again, housewives usually have completed their work in the morning and are better able to receive callers in the afternoon. Also, in the latter part of the afternoon the pastor will be able to meet the children who will be coming home from school. This is an advantage, for the pastor should become a real friend of the children in his parish. According to this plan no numerical goal is set. The pastor makes as many calls as he can between the hours of two and four-thirty.

In these complex times the pastor will have to make a good many calls in the evenings or at other times if he is to reach a certain segment of his congregation.

Some wide-awake pastors have found it profitable to set aside regular times each week when interested persons may call upon the pastor for counseling. For instance, one pastor has set aside Tuesday from two to four in the afternoons and Wednesday at seven in the evening for such calls. Usually appointments are made for these calls.

Some ministers have followed the *alphabetical* plan, calling upon the membership according to the order of the alphabet. They begin by calling upon all the members whose names begin with *A.* Next they call on those whose names begin with *B,* and so on until the whole membership is covered. This method employs one of the preceding plans in its execution. Such a plan possesses definiteness and order, but usually it is found to be very impractical because of the unnecessary travel it often entails. It seems like a waste of gas or shoe leather to pass up calling on the Browns who live next door to the Adams and go across town to call upon the Allens just because their name begins with *A*. This plan also has this disadvantage: certain members who may not desire a visit from their pastor may arrange to be absent from their homes if it becomes known that the pastor is calling upon a certain group in his congregation at a particular time. These folk may be the very ones who most need a call from their pastor.

Still another plan which may be used is the *sectional* plan. This method requires listing the membership of the congregation according to their location in the community in order that the pastor may do his calling by districts, thus saving time and travel. A map of the area served by the church will prove of real help in setting up this plan. Pins with colored heads may be used to indicate the locations of the members, making it easy to tell where the membership is located. Under this plan, the pastor, on an afternoon set aside for calling, will have in his possession the names of members in a certain locality. By spending his time on this occasion in that area, he avoids backtracking and loss of time.

Each pastor will be wise to select a plan for visitation which most appeals to him and which seems to him most practical. He should give it a fair trial before changing to another. Any plan, of course, will have to be flexible enough to allow for interferences. But if the minister does not have a plan to work by, he will probably get about as far as the builder with no blueprint. The biggest business in the world deserves careful planning.

Some pastors make use of a *calling committee* as an effective supplement to the minister's calling. According to this plan the parish is divided into districts with a responsible person in charge of each. Monthly or weekly meetings are held for the purpose of making calling assignments, giving reports, consultation, and encouragement. Eugene Dolloff has some interesting things to say about the calling committee in Chapter 13 of his splendid book entitled, *The Romance of Doorbells.*

Results of Pastoral Visitation

The ministry of pastoral visitation pays rich dividends. It helps the pastor first of all. It enriches his own life and testimony. It keeps his ministry down to earth. It gives him illustrations from life. It helps him to preach and pray more sympathetically. Sometimes when the minister feels dry and all "preached out," if he goes out into his parish and into some of the homes of his membership for an afternoon he will come back to his study full of sermons and with his heart renewed with zeal to serve his people.

Such a ministry will increase church attendance. There are cases where men who do not give themselves to this ministry have large audiences because of their pulpit brilliance. On the other hand, there are ministers who do much calling (maybe little else!) and who preach to small audiences. But these are the exceptions. Pastoral visitation will normally increase attendance.

Pastoral calling will help the pastor win the confidence of the people he serves. The pastor who is interested enough in the welfare, burdens, and problems of his members to call upon them and counsel and pray with them will develop a confidence on their part which will prove invaluable in his ministry. Having obtained this confidence, he will be able to perform a spiritual service for them which otherwise would not be possible.

Dr. Theodore Cuyler of Lafayette Avenue Presbyterian Church, Brooklyn, New York, was in many respects a model pastor, according to Dr. W. B. Riley. He grasped the opportunities that offered themselves in his calling for personal witnessing. He tells that one time he spent an evening in what seemed a vain endeavor to bring a fine young man to Christ. Just as he was leaving, this young man invited Dr. Cuyler to go with him into the nursery to see his children. As he went around and looked at them as they lay peacefully sleeping in their cribs, Dr. Cuyler asked, "Do you mean that these sweet children shall never have any help from their father to get to heaven?" The arrow struck the father's heart. A month later he made his decision for Christ and remained faithful to his Lord.[2] The faithful pastor never forgets the word from the Scripture which says, "He that is wise winneth souls" (Prov. 11:30, A.S.V.).

Finally, pastoral calling provides an opportunity for imparting spiritual truth in a most direct and effective way. From the pulpit, applications are often rather general. In the homes they can be particular. There the pastor can come to grips with need exactly as he

[2]Theodore L. Cuyler, *How to Be A Pastor* (New York: The Baker and Taylor Co., 1890), p. 34.

finds it. He can answer the questions that perplex the individual. He can sow the seed of the Word in a single plot that is well prepared, whereas in the public service the sowing is broadcast and may fail to meet the particular needs of many of his people.

Pastor, do not discount the value of getting into the homes of your parish.

RECOMMENDED READING

BLACKWOOD, ANDREW W. *Pastoral Work.* Philadelphia: The Westminster Press, 1945. Chap. 7.

CUYLER, THEODORE L. *How to Be a Pastor.* New York: The Baker and Taylor Co., 1890. Chap. 2.

DOLLOFF, EUGENE D. *The Romance of Doorbells.* Philadelphia: Judson Press, 1951.

GOULOOZE, WILLIAM. *Pastoral Psychology.* Grand Rapids: Baker Book House, 1950. Chap. 3.

HARRAL, STEWART. *Successful Letters for Churches.* Nashville: Abingdon-Cokesbury Press, 1946.

HOPPIN, JAMES M. *Pastoral Theology.* New York and London: Funk and Wagnalls, 1901. Part V. Sec. 23.

JOWETT, JOHN H. *The Preacher, His Life and Work.* Garden City, N. Y.: Doubleday, Doran & Company, Inc., 1929. Chap. 6.

RILEY, WILLIAM B. *Pastoral Problems.* New York: Fleming H. Revell Company, 1936. Chap. 12.

SHEDD, WILLIAM G. T. *Homiletics and Pastoral Theology.* New York: Charles Scribner's Sons, 1895. Pp. 389-406.

Chapter 25

SICKROOM VISITATION

FROM THE LIPS OF THE SAVIOUR one day came these words, "I was sick, and ye visited me" (Matt. 25:36). The context from which these words are taken shows that the ones who did the visiting received divine blessing. Though this quotation no doubt has primarily a dispensational application, it is clear that the ministry of visiting the sick meets with the approval of the Lord. Coupled with the thought contained in the words of the quotation should be the fact that our Lord spent much of His time in His earthly ministry dealing with the sick and those who were otherwise physically disabled. Those who are His undershepherds dare not neglect this phase of Christian service if they are to be like their Lord.

The Importance of Sickroom Ministry

In a consideration of the importance of visiting the sick, a number of things need to be observed if this ministry is to occupy the place in the pastor's program which it deserves.

1. For one thing, it is one of the most precious privileges of the pastor. During a time of illness, folk need sympathy and help in a very definite way. They are responsive. The veil between earth and the great beyond is not nearly so thick as when the individual is well and strong. There is often a willingness to consider eternal matters which the pastor does not find when the situation is normal. Here is the pastor's golden opportunity to point the soul to God, the One who is sufficient for every circumstance.

2. Visiting the sick is one of the most urgent tasks of the minister. Sick calls dare not be neglected.

For the sake of the sick, such calls should not be neglected. According to the New Testament, sickness is sometimes allowed in the lives of God's children as a disciplinary measure (e.g. I Cor. 11:30). It may be that the minister's help is needed at such a time to aid the sick one to a spiritual restoration. Of course, great tact and wisdom must be used in dealing with such cases. It is always proper for the minister to call the sick person's attention to the uses of adversity and to pray for his recovery. Often a pastor's words of counsel and encouragement mean as much as medicine in bringing back the health of a sick person.

For the minister's own sake, sick calls should not be neglected. He will suffer in his own nature from the lack of the sympathetic touch. He will also lose the confidence and love of his people if he fails in this part of his ministry. If sick ones cannot count on their pastor in times of sickness, they will be inclined to wonder if they can count on him at any time. Faithfulness in this phase of his work will make him a more compassionate and warmhearted preacher. It is said of Robert Murray McCheyne, the great Scottish preacher, that before preaching on Sunday morning he sometimes visited a parishioner who was lying extremely low because he found it good "to take a look over the verge."

3. Visiting the sick is a ministry that should elicit the support of the entire congregation. The pastor will do well to ask his church membership to let him know when there are sick folk whom he should visit. Some churches have special cards available in the back of the pews which can be filled out and dropped into the offering plate to notify the pastor of sick ones who need pastoral care.

4. It is important that this ministry should be attended to promptly. It is a sad state of affairs if the pastor waits until after the person is dead before he calls! He will find himself greatly embarrassed, to say nothing of the opportunity he has lost for a spiritual ministry.

5. This is a ministry that sometimes calls for repeated attention. There will be cases where for a time a daily call will be necessary. "Ye are not your own" is a truth that applies to the ministry in very definite ways. It is especially true when care of the sick is involved. At any hour of the day or night the faithful minister will be ready to respond to the call of human need. There are still many doctors who will call even in the middle of the night when the case is urgent. Will the minister be less responsive to spiritual need than the physician is to physical need? The answer is self-evident.

6. Then, too, the pastor's ministry to the sick sometimes will demand extended attention. Some cases of illness last for weeks, months, or even years. The pastor must not suppose that such people become

accustomed to their suffering and therefore can get along without his ministry. Such a situation is a definite challenge to the pastor's persistent faithfulness, and in the day of reward such fidelity will not be forgotten.

Preparation for Sick Visitation

Because of the opportunities afforded for a spiritual ministry in calling upon the sick and because of the possible far-reaching results, it stands to reason that some preparation ought to be made before engaging in this kind of visitation.

1. Surely the pastor ought to prepare his own heart by asking the Lord for guidance and help as he ministers to the sick. He ought to consider the spiritual need of the one upon whom he is to call. He will do well to have in mind a fitting Scripture to read if he has opportunity. He may also want to consider what remarks he ought to make in conection with the reading of the Scripture. The decision he makes in these matters will largely depend upon the spiritual condition of the individual being called upon.

2. In calling upon sick persons, the pastor, if he does not already know, ought to find out as much as possible about the nature of the illness. He will then be kept from making embarrassing blunders and will have greater liberty in conversation.

When visiting in a hospital, he should respect the authority of the nurses and ask if it is all right to make the visit, unless it is perfectly evident that the way is clear. When the patient's door is closed it is always wise to find out the exact situation. Even though ministers are given special privileges in calling upon the sick in hospitals, they should not take advantage of these privileges to the utter disregard of those in charge. Some ministers have been very inconsiderate in this regard and have irritated the nurses and embarrassed those called upon, as well as themselves. Such conduct is unbecoming the minister of the Gospel. Tell the nurse who you are and whom you would like to visit; usually you will find her very cooperative.

3. In sick visitation it will be well for the minister to carry with him some helpful literature, such as tracts and pamphlets written especially for the benefit of those going through distressing circumstances. Selected portions of God's Word, such as the Gospel of John or the Epistle to the Romans, may be given. Such literature is particularly helpful in cases where the sick one is convalescing. Some-

times a book with a helpful message will be very much appreciated in such cases.

4. The pastor should be willing to visit the sick at any time he is needed whether it be day or night. If he possesses the compassion of the Master, he will not find this difficult. In extreme cases a desire may be expressed for the minister to remain with the sick for some time. He should not hesitate to do this. There will be times when the pastor will be present when the sick one is ushered into eternity. At such a time the pastor's ministry will prove of inestimable comfort to the loved ones. He will be able then to exert an influence which will multiply the effectiveness of his ministry in future days.

The Character of Sickroom Visits

In describing the sickroom call, we may look at the experience both negatively and positively. There are some things which should be guarded against in this ministry; and there are some characteristics that should certainly prevail.

1. Usually the visit should not be long. Often patients are worn out by long visits by well-meaning friends who seem to know no better. But the pastor should know better and act accordingly. The success of a call is determined not by its length but by the manner and the message of the minister. It is possible to perform a vital ministry in ten minutes or even less. On the other hand, it is possible to weary a patient into a relapse by an hour of useless talk. Happy is the minister who senses the right time to bring a sick call to a close.

2. The call should not be hasty. Although it is true that ordinarily the call should not be long, yet the pastor should not give the impression that he is in a hurry to get away. By a nervous, fidgety manner, the minister may cause the sick one to feel that the call is made out of necessity and not out of concern. Let the minister be at ease, perform his ministry, and then be on his way. The patient may have a dozen other callers before the day is over.

3. Neither should the call upon the sick be professional in its character. The minister should seek deliverance from professionalism. The holy tone, language that is stiff and stilted, and a somber facial expression should be avoided. He should manifest the radiance of Heaven and show a vital interest in each individual visited, and a concern for his physical and spiritual welfare. Unless the minister has this interest and concern, he does not have the shep-

herd heart and hence is not a true pastor. The patient should sense this interest, and he will when the pastor walks close to his Lord and sees through His eyes and feels through His heart.

4. Coming now to the more positive aspects of sickroom visitation, let it be said that the minister's bearing in such visits should be calm and cheerful. It will not help the patient much if the pastor acts nervous and disturbed. He should be assuring and hopeful. His hope and trust is in the Lord, not in present circumstances. It should be his prayer that he will be able to transfer some of that hope and trust to the patient. With faith in a great God, the true pastor should be able to smile and speak confidently. Let him be a messenger of encouragement.

5. When the minister calls upon the sick he should exhibit the grace of sympathy. The sick one should not be expected to talk a great deal. Sometimes the minister will need to insist that the patient not talk much, and sometimes the minister himself ought not talk very much. It has been noted that Job's friends comforted him most when they kept silent! But by the minister's attitude and the words he does speak the sick one should be made to feel that the pastor really cares. This will accomplish more than a fine speech. Often a few words of sympathetic interest and a short prayer are all that the sick one needs to lift his spirits.

6. The pastor's visit in the sickroom should be primarily spiritual. The pastor is Christ's representative, sent forth to minister, and his calling should never be more evident than when dealing with the sick. He should engage in spiritual conversation, talking much about the goodness of the Lord, His faithfulness, His forgiving grace, and His fatherly care. There will be times when he ought to talk about the lessons of adversity. He may wish to remind the afflicted one of experiences like that of the Apostle Paul, who saw abundant reason to thank God for his "thorn in the flesh" (II Cor. 12:7), for through it he came to a fuller appreciation of the grace and strength which the Lord supplies to those who are called upon to undergo trial of one kind or another. Each case of sickness will have to determine how much and what kind of conversation there should be. But surely it should be of such character as to point the ill one away from himself and the distressing circumstances in which he finds himself to the Lord, who is sufficient for very circumstance.

In his visit the pastor will make much of the Word of God. Depending upon the situation, he may read a verse or a chapter. Such passages as Psalms 23, 91, and 103, II Corinthians 12, Romans 8, Hebrews 12 and I John 1 and 2 are suggestive of the many precious passages which may be read with great comfort and profit.

The Scripture reading should usually be followed by prayer, in which the pastor should ask the Lord to make precious the words from the Scripture which have just been read. It will also be fitting to pray that the Lord's presence may be felt in the individual's life, that His grace may be found sufficient, that the Lord's purpose in the illness may be realized and responded to, and that the Holy Spirit may do His comforting work in the life. He will doubtless also pray that healing may be experienced in the sick one's body if that be within the will of God. In this ministry of intercession the pastor needs to be at his best.

In cases where the sick person is not a Christian, the minister will surely want to bear a faithful witness for His Lord. This should be done tactfully, but let the minister be faithful! This is a door of opportunity flung wide open.

Safeguards in Sickroom Ministry

As the pastor engages in the ministry of calling upon the sick, he will sometimes be called upon to minister to those who have contagious or infectious dieasess. In such cases he ought to be willing to be of service as far as possible, but for the sake of his family, for the sake of all the people to whom he ministers, and for his own sake, he must exercise some precautions. He dare not be presumptuous. Ministers have been known to fall prey to certain diseases through their contacts in visitation or perhaps through their own carelessness with the result that their ministry has been curtailed at least for a time. In view of this possibility, a few pertinent suggestions are offered.

The minister ought to heed the laws and regulations which have been established for the welfare of society. Among these are quarantine regulations and vaccination requirements when certain diseases are prevalent. Such provisions are made for the protection of every one in the community and the minister, being called to serve others, should gladly comply with these regulations.

Sometimes he should consult the attending physician to find out the exact status of things. It is a happy situation when the pastor and the physician are congenial and work together in ministering to the sick. Many times the physician can be of definite help to the pastor as to how he may best minister to those who have contagious or infectious diseases. A book entitled *The Art of Ministering to the Sick* has been written about the relationship of ministers and physicians in the care of the sick. A minister by the name of R. L. Dicks and a physician by the name of R. C. Cabot collaborated in the production of this work. (See the recommended reading list at the end of this chapter.)

In visiting the sick, especially in hospitals, the minister should be glad to cooperate with the authorities in the matter of precautionary measures which have been provided to guard against the spread of disease. These include the wearing of a mask in some cases, the changing of clothing before and after visiting, prescribed washing and gargling, and other practices in various places. It is widely recognized that profuse use of soap and water after visiting the sick is one of the best precautions against contracting disease.

In such cases as we have been considering, the minister should not remain close to the patient longer than is necessary. Moreover, he should exercise care not to inhale the patient's breath nor touch his person unless it is absolutely necessary. When in doubt as to what to do, it will be well for the minister to consult the doctor or nurse in charge. They will be glad to advise him.

The pastor should make it a rule in his sick ministry not to expose himself when greatly fatigued. For the sake of his family, his church, and the community in which he ministers, as well as for his own sake, he should protect himself to this extent. If greatly fatigued the pastor had better delay the call until a later time when he is more rested. This is especially true when sick folk have communicable diseases. Such a practice may not always be possible but if the minister is very tired he should try to get some rest before he makes a sick call. He may save himself the experience of contracting some ailment.

Last, but not least, the minister should engage in this sort of ministry with the assurance that God will take care of him. If statistics were available, doubtless they would reveal that few ministers succumb to sickness as the result of calling upon the sick. While the minister has no right to be presumptuous and assume that because he is engaged in the Lord's work illness will never befall him, yet he is justified in trusting God to keep him as he pursues his ministry among the sick.

Benefits of Sickroom Ministry

A faithful ministry to the sick will without fail produce beneficial results.

Such a ministry *will strengthen the faithful.* Those who are ill, even though they are God's children, often become discouraged. They may experience doubts of one kind or another. In such cases the pastor can be the messenger of God to show the sick one that God makes no mistakes, affliction is like a refiner's fire used to bring forth the pure gold, God's grace is sufficient, no matter what the thorn in the flesh may be, and—most important of all—God knows all about the present situation, and He cares.

This ministry frequently *restores the careless.* As previously suggested, sometimes God allows affliction to be experienced for the purpose of bringing the wayward into conformity to the divine will. Many have testified that in times of prosperity and good health they have forgotten God and lived for themselves. But when God permitted sickness or some other affliction to lay them low, then they turned back to God. If such be the case, affliction becomes a blessing. God thinks too much of His children to allow them to go on in their waywardness without doing something about it. "Whom the Lord loveth he chasteneth" (Heb. 12:6).

It is the pastor's privilege from time to time to call attention to these matters, often with good response. When people are flat on their backs with illness or suffering from some other deprivation, they are usually ready to listen to God's message.

Sickroom ministry *will reach the unsaved.* Many people have been plucked as brands from the burning while lying upon a sickbed. True it is that some who make professions of faith at such times do not follow through with their profession when they are restored, but there are many who are sincere and live for God after their recovery. The minister should go to the bedside of sick folk who are unsaved with the assurance that God can save even in extreme circumstances. He saved the thief who repented "on his deathbed." God can do the same today. Let us not limit His power by our unbelief.

A ministry of visiting the sick will win friends for the church. The family of the sick person will become more intimately tied to the church. Moreover, when it becomes known in the community that the pastor is faithful to the sick in his parish, folk will be attracted to that kind of a minister and to the church of which he is pastor.

Finally, ministering to the sick is bound to *develop the pastor's sympathetic nature.* Our Lord was able to minister to the exact need of men's lives because He knew all about them. He looked upon the multitudes and had compassion upon them because He knew their burdens, their sorrows, their sicknesses, their sins—everything. Visiting the sick will reveal to the minister much about the need of his parishioners, and he will find his heart moved toward them in sympathetic concern. He will then preach with a warmer heart and with a content in his message that will meet human need.

RECOMMENDED READING

BLACKWOOD, ANDREW W. *Pastoral Work.* Philadelphia: The Westminster Press, 1945. Chap. 12.

CABOT, RICHARD C. and DICKS, RUSSELL L. *The Art of Ministering to the Sick.* New York: Macmillan Co., 1936; reissue, 1947.

CUYLER, THEODORE L. *How to Be a Pastor.* New York: The Baker and Taylor Co., 1890. Chap. 3.

DOLLOFF, EUGENE D. *The Romance of Doorbells.* Philadelphia: Judson Press, 1951. Chap. 5.

ERDMAN, CHARLES R. *The Work of the Pastor.* Philadelphia: Westminster Press, 1924. Chap. 4.

HOPPIN, JAMES M. *Pastoral Theology.* New York and London: Funk and Wagnalls, 1901. Part Five, Sec. 24.

Chapter 26

PASTORAL COUNSELING

ONE OF THE NAMES given to our Lord Jesus Christ by the prophet
Isaiah was that of Counselor (9:6). He was the exemplary counselor.
During His earthly ministry much of His time was spent in counseling individuals as well as groups. Large portions of the Gospels
are devoted to the records of these counseling experiences. Some of
those to whom He ministered in this way were Nicodemus, the
woman of Samaria, the rich young ruler, Zacchaeus, the blind man
of John 9, Simon the Pharisee, the demoniac, the palsied man of
Mark 2, the woman who touched the hem of His garment, the lame
man at Bethesda's pool, Martha, and the Syrophenician woman. Before Christ's apostles were sent forth to minister, they were called
into His presence that He might counsel with them concerning their
ministry (Mark 3:14).

Since counseling was such an important part of Christ's work during His earthly sojourn, it follows that those who are His undershepherds should also give attention to it. It is the business of the
pastor to deal with the spiritual needs of his constituency even as
the shepherd cares for his flock. This includes care for the flock of
God as a whole and for the individuals who compose the flock. It
is with the latter that the ministry of counseling is mainly concerned.

The Nature of Pastoral Counseling

According to the dictionary, a counselor is "one who gives advice,
suggestions, recommendations or intellectual instruction." Often the
word counselor is used to refer to one who gives legal advice. In
these days the word has often been applied to the pastor who gives
spiritual advice, suggestions, or aid to individuals who have problems. In order that this latter type of counseling be of the right kind,
it should be based upon the teaching and principles of the Word of
God.

287

In its larger connotation pastoral counseling can be done in many different spheres. It can be done from the pulpit as the pastor instructs his people in the way they ought to live. It can be done in Bible classes, Sunday school classes, new converts' classes, in pastoral calling or by manner of life.

In these days, however, pastoral counseling is becoming more personalized and includes those experiences when folk with problems of one kind or another come to the pastor, often by appointment, and unburden themselves; in turn the pastor seeks to help them find a solution to their problems. These are days when much attention is being given to psychiatry, psychology, mental therapy, psychosomatic illness, psychoanalysis, and the like. Many people with problems are seeking out those who are expert in these matters to help them. Sad to say, many such "experts" have not vital Christian faith. They do not approach the solution in a Biblical way. They fail in many cases to deal adequately with the problem of sin, which is basic to all human difficulty. Their efforts are humanistic, laying emphasis upon man's potentiality instead of upon God's power. What an opportunity therefore for the minister of the Gospel with the Bible in his hand to deal with such as these!

While physiological problems requiring medical attention sometimes lie at the base of difficulties which counselees bring to the minister, most of their problems issue from the fact of sin. The minister of the Gospel therefore should be the best counselor in the world, for he possesses the Gospel, which is the answer to the sin problem. This Gospel message includes not only a proclamation of salvation from the penalty of sin but also deliverance from its power.

One of the greatest needs of man is peace with God. If he has this, many of his other problems vanish. The Lord Jesus Christ is the answer to this need, and only the individual with the Christian message can proclaim the supply of this need. This is the supreme advantage that the minister of the Gospel has.

Pastoral counseling, then, is the experience of meeting face to face with individuals who have problems. The good pastoral counselor will listen carefully as the burdened one tells his story. Then in the spirit of prayer and by the guidance of the Holy Spirit he will seek to point out the difficulty and show how it may be solved. The true minister of the Gospel will keep in mind that the basic need of people is to be born again or regenerated. Once this experience has been theirs, they need to be instructed toward Christ-centeredness in all their living. Life on such a plane will lift them out of themselves and will dissolve many problems. Self-centeredness results in all sorts of problems—jealousy, inferiority complex, self-pity, pride, tension, ulcers, and the like. When this mean enemy of the soul is conquered, a host of problems are solved.

Pastoral counseling in its ideal sense is that ministry of the pastor in which, by personally dealing with folk, he gets them to apply the sufficiency of Christ to their mental, physical, emotional, and spiritual hunger. Christ is able to "heal the brokenhearted, to preach deliverance to the captives" of sin. He is still the power of God unto salvation, and it is the glorious privilege of ministers to get men to apply this power to meet their needs.

The Types of People Who Need Counseling

Stanley E. Anderson in his excellent book *Every Pastor a Counselor* refers to the following classes of people who need counseling—disturbed people, perplexed students, those who are vocationally uncertain, newcomers to a community, convalescents, the aged, potential divorcees, quarreling church members, and returned service personnel. These classes form a very good cross section of the many people who will confront the pastor with their problems. If he can become expert in dealing with these, he will have a very fruitful ministry.

The Word of God has answers for all of these problems. It remains for the pastor to know such answers, to be acquainted with Biblical principles which might apply in each case so that the Spirit of God can apply them to the healing of the individual. The pastor will doubtless discover some cases where there is mental or physical sickness which should be referred to the proper specialists in these fields. However, even in some of these cases, it may be discovered that back of the mental or physical disturbances there is a spiritual problem which, if cured, will bring remarkable relief to the mind and body. For instance, it is possible for a person to worry himself into a bad case of ulcers or nerves or serious headaches. The minister has the answer to the malady of worry, namely, complete trust in God (Phil. 4:6-7). There are other folk who have no assurance of salvation. As a result, there is fear for the future, emotional upset in times of failure (thinking that salvation has been lost), discouragement and constant unrest. They do not appreciate the joy of their salvation and are always disturbed about their spiritual condition. Some have worried themselves into a state of insanity over their uncertainty. Passages useful in dealing with such individuals include John 3:36, 10:28-30, and I John 5:12-13.

Doubtless the pastor will need to counsel with his young people from time to time about such matters as their life's work, their amusements, unbiblical teaching in their schools, their companions, the choice of a marriage partner, and so forth. The pastor has some answers to all of these problems in the Word of God. To the vocationally uncertain, the minister will make clear from the Word of God that the Lord has promised to guide the steps of His own (Ps. 37:23). To those ensnared by worldly allurements, he will show that God has declared the way of victory to be the way of separation from the world (II Cor. 6:14-18). To those considering marriage, the pastor should point out that the Scriptures have definitely shown the importance of marrying "in the Lord." He will not only show God's will from the Scriptures but he will be able to present illustrations of the tragedy which results when God's way is forsaken.

The pastor, in dealing with his young people, as well as with others, should take plenty of time to listen to their telling of their problems. Some ministers talk too much and listen too little. Being in the habit of preaching and teaching they find it difficult to let others talk. But careful listening is one of the essentials of good counseling.

The pastor can be of inestimable aid to his young people in showing them the importance of preparing for some useful calling in life. He can point out the advantages of a proper education and direct them to the right schools. He can cite good books on the subject of vocational guidance. As he helps them in these matters, he will gain their confidence and they will likely listen to his spiritual message more readily.

The ever present problems connected with marriage, divorce, and the home will most certainly require much of the minister's attention in counseling. Again, he has the Word of God as his authority. He will be wise if he preaches from time to time on such subjects as courtship, marriage, divorce, the home, the blessing of children, and the like. It will make his counseling easier, will save himself a lot of embarrassment in following days, and will alleviate some heartbreak if he will publicly declare what God has to say on these matters.

Then, in private consultation with those contemplating marriage, he should make clear the high esteem in which marriage is held in the Bible (Eph. 5:25-33). He should set forth the grave responsibilities of marriage as well as its incomparable blessings. Premarital counseling is being more and more recognized as essential by faithful pastors. What the Word of God has to say on the subject of divorce should be pointed out (e.g. Matt. 5:31-32; 19:3-11; Mark 10:2-12; Luke 6:18; I Cor. 7:10-15). If Protestant ministers had been more faithful in their counseling on this matter from the pulpit and in private, very likely the divorce rate would not have reached such alarming proportions as exist at the present time. There is now available an abundance of good books and pamphlets on marriage and the home. The pastor should be prepared to put such literature into the hands of those contemplating marriage.

There often arise within churches instances of church members who are at swords points. There are cases where members will not so much as speak to one another. These are ugly matters to handle, but they should not be allowed to continue with no action by the pastor or church. Such troubles usually become more deep-seated with the passage of time. The pastor should call the involved persons into his study to pray and counsel with them. He will have abundant material from the Word of God on the awfulness of the sin of hatred and the willingness to forgive which the child of God should manifest (e.g. I John 2:11; 3:14-15; 4:20; Matt. 18:21-22). He may want to call them in one at a time at first; then for a final reconciliation to be made it may be necessary to call in the offending parties in order that they may face each other and that prayer and counsel may be experienced by both or all of them at the same time. Too often situations like this have been allowed to smolder through the years when they might have been cleared up early and a Christian testimony preserved.

Stanley Anderson, in his work previously referred to, calls attention to an often neglected area where counseling can avail much, that is, returned service personnel. Many of these lose their spiritual fervor while in service, form bad habits, and come back into civilian life maladjusted. A little special interest shown by the pastor doubtless will save a lot of these men for the church and help them to make the adjustments involved in coming back into civilian life.

In counseling with all these various types and others not mentioned, the pastor should make much of prayer both before and during his counseling, depend upon the Word of God for answers to the problems involved, and lean heavily upon the guidance of the Holy Spirit to apply the truths of God's Word to the individual life. Moreover, let him learn to be an attentive listener and pray that he may have a heart of compassion toward those who are burdened and perplexed. In most cases he will find that if he can get those involved into a right relation with the Lord Jesus Christ the difficulties will vanish as dew before the summer sun.

The Advantages of Pastoral Counseling

The main advantage of pastoral counseling is that it enables the pastor to deal directly with the particular need of the individual. More than this, when one takes the trouble to come to a pastor for counseling, that one is conscious of need and is ready to listen.

Often when the minister preaches from the pulpit, he scatters his seed broadside. That is, he tries to interest those of all ages, with all sorts of needs and problems, the saved and the unsaved, mature Christians and immature. It is difficult for him to come to grips with the particular need of every individual. But this can be done when he sits across the desk from the person who has come to him for help. He can concentrate upon making the Word of God fit the need that is represented. On a given Sunday morning there may be someone in the congregation who has a heavy burden or emotional stress. The sermon may be good, but somehow it does not fit the particular need of this distressed soul. If this person will seek out the pastor and make an appointment with him to discuss the matter, very likely the need will be met with most happy results.

Then, too, pastoral counseling can help the pastor in his pulpit ministry. It will enable him more adequately to see just what are the needs of his people and thus to meet those needs in his preaching. It will keep him from aimless preaching. Of course, he will beware of dealing with particular cases of counseling from the pulpit, but continuous counseling will give the pastor a more intimate view of the needs of his people.

This sort of ministry will gain friends for the church and thus enlarge its influence. When a broken home is restored or an alcholic finds victory or a depressed individual is kept from suicide by the counseling ministry, it is bound to increase the influence of the church in the community. It will become obvious that the church is in business to help people in their need.

The Pastor's Preparation for Counseling

If a pastor is to be a good counselor, he himself must be a living example of a life well matured spiritually, physically, and socially. He ought to be Exhibit *A* of the thing he is trying to bring about in the lives of others. He will have little effect if he tries to get people to stop worrying but allows the problems of the church to bring about a case of ulcers in himself. Or his counsel as to how to have a happy homelife will fall on deaf ears if it is known that his own homelife is not what it ought to be. Let the pastor be as much like the Great Counselor as it is possible for him to be, and his parishioners will have confidence in his words of counsel.

The counselor must know the heart of God. God's heart is full of compassion and concern for men, even though they are full of sin. The pastor-counselor will seek to minister to those in need as one who sees, in a limited sense to be sure, as God sees and to have the attitude and concern for them that He has. In a remarkable Old Testament passage we read, "In all their affliction he was afflicted, and the angel of his presence saved them: in his love and in his pity he redeemed them; and he bare them, and carried them all the days of old" (Isa. 63:9). Unless the pastor has something of this conception of the loving heart of God, he is not likely to be successful as a counselor. Without such a conception his patience will become exhausted many times. With it he will exercise forbearance and unfailing kindness.

The following passages setting forth the heart of God are worthy of careful study on the part of the counselor before he undertakes this work: Psalm 78:36-39; Lamentations 3:22-23;Matthew 9:36; Luke 15:20; Hebrews 5:1-2; and Micah 7:18-19.

To be an effective Christian counselor, the pastor must also know the Bible. In this book he will find situations parallel to many of those with which he will be confronted today. In addition to this, definite statements and principles are laid down which meet the basic problems that face man. Let the counselor remember such passages as Hebrews 4:12 and I Corinthians 10:11, which set forth the power of the Word of God to achieve results and indicate that the experiences of those in Old Testament times are aids to correct conduct today. Advice backed with the Word of God is certain to carry weight.

In counseling, the pastor should be especially versed in the Scriptures on such matters as the assurance of salvation, the unpardonable sin, the place of sex in the married state, the Biblical teaching on the subject of divorce, the cure for worry, the means for victorious living, and worldliness.

For effective counseling the pastor must depend upon the Spirit of God for guidance. The Holy Spirit is a divine person who indwells every believer. His ministry is to give wisdom, to comfort, to reveal Christ to men and to prepare hearts for the reception of the Word. Before every counseling experience, let the pastor ask the Spirit of God to prepare the heart of the individual and to give the proper words in counseling. The Spirit should also be depended upon to bring to remembrance just the right Scriptures to be used in counseling. Let the pastor study carefully what Christ has said about the Holy Spirit's ministry in John's Gospel, chapters 14, 15, and 16. When the Spirit of God prepares the way in counseling, the results are amazing and the work is made much easier.

The counselor needs also to know as much about life as it is possible to learn. The better he understands the workings of the human mind, the background and environment related to each counseling experience, and the particular circumstances in each case, the better he will be able to counsel with people in their problems. It is important to have a knowledge of the homelife of counselees as well as the conditions under which they work. For instance, it is difficult to understand some of the reactions of young people in the church until the homelife is understood. The writer vividly remembers one young person who came regularly to his church and earnestly desired to respond to the challenge of the church but refrained from doing so for many years. It was discovered that there was violent opposition at home to her doing anything but attend the services. Knowledge of the situation made it much easier to be sympathetic with her seeming indifference. The prophet Ezekiel, at the beginning of his ministry to his people, "sat where they sat, and remained there astonished among them seven days" (Ezek. 3:15).

The counselor can learn much in preparation for counseling by actual observation. Ezekiel is an example of one who did. It is also possible to learn much by studying the findings of others who have written books on psychology and psychiatry. One needs to read such books with discrimination because some writers on these subjects have no knowledge of God and His Word. Within limits, however, they have a contribution to make.

The counselor needs to learn, as far as is possible, to look out of the counselees' eyes, to see as they see, and to feel as they feel. This sympathetic attitude will mean much in gaining rapport. It may be difficult to achieve at first, but it can be cultivated. See Ezekiel 3:15, Proverbs 18:24, Phillippians 2:4-5.

This leads to the matter of the love which a counselor must have for people. If the pastor has a generous amount of this, it will cover a multitude of other failings. This is imperative. He must have something of the spirit of Paul, who said, "But we were gentle among you, even as a nurse cherisheth her children: so being affectionately desirous of you, we were willing to have imparted unto you, not the gospel of God only, but also our own souls, because ye were dear unto us" (I Thess. 2:7-8).

If a pastor does not love people, he will never be a success. He had better seek another calling. He may not love them as much as he ought, but he must love them and pray for an increase of this love, for "love never faileth." When folk see in the counselor's face and eyes the sort of love which Jesus had, confidence will be produced and half the battle will be won.

Charting a Counseling Program

A vital counseling program is not something which can be started in full swing all at once. It is a ministry that develops in the course of time. When it becomes known that the pastor is available for this sort of ministry, those in need will seek him out. If one person is helped, that one will tell others. And in time a full-scale program is under way. A physician or a lawyer does not develop a flourishing practice all at once. The ability and reputation of either becomes known as one person after another receives help. So it is with the pastor in his counseling program.

At the beginning he may want to declare his availability for counseling from the pulpit and in the church bulletin. Folk who desire his help should be asked to make an appointment for consultation. Then, as the ministry increases, he likely will want to set aside definite hours in the week for this purpose and designate them "Hours

for Counseling," "For Private Interviews," "For Personal Conferences" or the like. One pastor known to the writer set apart certain
hours of one afternoon in the week (2:00 P.M. to 5:00 P.M.) and one
evening for this purpose. This pastor had a large church and found
he needed two periods a week to care for this work. Each pastor will
need to regulate this matter according to the size of his church and
the press of his other duties.

As aids toward forwarding this program, the officers of his church,
such as the deacons, deaconesses, and ushers, should know of the
availability of the pastor for this service and refer needy folk to him.
Sunday school teachers should be cognizant of the pastor's readiness
to help in time of need among their pupils. Certain young people
in their classes may need direction in their lives. What could be
better than to send them to the pastor for his counsel?

Then, too, as the pastor makes contacts in hospitals, public schools,
the Red Cross, service clubs, and other community institutions he can
let it be known that he is available for counseling. In these and
other ways, folk will become aware of the pastor's availability for
help in their varied problems. In time the response likely will tax
the pastor's time and energy to the maximum, but the service will
pay rich dividends.

The Aim of Pastoral Counseling

The pastor needs ever to keep in mind his supreme aim in the
ministry of counseling. In the technical sense he is not a psychologist
or psychiatrist or physician. He is a minister of Christ. Therefore
his main objective is to get people into a proper relationship with
Him. Whether he is dealing with a person with a marriage problem,
with a person on the verge of suicide, with one who is filled with
hatred against another, or with one who is not sure of his salvation,
the aim in each case should be to get the counselee into a right relationship with the Lord Jesus Christ. When this is done, there are
very few problems which will not eventually right themselves. However, very earnest Christians do have problems which the pastor can
help to solve. These problems can usually be solved by getting such
as these to appropriate fully Christ in all His ability to save, keep,
and satisfy.

Let the minister be persuaded that Christ is the answer to man's total need. The Psalmist David said, "He restoreth my soul" (Ps. 23:3). Those who come to the pastor for counseling will usually be those who need restoration in some area of their lives. It will be the happy privilege of the pastor to point those who come to him to One who is fully able to provide this restoration, even the Lord Jesus Christ.

RECOMMENDED READING

ANDERSON, STANLEY E. *Every Pastor a Counselor.* Wheaton, Ill.: Van Kampen Press, 1949.

BLACKWOOD, ANDREW W. *Pastoral Work.* Philadelphia: Westminster Press, 1945.

BONNELL, J. S. *Pastoral Psychiatry.* New York: Harper and Brothers, 1938.

BURKHART, ROY A. *The Church and the Returning Soldier.* Harper and Brothers, 1945.

BURT, JESSE C. *Your Vocational Adventure.* Nashville: Abingdon-Cokesbury Press, 1959.

CAPPER, W. MELVILLE and WILLIAMS, HUGH MORGAN. *Toward Christian Marriage.* Chicago: Inter-Varsity Press, 1958.

CHRISTENSEN, JAMES L. *The Pastor's Counseling Handbook.* New York: Fleming H. Revell Co., 1963.

CUBER, JOHN F. *Marriage Counseling Practice.* New York: Appleton-Century-Crofts, 1948.

DICKS, RUSSELL L. *Pastoral Work and Personal Counseling.* New York: Macmillan Co., 1944.

GOULOOZE, WILLIAM. *Pastoral Psychology.* Grand Rapids: Baker Book House, 1950.

HILTNER, SEWARD. *Pastoral Counseling.* Nashville: Abingdon-Cokesbury Press, 1949.

———. *The Counselor in Counseling.* Nashville: Abingdon-Cokesbury Press, 1952.

HULME, WILLIAM E. *How to Start Counseling.* Nashville: Abingdon Press, 1955.

LEACH, WILLIAM H. *Handbook of Church Management.* Englewood Cliffs, N. J.: Prentice-Hall, Inc., 1958. Chap. 22.

MACE, DAVID R. *Success in Marriage.* Nashville: Abingdon-Cokesbury Press, 1958.

MAY, ROLLO. *The Art of Counseling.* Nashville: Cokesbury Press, 1939.

OATES, WAYNE E. *An Introduction to Pastoral Counseling.* Nashville: Broadman Press, 1959.

SPANN, J. RICHARD. *The Ministry.* New York and Nashville: Abingdon-Cokesbury Press, 1949. Pp. 94-102.

INDEX